FASHION'S
DOUBLE

Dress, Body, Culture

Series Editor: Joanne B. Eicher, *Regents' Professor, University of Minnesota*

Books in this provocative series seek to articulate the connections between culture and dress, which is defined here in its broadest possible sense as any modification or supplement to the body. Interdisciplinary in approach, the series highlights the dialogue between identity and dress, cosmetics, coiffure and body alternations as manifested in practices as varied as plastic surgery, tattooing, and ritual scarification. The series aims, in particular, to analyse the meaning of dress in relation to popular culture and gender issues and will include works grounded in anthropology, sociology, history, art history, literature, and folklore.

ISSN: 1360-466X

Previously published in the Series

Helen Bradley Foster, *'New Raiments of Self': African American Clothing in the Antebellum South*
Claudine Griggs, *S/he: Changing Sex and Changing Clothes*
Michaele Thurgood Haynes, *Dressing Up Debutantes: Pageantry and Glitz in Texas*
Anne Brydon and Sandra Niessen, *Consuming Fashion: Adorning the Transnational Body*
Dani Cavallaro and Alexandra Warwick, *Fashioning the Frame: Boundaries, Dress and the Body*
Judith Perani and Norma H. Wolff, *Cloth, Dress and Art Patronage in Africa*
Linda B. Arthur, *Religion, Dress and the Body*
Paul Jobling, *Fashion Spreads: Word and Image in Fashion Photography*
Fadwa El Guindi, *Veil: Modesty, Privacy and Resistance*
Thomas S. Abler, *Hinterland Warriors and Military Dress: European Empires and Exotic Uniforms*
Linda Welters, *Folk Dress in Europe and Anatolia: Beliefs about Protection and Fertility*
Kim K.P. Johnson and Sharron J. Lennon, *Appearance and Power*
Barbara Burman, *The Culture of Sewing*
Annette Lynch, *Dress, Gender and Cultural Change*
Antonia Young, *Women Who Become Men*
David Muggleton, *Inside Subculture: The Postmodern Meaning of Style*
Nicola White, *Reconstructing Italian Fashion: America and the Development of the Italian Fashion Industry*
Brian J. McVeigh, *Wearing Ideology: The Uniformity of Self-Presentation in Japan*
Shaun Cole, *Don We Now Our Gay Apparel: Gay Men's Dress in the Twentieth Century*
Kate Ince, *Orlan: Millennial Female*
Ali Guy, Eileen Green and Maura Banim, *Through the Wardrobe: Women's Relationships with their Clothes*
Linda B. Arthur, *Undressing Religion: Commitment and Conversion from a Cross-Cultural Perspective*
William J.F. Keenan, *Dressed to Impress: Looking the Part*
Joanne Entwistle and Elizabeth Wilson, *Body Dressing*
Leigh Summers, *Bound to Please: A History of the Victorian Corset*
Paul Hodkinson, *Goth: Identity, Style and Subculture*
Leslie W. Rabine, *The Global Circulation of African Fashion*
Michael Carter, *Fashion Classics from Carlyle to Barthes*
Sandra Niessen, Ann Marie Leshkowich and Carla Jones, *Re-Orienting Fashion: The Globalization of Asian Dress*
Kim K.P. Johnson, Susan J. Torntore and Joanne B. Eicher, *Fashion Foundations: Early Writings on Fashion and Dress*
Helen Bradley Foster and Donald Clay Johnson, *Wedding Dress Across Cultures*
Eugenia Paulicelli, *Fashion under Fascism: Beyond the Black Shirt*
Charlotte Suthrell, *Unzipping Gender: Sex, Cross-Dressing and Culture*
Irene Guenther, *Nazi Chic? Fashioning Women in the Third Reich*
Yuniya Kawamura, *The Japanese Revolution in Paris Fashion*
Patricia Calefato, *The Clothed Body*
Ruth Barcan, *Nudity: A Cultural Anatomy*
Samantha Holland, *Alternative Femininities: Body, Age and Identity*
Alexandra Palmer and Hazel Clark, *Old Clothes, New Looks: Second Hand Fashion*
Yuniya Kawamura, *Fashion-ology: An Introduction to Fashion Studies*

'*Fashion's Double* is an outstanding contribution to the fast growing field of transdisciplinary literature on fashion theory. While the book deals primarily with fashion at the end of the twentieth century and into the new millennium it does offer a historical framework on the origins of fashion in the West. It is a clever, brilliantly researched book that draws on the politics of class, sociology and the histories of the image. Importantly, the writing is crisp and without jargon making it indispensable reading for scholars and fashionistas alike.'

BRAD BUCKLEY, *Professor of Contemporary Art and Culture at The University of Sydney, Australia*

'An excellent study not only on fashion as visual culture, but also on what fashion reveals about the social and cognitive role of both representation and imagination. Painting, illustration, photography, cinema, as well as music, are the fields where fashion signs create our "double" world – *the world*.'

PATRIZIA CALEFATO, *Associate Professor at the Università degli Studi di Bari Aldo Moro, Italy*

'*Fashion's Double* is a welcome addition not only to the growing scholarship in the field of Fashion Studies, but also to other fields such as Visual Culture, Film and Media Studies, Photography, Feminist and Gender Studies. The book shows clearly how different arts and media overlap in a complex circuit with the material and immaterial, yet connected, sides of fashion.'

EUGENIA PAULICELLI, *Professor of Fashion Studies at Queens College and The Graduate Center, City University of New York, USA*

'Articulate, engaging and profound, *Fashion's Double* is surely to be essential reading for all students and academics in the field of cultural history of fashion. Exploring representations of fashion in painting, photography, film and internet Geczy and Karaminas expertly navigate fashion's 'room of mirrors'. Thought-provoking historical case studies and subtle analysis of contemporary visual material make it a joy to read.'

OLGA VAINSHTEIN, *Senior Researcher at the Russian State University for the Humanities, Russia*

'This is a fascinating and at times provocative intervention in the field of fashion scholarship, constructed around a series of case studies which move in a historical arc from nineteenth-century portrait painting to online fashion film. The book effectively underwrites the rationale for locating and studying fashion in the context both of the visual culture contemporary with it, and of other academic disciplines.'

PAMELA CHURCH GIBSON, *Reader in Cultural and Historical Studies at London College of Fashion, UK*

FASHION'S DOUBLE

Representations of fashion in painting, photography and film

ADAM GECZY
AND VICKI KARAMINAS

Bloomsbury Academic
An imprint of Bloomsbury Publishing Plc

B L O O M S B U R Y
LONDON · OXFORD · NEW YORK · NEW DELHI · SYDNEY

Bloomsbury Academic

An imprint of Bloomsbury Publishing Plc

50 Bedford Square	1385 Broadway
London	New York
WC1B 3DP	NY 10018
UK	USA

www.bloomsbury.com

BLOOMSBURY and the Diana logo are trademarks of Bloomsbury Publishing Plc

First published 2016

© Adam Geczy and Vicki Karaminas, 2016

British Library Cataloguing-in-Publication Data
A catalogue record for this book is available from the British Library.

Library of Congress Cataloging-in-Publication Data
Geczy, Adam, author.
Fashion's double: representations of fashion in painting, photography and film / by Adam Geczy and Vicki Karaminas.
pages cm
Includes bibliographical references and index.
ISBN 978-0-85785-634-0 (hardback) — ISBN 978-0-85785-711-8 (paperback) 1. Fashion in art. 2. Fashion—Psychological aspects. 3. Fashion—Social aspects. I. Karaminas, Vicki, author. II. Title.
NX650.F37G43 2015
746.9'2—dc23
2015020562

ISBN:	HB:	978-0-8578-5634-0
	PB:	978-0-8578-5711-8
	ePDF:	978-1-4725-1929-0
	ePub:	978-1-4725-1928-3

Typeset by RefineCatch Limited, Bungay, Suffolk
Printed and bound in Great Britain

Dedicated to

Dante, Julian, Justine, Marcel and Ulrika

CONTENTS

List of illustrations xi

Acknowledgements xii

Introduction: Doubling xiii

1 Painting fashion 1

Winterhalter and Worth 2

Academicians and Impressionists 5

John Singer Sargent's *Madame X* 8

Fashion, painting and the fall of the old world order 13

2 The model image: From illustration to photograph 15

The transition from graphic imagery to photography 18

Edward Steichen and the birth of the fashion shoot 23

Fashion photographers in the first half of the twentieth century 27

   Adolph de Meyer 27

   George Hoyningen-Huene and Horst 27

   Cecil Beaton 30

   Richard Avedon 32

   Lee Miller 34

After the Second World War 35

3 The little black dress and *Capitol Couture* 43

The little black dress 45

Breakfast at Tiffany's 48

That's entertainment: *The Hunger Games* and *Capitol Couture* 50

4   Perverse utopias: Helmut Newton 65

Formalism in photography 70
Woman doesn't exist 73
Excess and Eros 81

5   Music video, pornochic and retro-elegance 85

Pornostyle and the pornification of fashion 87
Unwieldy fashion in representation 89
Madonna's Blond Ambition 93
'Girl Panic' 96
Gendering pornochic and SM style 104

6   Fashion film, or the disappearing catwalk 111

Early days of fashion film 113
Moving fashion 118
The democratization of fashion 120
Brothers of Arcadia: Homotography, or the meeting of fashion film and
pornochic 123

Conclusion: Conditions of impossibility 129
Bibliography 133
Index 141

ILLUSTRATIONS

1 *Madame Rimsky Korsakov*, Franz-Xaver Winterhalter. 5

2 *Femmes au jardin, a Ville d'Avray*, Claude Monet. 6

3 *Réunion de famille*. Terrasse de Méric. Frédéric Bazille. 7

4 *Madame X,* John Singer Sargent, 1883–84, oil on canvas. 9

5 Alphonse Mucha, *Job*. Art Nouveau Poster. 19

6 Georges Lepape, Couverture du magazine *Vogue*, 1928. 21

7 Edward Steichen, *Gertrude Lawrence*, 1928, gelatin silver print. 25

8 Model Lisa Fonssagrives in blue-and-white bathing suit by Brigance, seated in V position and spelling out VOGUE above; Cover of the 1 June 1940 issue of *Vogue*. 29

9 Audrey Hepburn looking into the window of Tiffany and Co. *Breakfast at Tiffany's*. 49

10 Audrey Hepburn looking into the window of Tiffany and Co. *Breakfast at Tiffany's*. 49

11 Peeta Mellark, Effie Trinket and Katniss Everdeen at the Reaping Ceremony. *The Hunger Games*. 56

12 Katniss and Peeta wear matching black garments with flaming fire and capes for The Chariot Rides. *The Hunger Games*. 60

13 Retro-Verseau, YSL, *Vogue* France, Paris 1979. 66

14 *Le Smoking* (nude), Yves Saint Laurent, Rue Aubriot, *Vogue* France, Paris, 1975. 69

15 'Self Portrait' with wife and models, Paris, 1981. 81

16 Cindy Crawford, Helena Christensen, Naomi Campbell, Eva Herzigova and Yasmin Le Bon. 97

17 Nick Rhodes and Eva Herzigova. 98

ACKNOWLEDGEMENTS

We would like to thank Anna Wright, Emily Ardizzone and Hannah Crump from Bloomsbury for their unwavering support. A special thank you to Jonathan McBurnie for his research support. Vicki Karaminas would like to acknowledge Professor Sally Morgan, Professor Claire Robinson, Professor Tony Parker, Jess Chubb and her colleagues at the College of Creative Arts at Massey University Wellington for their warm welcome, enthusiasm and creative and intellectual energy. Vicki would also like to thank her special chef and sous-chef for spoiling her with all those delicious meals and for the strange hours that she kept whilst writing this book. You know who you are. Adam would like to thank Sydney College of the Arts, the University of Sydney, Jennifer Hayes and Domenica Lowe of the library there, his parents (as always), and all those who continued to ask and show interest in the project.

INTRODUCTION

Doubling

[T]o achieve self-identity, the subject must identify himself with the imaginary other, he must alienate himself, so to speak, into the image of his double.

SLAVOJ ZIZEK[1]

This world of ours, which alone makes no sense, gets its signification and its being from another world that doubles it, or rather of which this world is but its sham double.

CLÉMENT ROSSET[2]

Fashion has always embodied the paradox of replication for the sake of appearing different. One follows certain forms and representations in order to fashion the self. Hence the appearance of a true, internal self is constituted from external signs. What determines these signs is similar to the evolution of language itself; an unaccountable tissue of physical inference and association (onomatopoeia), invention and appropriation. On the one hand, in its unambiguous suggestion of the body, closely fitting clothing is sexual, while, on the other, the necktie is a convention that grew from the neckerchief whose primary function was to keep the neck warm. Some signs retain their material, commonsensical reference, others gesture to a past when these references were there but are now lost. In the history of modern fashion, understood as a Western notion, the invention of increasingly sophisticated forms of representation has played an integral role in the way fashion has evolved, how it is consumed and in the regulation of society, the body and the self. Consider how we reflect on preparing for a dinner date or a special function: we negotiate between how we want to be perceived and the expectations of those around us. And this is done according to class, gender, genre – and whim. To be *à point* in one's dress sense is to have successfully gauged the two registers of self and society so as to become one with it while also standing out. This self-fashioning is a modern phenomenon, when people had the agency to play with signs rather than act under mythic universals such as kingship or the clergy. The negotiation of personal image, be it self-conscious or otherwise, is mediated at more than one level by a silent other. This other is a ghost or double that looms from an image that we might picture in our minds or which is deeper for how it unconsciously moulds our preferences and shapes our responses.

Despite fashion being an embodied practice, embedded in life and inextricable from life's performance, it is stalked by its double, which is how it is represented in photography, drawing, painting and film. Representation is fundamental to the transition from clothing to fashion as it marks the change from utility to sign (this is a central insight of Roland Barthes). Thus fashion, as opposed to mere clothing, is a matter of image. Image is to be understood as what the wearer seeks to project. But this intention is the result of the inherited meanings that have been projected onto the wearer. These largely come from the way fashion is marketed and displayed, from the photograph in fashion magazines to films. The powerful dissemination of fashion imagery determines what is most desirable. These paradigms are far more complex than simply the look of a season, or rhetoric about 'what's in'. Rather they are shaped from a multiplicity of sources; they haunt those more or less interested in fashion, as a representational super-ego, the silent voice of 'should' and 'could'. It is the representation, not the garment, that goads our desire.

It is no small irony that the birth of fashion in the mid-nineteenth century coincides with that of photography and cinema. Or should we say one of the births of fashion, since clothing, identity and self-representation have always been intertwined with earlier developments in representation, especially the printing press and engraving in the sixteenth century. *Feuilletons* and *affiches* in the eighteenth century were ways of circulating information from gossip to dress, make-up and various other integers of public image. What is therefore of interest is the imbrication of technology, identity and fashion and the back-and-forth movement between representation and self that such technology affords.

It is a commonplace that the invention of movable type around 1440 by Johannes Gutenberg in Mainz in Germany revolutionized the spread of information and was responsible for the changes in religious and political beliefs that gave rise to Protestantism, which in turn led to the separation of church and state, and ultimately to the birth of the modern individual. But in the discussion of the flows of information and how this helped to form the modern individual, the growth of self-image with respect to dress and deportment is largely limited to specialist scholars. True enough, the ideas propagated by Luther and Erasmus discouraged profligacy of all kinds, including dress. But what is noteworthy is the extent to which appearance, accoutrements and the signs of wealth in the individual and in the institution are opened for discussion through the dissemination of print. Prior to the sixteenth century, the body and the self were sites of subjection, component parts to a larger, inexplicable cause. This had changed profoundly insofar as there was now responsibility to appearance that had to do with the circulation of ideas. What this shared with the previous era is that clothing was about belonging, but in the early modern era it could also become a matter of resistance.

By the eighteenth century printing and engraving had evolved substantially to become melded into any person's everyday life. Given the unevenness of literacy, images were important. The industrial revolution that began at the end of the previous century had increased the size of the middle class whose status was now based more on wealth than on education. It was also due to the reorganization of wealth that a new disparity became noticeable, since members of the middle classes could be wealthier than their noble counterparts. The rise in the sense of entitlement, both in terms of material wealth and of the abstract ideology of individual right, reached its cataclysm in the French Revolution of 1789–94. Unlike its American counterpart fifteen years before, the French Revolution was far more about internal class tensions relating to status in which the nobility were a club whose membership had become more and more tenuous. The power of the older nobility, the *noblesse d'épée*, as the name suggests, had its basis in the military creation and protection of France. The more recent contingent of the nobility (from roughly the late Renaissance onwards as distinct from the age of Charlemagne – so went the myth), called after an item of clothing, was the *noblesse de robe* and were made up of high-ranking civic advisors and advocates. These finer distinctions bespoke a greater fluidity of status, class and their outward signs in clothing. By the middle of the eighteenth century, the middle class and intellectuals consorted far more openly and frequently with the nobility. And it was in small publications available in clubs and on the street that the activities and appearances of important and interesting people were circulated. For the sense of entitlement that forced itself heavily on the years pending the Revolution (this is not to discount other factors such as national debt and failed crops) was generated through the intangible quality of perception. People in the middle class began to *project* themselves into an image that best reflected their upward mobility. In an age where pornography was as prevalent as news, representation of actual people or types in a state of fashionable grace or *in flagrante delicto* had a cardinal effect in how people with means wanted themselves to be seen or not to be seen. It was at this time that we see the conundrum that is the soul of fashion – namely that image and truth, while separate, act on one another constantly. In fashion it is only through replication that one becomes the self.

When we turn to the nineteenth and early twentieth century, when the fashion system and industry takes root, it is also curious to observe the extent to which the double resurfaces in the respective histories of photography and film. For photography's birth was a lot like that of calculus, in that it was invented at roughly the same time by two very different people. Newton is said to have just beaten Leibniz to the mark; so too the Niépce brothers in France beat Fox Talbot in America. Like photography before it, film was invented by two brothers, ironically named Lumière (light). Film's flight into popularity was understandably swift, typically viewed in what were more akin to circus pavilions or makeshift halls as opposed to theatres, which came only when film began to harness narrative. When film took root as a feature industry in Germany, the spectres and doubles loomed large in its narrative repertoire, from the *Cabinet of Doctor Caligari* (1920) to *The Golem* (1915) to *The Student of Prague* (1913). Film's love affair with doubles does not stop there, for by the postwar era it became evident that at its heart it was, in more recent film theory parlance, an intertextual medium. That is, it thrived not only off quotation and pastiche, but also remakes – which had already happened much earlier when *The Student of Prague* was remade in 1926. And we should also not forget the important role of the body double. In the opening of the eponymous 1984 film by Brian de Palma, it is not insignificant that the protagonist Jake Scully (Craig Wasson) has just lost his role as a vampire in a C-Grade film – the vampire being the undead double of the formerly living. We can also not forget that film vampires have also stalked the living: the first famous actor to live in the shadow of his role was Bela Lugosi whose career never outlived *Dracula*, the 1931 Todd Browning classic. His demise is dramatically reprised by Martin Landau in a film about a filmmaker making a film: *Ed Wood* (1994) by Tim Burton.

And it is no small irony that the birth of fashion in the mid-nineteenth century coincides with that of photography and cinema. While studies of fashion have relied on painting, and while it is also true that developments in painting are attributable to the need to represent the lavishness of surfaces and garments, it is with photography and film that fashion becomes mainstream. Both fashion and photography became European and American society's vehicle for self-promotion. And both fashion and photography are defined by transience but in opposing ways. Fashion is part of the lived body and is therefore mobile and active, while photography is a static fragment of the past, a ghostly memorial. Photographic representation is always a disembodiment; with fashion this absence if of course acute, since fashion cannot divest itself of the body.

Aside from a prelude on painting, photography and the birth of haute couture in the latter half of the nineteenth century, this book deals principally with the end of the twentieth century and the new millennium. This is not just to make the content engaging through relevance and currency; this choice primarily has to do with the extent to which, thanks to mass and global media, fashion imagery has permeated into all facets of life in the developed world. Since the late 1970s, with the mass-marketing of perfume, and then the 1980s, with the corporatization of the fashion world, with the inception of world-wide branding strategies, and the birth of the supermodel, fashion has evolved into an industry of multiple facets in which the garment and the person become consumed by the more impalpable quality of image. True enough, there has always been an indissoluble relationship between body and image in the previous century, but the growth of mass imaging is critical here. After the introduction of television into American households in the 1950s, the distribution of information, image and desire accelerated in an untold fashion and literally melded into the fabric of the household. Just as the video artist Vito Acconci once remarked that the introduction of the television unit altered forever the way lounge rooms were arrayed, so too did it change the subject's perception of space and world. The television was literally a window to countless image-worlds (to use the term of Ron Burnett),[3] and hypothetical sites of possession and desire. More decisively than ever before, by the 1960s, the denizens of the developed world were increasingly to see their life, their conduct and their own image as continually mediated through models created through advertising and the media. Fashions of late modernity are not only the expression of aspiration and belonging, they become discursive on two levels: one, the projection of the lived self to the outside world; the other a reflection coloured by an imaged world. Which one comes first? Precisely: they are reciprocal and mutually exclusive.

The cross relation between body, identity, image and representation was prophetically expressed by Barthes in a comparison he made between Chanel and Courrèges in *Marie Claire* in 1967, in which he comments that

the Chanel–Courrèges context teaches us – or rather confirms to us – the following: today, thanks to the formidable growth of the means of communication such as the press, television, the cinema even, fashion is not only what women wear, it is also what all women (and men) look at and read about: our fashion designers' inventions please, or annoy us, just like a novel, a film or a record. We project on to Chanel suits for women, and on to Courrèges shorts everything that is to do with beliefs, prejudices and resistances, in short the whole of one's own personal history, what we call in one (perhaps simplistic) word: taste.[4]

Roland Barthes famously argued for the linguistic structure of the fashion system. Fashion, as distinct from clothing and dress, transpires as a result of representation. It is inscribed by, and created out of, the system of representation. So the representational system is inextricable from the fashion system. As Barthes wrote in an early preface to *The Fashion System*:

One might conceivably suggest that the small-scale models used by the big fashion designers, such as those sent to the studio or presentational models, constitute a purer corpus since they are closer to the logo-technical act; but precisely, this act is never fully finished until it reaches the fashion magazine stage, because it is the language of the magazine which gives the clothing created by haute couture the structure of the signifier and the power to signify . . . and therefore it is Fashion magazines which constitute the corpus of our analysis.[5]

Although Barthes is far more interested in unearthing a general 'grammar' and 'syntax' of fashion, what is important here is the way in which magazines, the compounds or anthologies of numerous representations, supply a general surface by which fashion is absorbed and understood.

Fashion is therefore eminently relational. No fashion can be understood on its own lest it be seen as aberrant, which would make it not a fashion but an anomaly which would incite either confusion or disgust. Even one-off classics like Yves Saint-Laurent's Mondrian Dress bear a relation to the connected aesthetic modality of art. Fashion enjoys family relations with itself (a fashion 'line' or 'collection'), and according to what it is not (from the last season to an entirely different era). Further, once fashion is represented on a fashion model, and in a particular stylistic milieu, it is coloured by context and imbued with a narrative. As opposed to film, the narratives within photography are partial (synecdoche) or suspended (prolepsis). This is a particular trait of the work of Helmut Newton, to be examined in this book. Drawing subliminally from both painting and film, from Hitchcock to noir, Newton goads the viewer with a taste of something far greater than what the image itself contains. His photographs can be prelude, or event, or aftermath, but there is always something beyond them; their self-containment depends on their spillage. The viewer is invited to enter then teasingly rebuffed; the image plays the coquettish role that only sharpens our interest.

The seminal essay that considers our psychic as well as political relationship to images produced mechanically is Walter Benjamin's 'The Work of Art in the Age of Mechanical Reproducibility'. This extraordinarily influential and multi-layered text is difficult to gloss – however, several observations can be extracted for our purposes. The first is the best-known point, concerning the way in which photography diminishes the work of art's 'aura', denuding it of its sense of rarity by displacing it in form, space and time. Yet at the same time it is also because of a work of art's dissemination through reproduction that it is able to rise to have mystical power, since reproduction, especially when repeated, has a ratifying power over the art work represented, and embeds into the fabric of the present. The second, connected point, is best put by Andrew Benjamin, who states, 'In the shift from *poesis* to *techne,* the work of art does not prepare itself to be identified as something particular. In the move from *poesis* something else takes place. Henceforth, the work of art is always prepared for its absorption into the realm of continuity'.[6] While these observations concern the way art is conveyed to us, they have much to say about how fashion is conveyed as well. Fashion indeed benefits from the secondary after-effect of reproduction inasmuch as its presence is continually reaffirmed in proportion to quantity of images that are seen. While for Walter Benjamin it is the role of the critical eye to rupture, or interrupt, 'the realm of continuity', it is the ruse of fashion to be part of the very substance of this continuity whilst also occupying a space outside of it, actually or rhetorically.

To quote Andrew Benjamin again:

Fashion has the capacity to interrupt. The interruption occurs through the act of citation. Citation is decontextualization and thus recontextualization. And yet, the question that cannot be avoided concerns the extent to which citation on the level of fashion can be taken as the model. It is worth recapitulating at this point. Fashion has the capacity to establish an affinity between the dress or costumes of the past and the present. It does this by allowing for a form of repetition. What marks the realm of fashion out is that such a movement – the movement of repetition enables contexts to exert their hold – is unfettered. What fashion creates is that which comes to be à la mode; its becoming thus will have no real restriction other than the operation of fashion itself. What operates is an industry. Nonetheless, it is an industry in which the process of interruption can figure. *Rather than the historical moment, what occurs is its double*. However, the interruption does not take place in a neutral setting. While fashion may involve a 'tiger's leap', were that leap other than one occasioned by fashion for its own ends, then another state of affairs would have occurred. This is why Benjamin concludes Thesis XIV with an evocation of the 'open air of history'.[7]

The purported weakness of fashion in Walter Benjamin's eyes lies in its misperception that it is free to play with the matter of history for its own arbitrary ends. Its references remain as references of the past, which means that it disavows the possibility to use the constructive, ethical potential of history in favour of history as mere sign. Put another way, for Walter Benjamin, its references to the past leave the past inert and specular. Fashion is referential but not dialectical. It remains moored to the lived world and, to use his words, 'it awakes, for example, in advertising'.[8] It is a place of commonality unaligned to history. What is noteworthy is Benjamin's use of the word 'awake'. Although it is not an unfamiliar term for him, it is illuminating for our purposes, especially for the way in which fashion literally comes to life when it encounters its double in representation.

These points are taken up in the early work of Jean Baudrillard, in particular the essay 'Fashion or the Enchanted Fairy Land of the Code'. Here he elaborates on Benjamin by asserting that fashion is inscribed within modernity, its obvious manifestation of modernity's will-to-progress and its will-to-produce. The specious and arbitrary changes within fashion are there for the sake of market impulse. Fashion is the visualization of the market's need to change, to renew itself for the sake of profit. In this way it is an agent of death; its play of artifice and reference to models of form, image and body are 'the seizure of the living by the dead'.[9] We are uncannily close to the common myth of the double that ultimately murders its host. One famous example is Edgar Allan Poe's story 'William Wilson', when the protagonist finally faces his double, skewers him in a duel, only to find that he has consigned his own self to oblivion.[10]

We might even go so far as to insist that the phrase 'fashion's double' is next to redundant since the fashion system from its beginning has survived off representations of itself that help to assert the particular modality of the look that is then in favour. Fashion also survives off replications of itself, through the serialization of a ready-to-wear line, to the continual appeal to 'inspiration' (a euphemism for copying). In material form, the premature or pre-dated death that Baudrillard describes as central to fashion is carried out first in fashion's representation, which today is a falsified wearing before the appearance of the garment proper. By 'falsified wearing' we mean that a model (not representative of the everyday human but suggestive of a fictive ideal either of humanity or the look or both), styled in a premeditated fashion beyond his or her choice, is designated without choice to wear items of clothing that are not to be lived in, or part of lived activity. Rather, the model before the camera enacts a staging that anticipates the 'real' wearing, and yet when the garment is 'really' worn it is always in the shadow of the representation because the representation offers the ideal conditions. Yet these ideal conditions are shorn of reason and circumstance. How did the model get there? Why are the two models together? How did they meet, and what will they do after the photograph is taken? It is precisely the fictive nature of the fashion photograph that opens the insurmountable gap between hypothesis and actuality.

This gulf is so wide not only because of the fantasy nature of the fashion photograph, which – unlike art, which we know is fantasy – we are meant to apply to our own lives, but also because the photograph is multiple, and we are only singular. Using Baudrillard and Deleuze and Guattari as theoretical subtexts, Slavoj Zizek remarks:

> This is what the fashionable critique of binary logic gets wrong: It is only in the guise of the double that one encounters what is real – the moment indefinite multitude sets in, the moment we let ourselves go to the rhizomatic poetry of the simulacra of simulacra endlessly mirroring themselves, with no original and no copy, the dimension of the real gets lost. The real is discernible only in the doubling, in the unique experience of a subject encountering his double, which can be defined in precise Lacanian terms as myself plus that 'something in me more than myself' that I forever lack, the real kernel of my being. The point is thus not that if we are only two, I can still maintain the nondeconstructed

difference between the original and its copy – in no way, this is true, but in the *obverse* way: What is so terrifying in encountering my double is that my existence makes me a copy and it the original.[11]

Before the inception of photography, the same holds true for painting but in a slightly different way. The subsequent representations of people in fashionable dress, most of which was designed and worn for the sake of being embalmed in painting, live on through the representation. And if they are people of no great historical consequence beyond their wealth and title, dress is a key source of historical periodization. This will be the subject of the first chapter.

Chapter Two navigates the early stages of fashion imagery, from graphic representation to photography, until the postwar period. Chapter Three brings together two contrasting films in which clothing is central to both the visual texture and the overall content: aligning *Breakfast at Tiffany's* and *The Hunger Games* would seem rather far-fetched, but the contrast is intentional. While there are other citable examples of fashion playing a leading role in film, from *Blow Up* (Antonioni, 1966) to *The Devil Wears Prada* (Frankel, 2006), these films are notable because of the way fashion is imprinted into the very meaning and structure of the narrative and imagery. *Breakfast at Tiffany's* is the film synonymous with the classic styling of the black dress, the quintessential garment that all but disappears for the sake of accenting the individual, while *The Hunger Games* uses all manner of clothing, many of which point to excess and are near unwearable, to advance various forms of characterizations regarding class and gender, many of which devolve to typologizing. The following chapter is on Helmut Newton, whom we have already mentioned above. Newton is the watershed photographer of the present age, introducing oddity and intrigue into the realm of beauty. Chapters Five and Six follow the recent and risqué lines of pornochic, retro-elegance and BDSM styling through the lens of music video. Leading from this, the final chapter, 'Fashion Film, or the Disappearing Catwalk', deals with the virtualization of fashion through the Internet and the burgeoning new genre of fashion film, whose chief originator is Nick Knight and his affiliated organization, SHOWstudio. The overall structure of the book follows a general chronology, but the themes of the chapters are neither comprehensive, nor exhaustive. Following a case-study format, the content has been chosen for the way in which it admits entry to the most pertinent themes of what is a dynamically shifting and deceptive set of co-ordinates whose presence is visible everywhere in the developed world.

Notes

1 Slavoj Zizek, *The Sublime Object of Ideology*, London and New York: 1989, 116.

2 Clément Rosset, *The reel et son double*, Paris: Gallimard, (1976) 1984, 55.

3 Ron Burnett, *How Images Think*, Cambridge, MA: MIT Press, 2005.

4 Roland Barthes, 'The Contest Between Chanel and Courrèges', *Marie Claire*, September 1967, 42–44, reprinted in Roland Barthes, *The Language of Fashion*, trans. Andy Stafford, Andy Stafford and Michael Carter, eds., Sydney: Power Publications, 2006, 109.

5 Roland Barthes, 'An Early Preface to *The Fashion System*', *The Language of Fashion*, 78–79.

6 Andrew Benjamin, *Style and Time*, Evanston, IL: Northwestern U.P., 2006, 17.

7 Ibid., 33.

8 Cit. Andrew Benjamin, 36.

9 Jean Baudrillard, *L'échange symbolique et la mort*, Paris: Gallimard, 1976, 133.

10 See also Slavoj Zizek: 'This domain of the double provides the answer to this question: What is so unsettling about the possibility that a computer might really think? It's not simply that the original (me) will become indistinguishable from the copy but that my mechanical double will usurp my identity and become the original (a substantial object) while I remain a subject. It is thus absolutely crucial to insist on asymmetry in the relationship of the subject to his or her double: They are never interchangeable – my double is not my shadow; on the contrary, its very existence reduces *me* to a shadow. In short, the double deprives me of my being. My double and I are not two subjects; we are I as a (barred) subject plus myself as a (nonbarred) object. For this reason, when literature deals the theme [sic] of the double, it is always from the subjective standpoint of the original subject persecuted by the double – the double itself is reduced to an evil entity that cannot ever be properly subjectivised.' Slavoj Zizek in Slavoj Zizek and Mladen Dolar, *Opera's Second Death*, New York and London: Routledge, 2002, 183.

11 Ibid., 183–184.

1

PAINTING FASHION

The painter bit his lip and walked over, cup in hand, to the picture, 'I shall stay with the real Dorian,' he said, sadly.
'Is it the real Dorian?' cried the original of the portrait, strolling across to him. 'Am I really like that?'
'Yes you are just like that.'
'How wonderful, Basil!'
'At least you are like it in appearance. But it will never alter,' sighed Hallward. 'That is something'
'What a fuss people make about fidelity!' exclaimed Lord Henry.
OSCAR WILDE, *The Picture of Dorian Gray*[1]

It is well known that the invention of oil paint concurred with the rise of the imperial age. Trafficking goods was, and is, inseparable from trafficking rank and personality. These symmetries help to explain one of the highpoints in the history of the medium in sixteenth-century Venice, then a small superpower, the mercantile artery for silks, spices and exotic valuables between Occident and Orient. It is perhaps a commonplace to observe that grandees would dress up when they had their portrait painted, but it is a point that needs to be made when the focus is on fashion's representation. But it is with the birth of couture with Charles Frederick Worth that this simple relationship is added several more layers. For Worth not only plundered indiscriminately from historical paintings, but many of his gowns were expressly destined to return to the painterly form that had inspired them. Photography served as a go-between in this dynamic, in depicting the models or 'mannequins' who gave stylized life to the garment before it was worn by its 'patron' who would then commission a painting. Worth's foremost colluder in the passage from garment to its saccharine immortalization was the court painter to Napoleon III, Franz-Xaver Winterhalter.

Winterhalter and Worth

The word 'patron' is used above because Worth considered himself an artist and his designs creations; he was an independent mind and his 'works' were supposed to resonate as beautiful objects more than just decorate and clothe the body. Before him, women had seamstresses who would work from widely available style and pattern books of the latest fashions. Aside from the skills in sewing and the appropriateness of the fit, the prized aspect of a gown was the fabric. Seamstresses were typically inundated on two occasions: before a major social event like a marriage or ball, or when the latest shipment arrived from China or India, although by this time Britain had begun to rival the Orient in its ability to reinvent its designs. Unconventionally for a man – he was called the 'man-milliner' – Worth not only placed fabric at a premium but the manner of design itself. Whereas a woman could once encounter another with almost the same design but in a different cloth pattern, for the right price Worth could give assurance that a woman would never be embarrassed like this again. He thereby ushered in a new level of commodity to the codes of fashion and dress, in which desire, money and image were comingled more densely than ever before. A woman not only dressed well, she was the purveyor of a look that emulated, if not competed, with a painting, and preferably a great one. Since the proliferation of the masque in the 1500s, dressing up had always been a popular practice in court life. It was also a useful measure by which women could express themselves, either publicly or in their portraits (Joshua Reynolds frequently painted subjects dressed as a character, which was for surreptitious self-expression where the overt would have been unseemly). Now dressing up was more a matter of being, as it were, 'more than oneself', where a woman in a dress was not only an echo of a work of art, but also where art served their own ends. With Worth, it was typical for women to choose their dresses in anticipation of a portrait.

Before Worth's rise in the 1860s, art appreciation was something left to specialists. While the availability of photographs continued to increase, those reproducing paintings were still not so plentiful. It was primarily Worth who ushered in a literacy of art to the upper and upper middle classes that was normally the province of collectors, historians and connoisseurs. Since his 'inspiration' was interpolated onto the body and correlated to the person who wore the garment, the references he used were demystified and made more accessible. Worth was also promiscuous in his derivations, his criteria being according to whim rather than according to any academic or historical schema. Certain favourites were van Dyck, Velasquez, Watteau and Vigée-Lebrun, but he also drew from the deep Renaissance well, especially Venice: from Veronese to Titian and Carpaccio. Thus the sumptuous representations of cloths and stuffs resurfaced anew. (A little later the designer Mariano Fortuny would draw heavily from Venetian artists, especially Carpaccio – immortalized in the famous sequences toward the end of Proust's *À la recherche du temps perdu*, when the narrator dresses his lover Albertine in Sumptuous Fortuny robes.) This is what leads Diana de Marly to remark, 'The history of art and the history of costume were the twin foundations upon which modern dress design would rise, and from which it should draw its strength.'[2] So much so that it is safe to say that Worth's dresses were an intricate but arbitrary register of the history of Western art from the Renaissance to this day. Fashion was able to combine stylistic references that were both rhetorical and substantial in the literal sense of material habitation – and it did so well before this stylistic pastiche became the norm for art in the late twentieth century. Thus the notion of inspiration as it is used commonly within contemporary fashion parlance is synonymous with the birth of modern fashion, as is the arbitrary and constant repositioning of influences from season to season. It was Worth who made the marriage of clothing and representation decisive.

Like anything subject to the vicissitudes of taste and perception, Worth's success was catapulted with the patronage of Empress Eugénie shortly after he set up his fashion house in 1858 thanks to the backing of a generous Swede, Otto Bobergh. Worth soon became the couturier who clothed the most famous and fashionable women of the day: Pauline von Metternich, Countess Castiglione, Sarah Bernhardt and the opera diva Dame Nellie Melba. Many of these women are now remembered in paintings and photographs wearing Worth's dresses, something taken relatively for granted until fairly recently. Castiglioni (Virginia Oldoïni) was one of the most famous beauties of the day, and also a peripheral but not insignificant figure in the history of photography. From 1856 to the years leading to her death in 1899, she had the photographer Pierre-Louis Pierson take photographs of her in all manner of poses and outfits acting out theatricalized images symbolic of key moments of her life. Several images prefigure the avant-garde photography of Man Ray, especially those figuring only parts of her body, such as one of her crossed legs enframed by a miniaturized mock stage (c. 1861/67).

Worth's close association with the royal family inevitably brought him in close contact with the court painter Franz-Xaver Winterhalter, with whom he formed something akin to a de facto collaboration. Initially accepted into court of the 'bourgeois king' Louis-Philippe after the deposition of Charles X in 1830, Winterhalter was introduced to some of the most distinguished people of the day, including Queen Victoria who is said to have pronounced him the equal of van Dyck,[3] then considered one of the greatest portraitists in history. Victoria was perhaps a little overexcited in her judgment. Winterhalter was a consummate technician, and while some of his earlier works sing with some empathy and insight, dignity soon gives way to pomposity, and he quickly developed a love for doe-eyed womanhood swamped in finery. Very early in his career, clothing and fabric assume dominant roles in paintings; he clearly prided himself in the facility with which fabric texture, lustre and density could be replicated. It is an observation more than echoed by Aileen Ribeiro:

Winterhalter depicts textiles with virtuosic skill, whether it is the pleats and open-work on the shift seen in the *Young Italian Girl by the Well*, or the rich Brussels lace and embroidered net which dominate the costume worn by Queen Marie-Amélie. He dwells with pleasure on the tactile surfaces of velvet, fur, lace, foaming tulle, and on glossy wings of hair, decorated with flowers.[4]

Worth became introduced to the royal family in 1860 after Princess Pauline Metternich came dressed to court in an evening dress of white tulle woven in with silver thread; it had a daisy trim that had been finished with pink hearts. It immediately drew the attention of Empress Eugénie who summoned him to the Tuileries whereupon Worth began his sartorial monopoly. He was enlisted to design all the best clothing at court, including masquerade. Worth quickly lifted the standard of dress at court, something to which Winterhalter was eager to respond. In Ribeiro's words, 'At times, it seems as if Worth and Winterhalter were working as a team.' They were both also promiscuous appropriators. Like Worth, Winterhalter was a zealous plunderer of art history, as evidenced for instance in his pastiche of Raphael in his portrait of the Comte de Niewerkerke (1852), or of van Dyck (again) in his group portrait of the Royal Family (1846). He was also attentive to the work of great portraitists such as Lawrence and Ingres, as well as the facility with texture of Watteau, Fragonard and Boucher.[5] In 1854, before Worth's entry into court, Winterhalter had already painted Eugénie 'à la Marie Antoinette', standing in profile against a benignly saccharine, artificial, theatre-style ground or a tended garden in bloom, her hair whitened, with a sumptuously bulging dress of yellow silk giving way to a blue-trimmed white underdress. The lavishness of Napoleon III's court – including the work of writers such as the Goncourt brothers who wrote a history of eighteenth-century art – made a revival of the eighteenth century seem inevitable. Eugénie had her personal apartments decorated in the Rococo style as well. This trend meant that the stylistic references were like a multi-panelled chamber of mirrors: Worth borrowed from artists like van Loo, Nattier, Boucher, Lancret as well as others already mentioned, which were then translated into garments that were then retransposed to painting in which eighteenth-century pastiche was writ large.

One of the more famous portraits of the Worth era is the stately but coyly informal portrait of Barbe Dmitrievna Mergassov, Madame Rimsky-Korsakov (Figure 1). Wearing a *robe de chambre* of richly flowing tulle finished with blue facing and ribbons, she poses holding her hair, face askance, and in typical boudoir *désabille*, redolent not only of Boucher and Vigée-Lebrun, but van Dyck. It is also possible that Winterhalter drew from Courbet's erotic female figures of the 1850s and 1860s.[6] It is precisely the relaxed nature of the pose that masks its myriad references. She is at once in the moment

Figure 1 *Madame Rimsky Korsakov*, Franz-Xaver Winterhalter. Photo © Musée d'Orsay, Paris. RMN – Grand Palais / Patrice Schmidt.

and embedded in iconographic history. While not expressly about this painting, the words of James Laver on Winterhalter are strikingly apt:

> A head or at most a head and a pair of bare shoulders were all that emerged from the mountains of organdie, tarlatan, barege, grenadine and gauze with which the dressmakers of the 'sixties loved to envelop their clients. It is interesting to note the eagerness with which Winterhalter seized upon the bare shoulders. They were all he was allowed to show of the female figure, and he made them as expressive as possible.[7]

Academicians and Impressionists

Needless to say, depictions of Worth's dresses were not exclusive to Winterhalter. And it was not only that women wished to be wearing Worth gowns, but artists wanted to be seen painting them also. Worth gowns are immortalized in what is the roll-call of some of the technically brilliant painters of the time: Elven, Baron, Boldini, Compte-Calix, Carpeaux and the arch-academician Gérôme.

It was also more convenient to flatter the sitter through finery than to probe into character. There were huge financial incentives for this, as French artists vied with each other for medals at the Salon. Patrons were also inclined to offer huge bonuses – well beyond the original commissioning fee – to artists if a portrait of them was received for exhibiting there.[8] Again, fashion played a central part in dressing up, but in this case it was the representation, the highly refined and formalized facsimile that was doing the performing. The relationship between the double and death resurfaces again, with the sitter dressing in his or her best clothing as one would when embalmed and in a coffin for burial, the painting preserving the image for posterity.

The commitment of their academic nemeses to fashion did not mean that the Impressionists were uninterested in the same theme. This is more than evident once it is pointed out, but what is astonishing is the way in which this aspect has not been the subject of serious study until very recently; in particular with the exhibition at the Musée D'Orsay *L'Impressionisme et la mode*, renamed *Impressionism, Fashion and Modernity* when it arrived at the Metropolitan Museum of New York. Under the spell of Courbet and then Manet, artists such as Caillebotte, Bazille, Monet and Renoir triumphed, especially in their early years, at striking depictions of dress. Monet's *Déjeuner sur l'herbe* (1855–6) is worth citing in this regard as the grass is almost cloaked in women's dresses; three women are shown obscured or from the rear, masking their identity and turning them into bodies for the sake of showing off clothing. Monet's painting that comes a little after this one, *Femmes au jardin* (Women in the Garden), follows a similar theme (Figure 2). Four women are enjoying the spring sunshine in a state of bucolic placidity. With our own contemporary eyes trained by advertising to pick up pictorial references, this painting appears all too much like a fashion advertisement. The association of women and flowers, especially strong in art and poetry of the nineteenth century, is here demonstrated to the point of celebration. One woman hides her face in a bouquet; another reaches to a wild white rose bush, the dots in her white dress echoing the thicker dots in

Figure 2 *Femmes au jardin, a Ville d'Avray*, Claude Monet. Photo © RMN – Grand Palais (Musée d'Orsay, Paris) / Hervé Lewandowski.

bloom; the woman sitting evokes a huge splayed, open flower pod, and the bunch of flowers in her lap is like the seeds within the calyx.

Less lyrically suggestive, more austere, Frédéric Bazille's portrait of his family (*Réunion de famille*, 1867) on a garden terrace reads, from a fashion perspective at least, like a museum diorama of period dress (Figure 3). On this very large canvas (152 × 230cm), Bazille depicts several generations, and the clothing that pertains to them. The figure on the far left holding the cigarette is in more casual attire for the time, while the man left of centre arm in arm with his spouse is more formally dressed, with cravat and top hat. The paterfamilias, seated, is with bow tie and watch chain, while his wife's blue dress and black shawl fills the left quarter of the painting. The younger girls appear to be wearing the same spotted damask gown with silk sash. A slightly older woman sits behind the table, a little hunched wearing a folkish bolero jacket and a straw floral hat befitting the outdoors. Most of the sitters look earnestly and interrogatively toward us, addressing us as live, thinking, feeling subjects. However the dress also identifies their age, position and disposition. Indeed, how we apprehend them is a contest between their faces, their bearing and their clothing. Consciously or otherwise, the artist has used fashion to assert the status of his family, that they are well dressed and 'in fashion', and therefore have purchase, status and mobility in their world. Toward the end of his study of fashion, Barthes comments that

> it is easier to dream about *the dress that Manet would have liked to paint* than to make it. This law, however, does not seem infinite: cultural investment, for example, is possible only if its image is in fact within the means of the group to be offered: thus, connotation is strong where there is tension (and equilibrium) between two contiguous states, one real and the other dreamed.[9]

Figure 3 *Réunion de famille*. Terrasse de Méric. Frédéric Bazille. Photo © RMN – Grand Palais (Musée d'Orsay, Paris) / Hervé Lewandowski.

To draw from this statement, we might add that Bazille's group portrait is an example of these two states of conflict and balance. We are not only given an image of who these people are, but the degree of its formalization on the part of the sitters, their clothing, gesture and bodily distribution is a visualization of their aspiration of how they want to be seen. This image is both a description and an assertion. As provocative as this may sound, from this angle, it shares a good deal with advertising, only what is being sold to the viewer is the family *sui generis*, not a mass-marketed product.

Among the numerous other Impressionist paintings in which fashion plays a key role is *Chez la modiste* (1879–1886) by Edgar Degas. A female milliner (a tautology to someone of that period) sits contentedly to the right adjusting a hat. But the picture is dominated by the still life of hats arranged for display on their wooden stands. Playing visual games strongly influenced by both Japanese prints and photography, one hat with a thick green dangling ribbon slightly obscures the woman's head, making it look as if she is almost wearing it. The transitory, ostensibly unposed action of adjustment, captured like a photographic snapshot, is mirrored in the objects themselves, which as the objects of fashion are by nature transitory. The fleetingness of gestures is reiterated in the material soul modernity, the endless flow and revisioning of the new.

John Singer Sargent's *Madame X*

In terms of painting and fashion, a figure that stands out in the last decades of the nineteenth century is John Singer Sargent, a painter enormously successful in his day, but whose reputation has dimmed because his work has been viewed as a watered-down and socially pleasing form of Impressionism. Born in America and trained in Paris, Sargent was a close friend of Henry James – an important detail, since Sargent proved adept in representing the world, a world of finery and transition, which James described in words. Unlike many of the now-forgotten French academicians, whose work is more useful for costume history and for a record of painterly technique, Sargent's knack for psychological penetration was subtle and canny. While Sargent was drawn to Manet and Impressionism to some degree, the exuberant but still prudent painterliness of his style owes much to his teacher, Émile Carolus-Duran, who was one of the few prominent academicians whose finished work derived directly from tonal sketches. Carolus-Duran was also an ardent admirer of Velázquez, an artist of many virtues, the simulation of texture being high among them. While the ability of artists such as Ingres and Winterhalter to recreate textiles of all kinds can hardly be faulted, Sargent's ostensibly more spontaneous technique managed, in a different way, the richness of clothing, in all its worn, embodied materiality. As Carter Ratcliff remarks of an early portrait (*Madame Édouard Pailleron*, 1879):

'She faces forward, flouncing her skirt, her image made from bravura flurries of tone and texture. The high-keyed setting of branch, lawn, and distant terrace is a degree more agitated – sunlight in this painting falls through a breeze.'[10] While a virtuoso of the lush painterliness introduced by Manet, Sargent had a hedonist's taste for class and eminence; something the anarchist and socialist leanings of Impressionists like Pissarro would have found distasteful.

The most memorable, and scandalous, work of his early career is the enigmatic portrait *Madame X* (1884), the stately and fashionable Mme Gautreau, showing off her sharp profile with its sensually malevolent long nose and small pursed lips (Figure 4). Born in Louisiana, Virginie Avegno arrived at an early age in Paris where she eventually married a banker and ship owner, Pierre Gautreau. She inhabited the fringes of highest society Paris, although her spectacular and carefully studied appearance ensured that she was known by all. Her hair was kept a deep auburn by the use of henna, her eyebrows were kept dark and hard, and the tips of her ears were tinted pink. But the most striking part of her appearance, which made her appear like marble, was facilitated by a liberal application of powder on her face, shoulders and arms, which kept her skin a bloodless white. As Sargent's biographer Stanley Olson describes her, the

Figure 4 *Madame X,* John Singer Sargent, 1883–84, oil on canvas. Arthur Hoppock Hearn Fund, 1916, The Metropolitan Museum of Art, www.metmuseum.org.

'sarcophagal colouring had the effect of flattening the contours of her face and body, making her appearance two-dimensional, and accentuating the line of her profile.'[11] The artist himself was more flattering. In a letter to his friend Vernon Lee, he remarked that Mme Gautreau was like those *fardées* to the extent of becoming a uniform lavender or blotting paper all over . . . [with] the most beautiful lines'.[12]

She poses for the painter in the way that fashion models do for the camera: muscles tensed, her right arm tensed in a manner of contortion, the left gripping her dress, giving the net effect of eroticized grandeur, with the preening self-satisfaction that can make models so alluring. Her dress is a progenitor of the long black dress of the following century, with a generous butterfly-style bodice supported by golden chains over the shoulders. The boldness of her profile and the contortions of her arms generate an air of coquettish sensuality. Here the black dress is the support for everything else besides: the provocative stance and her uninhibited *décolletage*. Writing in *Le Figaro*, Albert Woolf remarked smarmily, 'One more struggle and the lady will be free.'[13] Even the sitter, known for her many infidelities, requested the painting to be removed from the Salon, but the artist steadfastly refused. Yet the arch-aesthete Robert de Montesquiou (himself painted with gloves and cane by Boldini, self-consciously playing the dandy) believed it to be the artist's crowning achievement. Whereas with Winterhalter the subject becomes a support for clothing and other decorative regalia, in this and other works, Sargent makes clothing the support for a wider set of values. Being black, the dress is turned into a suggestive cipher. The sitter's own remarkably stylized self-fashioning in life had the desired effect of placing her above fashion, to a figure *sui generis*, while the generic title of the painting, together with the artfulness of the pose thrusts the subject into the space of representation itself – that is, she exists for the sake of eliciting imaginative responses in the viewer. At a time when the most glamorous representations of fashion were still society portraits exhibited in the Paris Salon or London's Royal Academy, this work is remarkable for our subject insofar as it presages the work of fashion photographers like Helmut Newton in which the evocation is often placed above the subject or what (most often) she is wearing, engendering an erotic space in which perverse bodily desire is used to transcend the desire for the commodity since it remains an ungraspable idea. (In Lacanese, the subject is made into the *objet petit a*, the visual stand-in for unrequited desire.) Gautreau, transposed into elegant feline mystery is thus a double in more than one sense of the term: first she is represented, but second she is usurped by her representation, the floating signifier of free-wheeling allure. The contemporary corollary is perfume photography in which an abstract attitude is used, in the absence of the physical smell, to convey an 'air', a certain yet uncertain inclination that is coveted and intriguing.

To put this in different terms, what distinguishes Sargent's *Madame X* is the way it presages what in fashion-model parlance is known as 'the look' over the clothing. But it is also a visual marker of the new economic elite, the rise of the upper middle classes over the waning former feudal classes, a transition graphically described in the novels of James and Proust. Writing about Sargent's portrait in the conservative *Gazette des Beaux-Arts*, Louis de Foucard describes the new category of the *parvenu*, couched in far less derogatory terms than the word is meant today. The parvenu is instead as committed to the 'refinement of pleasures' and is a 'man of the world'; he is 'a newly rich man of affairs, roughed out on the wing, slicked up in a jiffy, to become suddenly, not a nobleman, but – as we say at present – a *gentleman*' (in English).[14] When he had his portrait painted, the purpose was primarily to convey an aura of astuteness, assurance and wealth. When it came to women, Foucard speculates, the air of specialness for this class of people becomes a more difficult affair. In the words of Albert Boime,

> Wives of industrialists, well-heeled notaries, fashionable physicians, nabob ambassadors, and *arriviste* painters, the actresses creating a storm, and the *demimondaine* in the limelight, all adorn themselves with similar gowns, diamonds, laces and frills – all made by the same firms and following the latest fashion. The attempt to recover 'the natural' under the artificial trappings, to bring out the authentic personality from beneath the various disguises, would drive anyone crazy. Few portraitists measure up to the task, and in an effort to find a way of pleasing clients most of them wind up adopting formula.[15]

Whereas the aristocracy did not have to prove itself – an aristocrat just 'was' – it was the obverse with the *nouvelle riche* bourgeois. In the era of frenetic upward mobility, it was imperative to represent, to characterize the *je ne sais quoi* of individual talent that thereby vouched for the sitter's indispensability over and above cold economics. In Boime's words again, '*Madame X* symbolically points to the ascendance of a new economic élite. Through the extraordinary display of purchasing power in the form of high fashion. She is the emblem of "conspicuous consumption".'[16] It is immaterial that Sargent was largely unaware of the implications of his achievement – he cowered from the attention it drew – although he had managed to isolate the quality needed for this new class: discernment. As distinct from the nobility who 'had it', the new class had to show that they comfortably had the power to 'get it'. It is an image that is a dominant precursor to the way in which fashion photography, to be successful, forces a distinction between success and the power to succeed, a quality over a substance. Another contemporary writing on this work picked up on this: 'A successful, or in current phrase a "professional" beauty, the lady herself was superficially a work of art . . . From any point of view the individuality of the sitter is quite lost, which is bad portraiture.'[17] The point lost here is that Sargent had dispensed with the single person with a name, personality and a history, to distil a certain quiddity of desirability. Turned away from the viewer, Mme Gautreau is haughty, arrogant and mightily self-assured, and all the more magnetic because of it. She has something we want that transcends her social or sexual entity.

The example of Sargent serves to suggest that he and other artists like him or in his circle, beginning with his teacher Carolus-Duran and contemporaries like Boldini, Tissot and Bonnat, have provided the most striking and memorable records of the fashion of their age, the end of the nineteenth and early twentieth century. It may be true that Impressionism played some role, but in a far more de facto fashion since it was the goal of Impressionism, at least at its most radical, to reduce the figure to the same status as other things, allowing for a more 'objective' summation of light and atmospheric phenomena. This era was an era of radically fluid class-cross-over. The aristocracy was on the wane; the feudal era all but dead, and the financial middle classes were taking hold. On one hand, the aristocracy sought in portraiture to assert their former glory, while the *haute bourgeois* used portraiture to insinuate himself in the older traditions. It was therefore not only through whim but because of this dynamic that the most sought-after portraitists cast out lines of affiliation with the great portraitists of earlier eras: van Dyck, Kneller, Reynolds, Romney, Raeburn and Lawrence. These artists were subtly 'modernized' – in the case of Sargent it was his fluid brushmanship that was an elegant amalgam of Lawrence and Manet – in pictures that could nonetheless stand amongst them in stately homes, be they crumbling or newly acquired.

In his portrait of the 9th Duke of Marlborough, Sargent was asked to straight out echo the Reynolds portrait of the 4th Duke. Thus Sargent

had to deal with four persons and three dogs, and cover a canvas eleven feet by eight feet. The Duke wore Garter robes, the Duchess a dress that Sargent had copied from a van Dyck in the Blenheim collection, their sons were in costumes he also designed, and they were craftily posed in such a way as to disguise the Duchess's height. His treatment of the dogs was borrowed from Rubens.[18]

Portraiture at this time was a studied business, a visual panoply of references, in which the artist also assumed the role of designer, and often on more than one level. What is important to emphasize here is that the interrelationships with art are intricate and many. Art not only conspired with fashion, but fashion 'borrowed' from art, not only in the most material way – as in the way Worth unflinchingly lifted designs from paintings – but in the respect of using art to add credence, value and dignity to fashion. It was art that allowed fashion to become its own commodity and to assume a role of its own autonomy, albeit rhetorical and fictitious, since fashion is always yoked to the historical circumstances that it also reciprocally helps to define.

Fashion, painting and the fall of the old world order

It was also fashion's covert collaboration with painting, its connivances with art, that reveals its emergence in the mid-nineteenth century as intimately bound to the demise of the old feudal class and the old world order. True, the aristocracy of the pre-industrial age, indulged heavily, and in the case of the Louis XIV, or the Marie de Medici of the massive cycle painted by Rubens (1622–1624) now in the Louvre, overwhelmingly in their own lionization in paint. After all, the popularity and pervasiveness of oil painting from the late fifteenth century onward owed itself in no small part to the way it could sympathetically convey the richness of all manner of materials of the aristocracy. It is a platitude to say that aristocrats dressed up when their portraits were painted. But clothing was but one of a set of registers of status and wealth that began and ended with the more impalpable abstraction of nobility and authority. Clothing was a key cause of contempt of the old nobility of the rising middle classes in the seventeenth and eighteenth century because of the way it was used to manipulate perception in what to an older age was *en soi*, essential and prior; dress was always only intended as an accessory to what was inviolably but intangibly there. It was a component of a celebration, not a ratification.

Worth's signal innovation was to harness this quality by confounding the dress with the person, both of which were to be found in painting, then, with the help of his artistic collaborators, to superimpose the person and the dress back onto the loaded semantics of painterly representation. Painting therefore becomes a vital means by which the status of the wearer and what is worn becomes socially endorsed, giving the subject a de facto stake within the arbitrary history as described by the history of painting. By the middle of the nineteenth century, the lines between old and new nobilities had become so muddled, and the middle classes had become so ubiquitous as to necessitate the upper classes to buy into this game as well. The cross-relation between fashion and painting was an intertextuality whose basis was on social value, occurring precisely at a time when these values became contested increasingly on the basis of perception than on progeniture.

When put to this service, painting, as we saw above, was ultimately condemned to the margins of mediocrity and was headed to its imminent dead end. Historically the paintings of this genre from Winterhalter to Boldini are the nostalgic last breath of the great European age. As opposed to status inhering in the individual, social class was more a matter of the ability to activate belief.

Fashion was at the epicentre of this change, and it was painting that helped to solidify these beliefs and to recast them into a fictive history.

Notes

1 Oscar Wilde, *The Picture of Dorian Gray, Complete Works*, London and Glasgow: HarperCollins, (1948) 1991, 36–37.

2 Diana de Marly, *Worth: Father of Haute Couture*, London: Elm Tree Books, 1980, 112.

3 John Hayes, 'Foreword', Richard Ormond and Carol Blackett-Ord, eds, *Franz-Xaver Winterhalter and the Courts of Europe 1830–1870*, exn cat., London: National Portrait Gallery, 1988, 8.

4 Aileen Ribeiro, 'Fashion in the Work of Winterhalter', Richard Ormond and Carol Blackett-Ord, eds, *Franz-Xaver Winterhalter*, 67.

5 Richard Stone, 'Winterhalter: London and Paris', *The Burlington Magazine*, 139 (1019), February, 1988, 152.

6 Richard Ormond and Carol Blackett-Ord, *Franz-Xaver Winterhalter*, 210.

7 James Laver, 'Winterhalter', *Burlington Magazine for Connoisseurs*, 70 (406), January 1937, 44.

8 As James Harding explains, 'success at the Salon ensured success with the buying public. Indeed, one patron agreed to pay 1000 francs for his portrait with a further 2000 francs to be added if the portrait was accepted at the Salon.' *Artistes Pompiers*, London: Academy Editions, 1979, 7.

9 Roland Barthes, *The Fashion System* (1967), trans. Matthey Ward and Richard Howard, Los Angeles and London: California U.P., (1983) 1990, 244.

10 Carter Ratcliff, *John Singer Sargent*, New York: Abbeville Press, 1982, 47.

11 Stanley Olson, *John Singer Sargent*, London: Macmillan, 1986, 102.

12 Cit. Marc Simpson, 'Sargent and His Critics', Marc Simpson, ed., *Uncanny Spectacle: The Public Career of the Young John Singer Sargent*, New Haven and London: Yale U.P. and Williamstown: Clark Institute, 1997, 50.

13 Cit. Ratcliff, *John Singer Sargent*, 85.

14 Louis de Foucard, 'Le Salon de 1884', *Gazette des Beaux-Arts*, 29, June 1884, 91, cit. Albert Boime, Patricia Hills, ed., *John Singer Sargent*, exn cat., New York: Whitney and New York: Abrams, 1987, 90.

15 Boime, 'Sargent in Paris and London: A Portrait of the Artist as Dorian Gray' in Hills, ed., *John Singer Sargent*, 90.

16 Ibid., 91.

17 W.C. Brownell, 'The American Salon', *Magazine of Art*, 7, London 1884, 493–494, cit. Marc Simpson, ed., *Uncanny Spectacle*, 141.

18 S. Olson, *John Singer Sargent*, 222.

2
THE MODEL IMAGE

From illustration to photograph

Masks offer themselves to us,
But beneath them we feel
Faces that pucker
And, feigning surrender, intimately satisfy
Their taste for avarice

All is double; an assumed
grace lends to all
this turbulent trouble
between two shores.

RAINER MARIA RILKE[1]

Today, the fashion photograph is something that is all but taken for granted. It is also the bedrock on which all of commercial photography is built, since it is the locus of imagination and desire. From these images we infer a complex language of gestures and facial expressions hinting at joy and satisfaction. As the French psychoanalytic philosopher Jacques Lacan proposes, the logic of desire is one of repeated non-fulfilment, a systematic failure. The logic of the fulfilment of desire – *jouissance*, which is also the French for 'orgasm' – is built on its rupture; that is, the sensation of fulfilled desire is only a factor in its eternal dissatisfaction. For desire is at its best in the passage of its own desiring; one desires to desire. The feeling of fulfilment is but a punctuation mark in a more profound process that has no end except death itself. The conundrum of the fashion photograph is that it posits itself at the Archimedean point of *jouissance*; it is the fictive utopia (*u-topos* – literally 'no place') that we know to be fictional yet find joy in believing it to be true. Yet the utopias of the fashion photograph are inscribed with a different ideological import from political ones, for the ideology of the fashion photograph is legible within its visual syntax, in making the implausible seem plausible. Only the most delusional or gullible believe that the fashion image – and related forms of advertising – is something within our grasp. Rather, the more skilful and arresting fashion images allow us to approximate ourselves to it, we project our own double over the representational double of the photograph.

In his recent meditation on literature, Terry Eagleton states:

> Fiction . . . is an event inseparable from its act of utterance. It has no support from outside itself, in the sense that what it asserts cannot be checked off in any important way against some independent testimony. In this sense, it is more like swearing than reporting an armed robbery. Fiction manufactures the very objects to which it appears to refer. It covertly fashions what it purports to describe. It looks like a report, but is actually a piece of rhetoric. In Austinian jargon, it is a performative masquerading as a constative. As the German critic Karlheinz Stierle illuminatingly puts it, it is the auto-referential in referential form. Its referent – a murder mystery, a political crisis, an adulterous affair – is purely internal, existing only in its own account of it. As Lamarque and Olsen put it, 'Fictive states of affairs owe their identity to their mode of presentation'. *Fictional narratives project an apparent outside to themselves out of their own internal activities.*[2]

This is a remarkably useful passage for the understanding of the fashion photograph for a number of reasons. To begin with, a fashion photograph is pre-eminently fiction; a fictitiousness that is sustained on the suggestion that it is part of a much larger, more intricate narrative. 'It looks like a report, but is actually a piece of rhetoric.' Similarly, the fashion photograph appears to enact a scene from life, with greater or lesser degrees of credibility, and yet the world it presents is not only constructed, but constructed around a set of co-ordinates established by the brand. The look of the photograph must be consonant (or consonantly dissonant) with the clothing it is its purpose to represent.

Thus the image's logic manipulates registers of the outside world to create a closed circuit that, in turn, anticipates what the world could become. The fashion photograph is made, fashioned from components of the outside world to create a visual hypothesis of what that world could become. Yet unlike a political message, the fashion photograph is oriented more toward particulars than universals. It presents an exclusive universe in the twin sense of the term – exclusive as in elite, but also what seeks to exist in isolation, at the expense of everything else. This is why early theorists of fashion like Simmel and Flügel equated fashion with femininity, since women were perceived as more 'emotionally frail, fickle and vain' than men. Even if, alas, we have not entirely divested ourselves of this prejudice, what remains compelling is the self-serving nature of the fashion image. Unlike art, which is meant to serve some higher purpose that extends beyond the material conditions of its making and what it represents, the fashion image's insistence on being special is written into the claims and rhetoric of the image itself. It is therefore supremely conscious of itself as a 'mode of presentation'. We shall develop this point in Chapter Four with respect to the formalism that may be deduced from the photographs of Helmut Newton.

Since its inception, photography has always been preoccupied with, and bedevilled by, notions of truth. It was reviled by some such as Baudelaire for its slavish relationship to the material world, leaving little room for imagination, the 'queen of the faculties'. Even though photography could be manipulated to lie, its ability to serve as evidence is self-evident. As Walter Benjamin observes at the beginning of his 'Short History of Photography', the first people that the new medium of photography put out of business were miniature-portrait painters. Photography has always been an invaluable tool for recoding and documenting, yet it has a curious double genesis in its use within the public sphere, especially as it began to be used in newsprint at the beginning of the twentieth century. Here photographs acting as evidence coexisted, as they continue to do, with others advertising and promoting people and objects. (We might be tempted to go down the line of argument to suggest that even the evidential photographs were covert forms of promotion, but that would be to digress too far.) In the latter, the factors of evidence and proof existed solely for the sake of presenting the object advertised; the rest was persuasion and seduction. One rests on the premise of believability, as we in principle like to trust in the news provider that it gives us something authentic, while in the other questions of authenticity are suspended as the advertisers vie for our belief in what they can offer. Hence Michael Carter asks the inevitable question about fashion photography, '*Why do people believe it*?'[3] Stressing that the answer to this question may tumble into abstract psychoanalytic explorations into representation and desire, Carter presciently considers that

> [a] more fruitful line might be to place the stress upon the word 'fashion' in the term 'fashion photography'. By this I do not mean that what we should look at is photographic documentation of something happening elsewhere – down in the streets or out in the world – but more in the set of operations that occur within the frame of the fashion photograph. We might say that fashion only really exists within the photograph at that moment where modeled clothing and medium collide. All that interests me about fashion in this piece [essay] are the exchanges that take place between it, as a point through which a particular type of ideal may be pictured, and that other place where we constantly suffer at the hands of our ability to represent this unattainable ideal. The fashion photograph is, *in potentia*, a place where there is a perfect equivalence between image and non-image. I must add that by the term ideal I do not mean beautiful, pure, good, nor something particularly immaterial, more the attainment of an absolute unity up to and including the grotesque and the idiotic.[4]

Fashion photography is therefore located in two places. Its data are taken from the world, but it is not that world. Its locus is always elsewhere, *hors champ*, a threshold ideality of desiring, that need not discriminate between beauty or its degradation. Although it is theatrical, it is unlike theatre. Theatre is metaphorical, a stylized extraction from life that causes relief (*catharsis*) or helps us see ourselves or social circumstances with greater clarity or complexity. Fashion photography may alight on all these characteristics, as indeed does most art; however, fashion photography reserves for itself the right to disavow metaphor for the sake of persuasion, namely that there may be a possibility that the viewer may enter the stage and participate in the drama (glamour) of the image. Hence Carter's 'absolute unity'; this is the unity of the self with its other, a unity in which the self is ultimately obliterated.

The transition from graphic imagery to photography

Fashion photographs are associated with models; however, the first models were not expressly dressed up to be photographed. It is testimony to Worth's ingenuity, insight and innovation that not only did he introduce a new way of thinking about fashion design – as creation – but with that more or less invented the fashion model, or *mannequin*, in the 1850s to entice prospective clients who visited his salon. She was the anonymous alias before the 'real' wearer, and a reminder once more of the curious reversal of the double, who comes first. In the main, the first models were women drawn from the workshop floor, or, like Degas's ballerinas, women of the lower classes seeking other occupations to supplement their incomes to keep them from the streets. Modelling was far from the sought-after occupation that it is today; its sexual undertones were suspect as opposed to desirable. In the mid-nineteenth century, the depiction of fashion was confined to engravings, disseminated in the *affiches* that had grown from the previous century. There was no suggestion yet of selling a lifestyle or a look, rather, the figures were imaginary generic armatures, and the backgrounds for the sake of continuity – much in the manner of the two-dimensional roll-call of images in a sales catalogue for Sears, Roebuck & Co. These illustrations featured in a rising welter of publications marketing fashion and good taste: in Paris one could choose from *Feminina*, *L'Album de la Mode du Figaro*, *L'Officiel*, the *Journal des Modes* or *La Mode Illustré*, while the first fashion magazine in the United States was *Harper's Bazaar*, issue number one published on 2 November 1867. First published in a more newspaper-like format, these presented an exhaustive taxonomy of fashions of the period. Style and type were of the order, the garment itself. Personality and aura were of next to no issue, except of course what permeated from the *artiste* Worth himself.

The invention of the box camera in 1890 by Kodak ushered in a decisive change in the rituals of representation that is commensurate with, say, the smartphone in the present era. With the famous slogan, 'You press the button, we do the rest', photography was no longer a debased art form confined in semi-artisanal fashion to photographic studios that had the requisite neck clamps to keep the head and body stable, it was transported into the fabric of everyday life. On a much smaller scale than today, taking pictures became part of everyday life, increasingly integrated into the circuits of communication. Such availability increased this overall visual literacy of photography – that is, people at large became more responsive to it as part of their lives, its abstract and concrete functions, its visual grammar. With this came the next major development in photographic history, which was pictorialism, the self-conscious construction of photographic images to rival paintings.

To be sure, photography from an establishment point of view was still a far cry from painting, but it did become a suitable alternative for those who could not afford painting – it was also slowly adopted by advertising. Although photography proper still retained a de facto relation to fashion – it showed fashion off as an image – photography was used plentifully as understudies for poster advertisements. One such example is a poster by the guru of Art Nouveau visual designs, Alphonse Mucha, advertising JOB cigarettes (1896) (Figure 5). There is little by way of clothing in this seductive image, but it is evident that he had absorbed some of the influence of *Madame X* wittingly or otherwise, as it is a

Figure 5 Alphonse Mucha, *Job*. Art Nouveau Poster. Private Collection. Photo credit: Art Resource, NY.

work that displays confidence and attitude. In the 1890s it was still considered risqué for women to smoke cigarettes. That Mucha worked closely from photographic studies is well established, and also evident in the rigidity of his figures, qualities ill-suited to painting but sympathetic to graphic advertising. His anonymous model is depicted in a swooning state of self-induced ecstasy, tendrils of smoke snaking around her like the spirit of Zeus around Danaë. While it may be convenient to place this image amongst those objectifying women, to smoke openly was one aspect of the rising independence of women, the suffragette movement (first decreed in New Zealand in 1893, with France coming very late in 1945) and bloomerism. Bloomerism, itself liberally treated usually through satirical engravings in the mainstream media, was an important step to the new wave of practical, pared-down fashions of Patou and Chanel at the beginning of the twentieth century.

Until the 1920s representations were still heavily reliant on illustrations to convey garments to the public. In 1912, the publisher Lucien Vogel developed a new kind of fashion magazine, *La Gazette du Bon Ton*. It distinguished itself from its predecessors by being less of a catalogue and more of a vehicle for selling the artistry of the doyens of fashion who sponsored it: Cheruit, Doeuillet, Doucet, Paquin, Poiret, Redfern and Worth. For the first time, the skills of the great illustrators were no longer subordinated to the designs but placed them into decorative tableaux. Thus these designers were paired with the elegant linear inventiveness of some of the foremost illustrators of the day: Georges Lepape, Georges Barbier and Paul Iribe, and Léon Bakst, best known for his designs for the Ballets Russes. These illustrations are classics in their own right, and helped to define the popular aesthetic of the era before the 1929 Depression, both defining an era of boom for high fashion while also retaining some independence as images in their own right, even overshadowing the garments they were intended to advertise. Hedonistic and graceful, the illustrative license taken by these artists was at times at the expense of the garment itself. Gustave Babin, writing *L'Illustration*, lamented the impracticability of some of the represented clothing. For instance, a winter coat in a picture by Georges Lepape was but 'a picturesque fantasy' (Figure 6).[5]

The conformity of the designers of this time with a particular style of visual design led by a handful of artist-designers was mirrored in the burgeoning industry of modelling. The first documented catwalks, or mannequin parades, occurred in London in the 1890s, but little is known of them. It was only with the couture houses of Patou and Poiret at the beginning of the next century that the use of models became more accepted. In Worth's day, before they became known as mannequins, they were called *sosies*, meaning 'lookalike' or 'double'. *Sosie* is also the name for an alter ego.

It is worth pausing to examine the origin of the term *sosie*, a word that has shifted from a character to a trait, something like the term 'patsy' in English. What

Figure 6 Georges Lepape, Couverture du magazine *Vogue*, 1928 © ADAGP, Paris, 2015 – Cliché: Banque d'Images de l' ADAGP.

is even more instructive, or ironic, is that Sosie was the name of a man, not a woman, specifically the servant of Amphitryon, the eponymous lead character of Molière's play, itself a rewriting of the classical play of the same name by Plautus. (That *sosie* should originally have been a man will gain resonance in the queering and bending of female models and celebrities to be discussed later in the book.) The story goes as follows: Jupiter desires Alcmena, the wife of Amphitryon. However, she is newly married to her husband and still full of ardour and love, and is unlikely to be won over in a hurry. As a result Jupiter decides to disguise himself as Amphitryon, a Theban general, when the real Amphitryon is away on campaign. In order to pull off this complex ruse, Jupiter asks the help of Mercury, who transforms himself into Amphitryon's servant, Sosie. Yet in a twist of events Amphitryon returns home earlier than expected. The 'real' Sosie is sent ahead to announce his return. Upon his arrival he meets his double, who is really Mercury. In the comic interchange that follows, Mercury, after telling Sosie some very intimate details about himself, causes him to doubt himself and therefore to think that the imposter Sosie is the 'real' him. Wracked with confusion, Sosie returns to his master and tells him that he had met himself: 'No Monsieur, it is the simple truth: this I was at your house sooner than I; and, I swear to you, I was there before I arrived.'[6] In her coruscating analysis of the comic intricacies of this play, Alenka Zupancic adds that 'in the very moment when the I/ego is stripped of all its properties, when it remains only as an empty word, as a pure signifying marker of the speaker, we see how – far from becoming free-floating monad within the multiplicity of others – the "I" is irreducibly *fastened* to the other (to the "I" of the other)'.[7] While there are many psychoanalytic ramifications here that Zupancic explores at length, what is important to extract is not only the way that *sosie* has become reversed sexually once she enters fashion discourse, but the psychological link that connects the model, via the double, to the individual who wears the fashion, and indeed, opens the question as to where the representation takes place. Is the wearer of fashion already now the double or the double's double?

The model in Poiret's time was expected to look identical, and when on tour, not wearing the garments in question, they would dress the same to stress their status as ciphers. As Caroline Evans comments, 'Her body was replicated in the commercial and social spaces of the city: she mirrored the inanimate dummies of the shop window, with whom she was often paired, and she herself was duplicated in the mirrors of the salon where she worked.'[8] A mannequin was meant to be demure and decorous – Chanel stipulated 'slenderness and good manners' – yet her apparent subservience to the designer and prospective buyer presented a problem. Echoing again the sosie problem, Nancy Troy in her book on Poiret locates a dilemma that lies precisely at the heart of the division between fashion model and individual subject: that of originality and replication. A haute couture piece, that was meant to grace only one body, was already worn by another.[9]

The gradual usurpation of the photograph over the illustration arrived together with the entry of photography into the artistic avant-garde. Until then fashion illustration was on two simple scales: specialized and élite, as exemplified by *La Gazette du Bon Ton*, whose name said it all, and the more pedestrian catalogues that littered the market along with the growth of Fordist production and department stores. With Poiret, Patou and Chanel, the notion of the celebrity designer was no longer a novelty as it had been in Worth's time, having become something expected, tied to commodity prestige. The rise of the modern designer and the marriage of name and label meant a closer allegiance to the cult of personality – both as reflected by the designer and what could be gained by the wearer – that emanated not only out of the way the clothing looked but where it manifested. Hence anything that captured the eye or intrigued the mind was put to photography's disposal. One need only think of Elsa Schiaparelli in this regard, whose Surrealist and avant-garde styles, cannibalized from the likes of Dalì and Cocteau, would only have looked too eccentric if transposed into illustration, since it was from art that the ideas had germinated; it made no sense to translate them back again.

Another component in the shift from graphic imagery to photography was the rising demographic of buyers. By the 1920s, far more than the affluent concerned themselves with fashion and fashion advertising. One of the twentieth century's first media moguls, Thomas Condé Nast, seized upon Steichen's innovations in fashion photography and knew that there was a rapidly rising audience, in his words, 'so literally interested in fashion that they wanted to see the mode thoroughly and faithfully reported – rather than rendered as a form of decorative art'.[10]

Edward Steichen and the birth of the fashion shoot

If the genealogy of fashion photography were said to have a point of origin it would probably be traced back to Edward Steichen. He was the most prolific contributor to Stieglitz's magazine *Camera Work* (1903–1917), itself the first serious journal devoted to establishing photography as an autonomous art. Born in Luxembourg in 1879, he and his family emigrated to the United States a year later. At age fifteen, Steichen studied lithography at the American Fine Art Company in Milwaukee. During this period he also preoccupied himself with drawing and painting, becoming an accomplished technician that led him to team up with friends to found the Milwaukee Art Students League. In New York in 1900, on his way to Paris, Steichen met the highly discerning Stieglitz, who had no compunction in buying three of his photographs for five dollars each. Shortly after Steichen was to become an integral member of Stieglitz's circle and eventually became the most published photographer in the magazine *Camera Work*. With Steichen's background in traditional art, and with Stieglitz's campaign to secure photography a place within the canon of fine art, perceptions about photography's limits and capabilities were suitably expanded.

As his biographer Penelope Niven recounts, in 1911 Steichen was offered a challenge by the editor of both the *Gazette du Bon Ton* and *Jardin des Modes*, Lucien Vogel, to push the status of photography to that of art.[11] Steichen's subsequent series of photographs published in the April issue of *Art et Décoration* that year have a discernibly austere and studied air. Arrestingly statuesque, they appear to glory in the literal meaning of the term *mannequin*, about which Evans comments, 'Derived from the word an inanimate dummy, *mannequin* seemed brutal and shocking when applied to the living woman, *le mannequin vivant*. It suggested an unwarranted passivity and that she was an object, yet it was also accurate and practical.'[12] Amplifying the sculptural and pictorial dimensions of his images, these photographs are widely considered to be the first instance of the fashion photographic shoot. There had already existed documentary photographs of models in fashion houses, and the transactions between models, couturiers and prospective buyers, but there had never been a suite of images with the same ambitious, scenic quality. Steichen's photographs have a decidedly dreamy air, as if extracted from an anterior world. But even if the birth of the first fashion shoot seems sudden and serendipitous, a glance at Steichen's earlier photography makes the progression seem more predictable. There are photographic works from 1899, for example, such as *Woods in Rain* and *The Pond*, that belong to pictorialist 'tonalist' school of American photography practised by the likes of Homer Martin and Dwight Tryon.[13] These are of subdued and atmospheric landscapes, purposely mildly out of focus, that evoke the work of painters like Daubigny and Corot, as well as the elegantly abstracted, stylized moodiness of the landscapes of Whistler and Klimt. Before he devoted himself almost solely to photography, his paintings of his twenties reveal a persistence with moody landscapes and portraits with mysterious chiaroscuro effects.[14] It was the feeling of mystery that he ably infused into his early fashion scenes, heightening the 'Oriental' allure of Poiret's designs.

In his essay on Steichen's formative years between Paris and New York, Joel Smith describes how Steichen grew up in the epicentre of cosmopolitan culture in which art and design were dynamically blurred. Having seen the developments of various secession movements in Munich, Berlin and Vienna, as well as the exhibition held at Siegfried Bing at his gallery, L'Art Nouveau, Steichen received a rich osmotic schooling on the way in which decorative objects, including furniture, interior panelling and architecture, could decoratively concatenate to form a stimulating and beautiful composite. Steichen became sensitive to the way in which 'a wide array of formats and materials' could form 'carefully arranged ensembles', thereby 'transposing composer Richard Wagner's dream of the *Gesamtkunstwerk* – a "total", all-embracing artwork – to the components of the bourgeois interior'. This was a period when 'the mysterious and the provoking defined the height of fashion. Objects of art were to complement one another yet allow for recombination, like accessories in a Parisienne's wardrobe.'[15] It was no doubt this instinct for decorative composition and adaptation that made him so sympathetic to the prospect of a fashion shoot, in which the models are like decorative dolls that share in their environment, complementing, rather than dominating, the lines, patterns and shapes around them. Hence fashion photography from the very beginning begins with fantasy; offering a pictorially stylized image of a world that is possibly not nearby, and possibly not inhabited by real sentient beings.

Until these images by Steichen, this different, appealing, intriguing, enviable world had not yet been conjured up. Hitherto these qualities inhered in the garment, the wearer, or the wearer's celebrity, to which was attached a train of associations provided by the still new medium of film. Magazines such as *Harper's Bazaar* had been publishing since the 1860s, yet it was only after Vogel's suggestion that fashion photography entered such magazines in earnest, not only as a way of beefing up content but also to attract advertisers. For these new kinds of fashion images were able to impart a sense of setting, and thereby to project luxury and lifestyle.

The momentum that these images produced was abruptly cut short by the First World War, where Steichen would produce many memorable images. Following the war, he returned to fashion imagery as chief photographer for

Figure 7 Edward Steichen, *Gertrude Lawrence*, 1928. Gelatin silver print. Thomas Walther Collection. Edward Steichen Estate and gift of Mrs. Flora S. Straus, by exchange. Acc. n.: 1869.2001. The Museum of Modern Art, New York (MoMA) © Photo SCALA, Florence.

Condé Nast, which published *Vanity Fair* and *Vogue*, *Allure*, *Brides*, *Glamour*, among numerous other non-fashion titles including *The New Yorker*. During this time Steichen produced an array of photographs, such as those of Gloria Swanson, Greta Garbo and Marlene Dietrich, that would become the definitive, iconic images. Steichen was later appointed as Director of Photography at MoMA, a position that he held until 1962. Despite this position, Steichen remained a lover of glamour and of the ability of photography to be both seductive and pervasive, qualities essential to fashion photography, although not limited to it.

Steichen's own reflections on fashion and commercial photography reveal his sharp pragmatism about what it entailed and what was specific to them. 'In the production of the fashion photograph,' comments Steichen in an article for *Vogue* in 1929,

> the given instant is not a normal happening – like the sunset, a landscape or a street scene – which may be photographed as the result of sensitive observation and patient waiting. The fashion photograph is more complex, as it is the picture of an instant made to order.[16]

What strikes us here is his assertion that the fashion photograph 'is more complex', whereas we, today, are traditionally made to believe that the opposite be the case. Steichen goes on to describe the complex orchestration of which the fashion photograph is the culmination. He stressed not only the variety of the skills it draws on to manage the sense of contrived verisimilitude, but the importance of the photographer (usually) himself in crafting the mood of the photograph:

> In addition to directing the activities of his assistants in the adjusting of the lights, camera angles and backgrounds, the photographer plays the clown, the enthusiast, the flatterer. He acts and talks all these things while his mind is watching the building up of the picture – its lights, shadows and lines, its essential fashion photograph requirements – distinction, elegance, and chic. He must instill a thrilling interest in himself, the model, editors, the helpers, so that all eyes and senses are in alert activity. A lapse into boredom is apt to prove fatal.[17]

Steichen offers a seldom discussed insight into the fashion photograph's genesis. In addition to the complex machinery and the contrivances of the photographer's personality, there must be energy. This is in direct contrast to artistic photography – if we can make a conventional, archaic distinction in the manner of Steichen and leave out the mass of art photography from then until now that is in a complex dialogue with commercial photography – in which the artist attempts to express himself through a subject by letting that subject disclose itself. Fashion photography on the other hand has a momentum that is not only the photographer maintaining a degree of intensity for an optimal result, but it must also take into account that the model, the make-up artists and other support staff are paid by the hour or the day. While all forms of representation involve manipulation and rearticulation, the fashion photograph discloses something assumed already given (the commodity) while the work of art something hidden.

When Steichen was appointed as the head curator of photography for MoMA in 1947, the librarian Beaumont Newhall resigned. Until then, no one in the museum made any great claims for photography, but Newhall's 'Photography 1839–1937' is widely considered to be a milestone in shifting the perception of photography in the direction of fine art.[18] To be sure, Stieglitz and other photographers had had their advocacy, but their voice could only carry so far, deprived of the weight and exposure that a MoMA exhibition could provide. When he offered justification for his resignation, Newhall explained that while he respected Steichen, he did not trust the prospects of working with him: 'My interests were simply in the art of photography; his were increasingly in the illustrative use of photography, particularly in the swaying of a great mass of people.'[19] This statement was both accurate and not, since it presumes a bifurcation in photography that is more coherent than it really is. However it does describe a difference between art and commercial photography, yet not allowing for the possibility that a photograph can enjoy success in both spheres. Steichen instinctively knew this, and he is the foundational example of how art and fashion photography constantly encroach on each other, by invitation, or trespass.[20]

Fashion photographers in the first half of the twentieth century

Adolph de Meyer

In 1913, *Vogue* appointed its first official fashion photographer, 'Baron' Adolph de Meyer. Born in 1869, de Meyer was very much a man who carried the nineteenth century with him, and like many upwardly mobile and eccentric figures of the time, had the audacity to dredge up an obscure, or possibly fictitious, aristocratic lineage to grant himself the auspicious credentials proportionate to his clients. The court flatterer of photography, de Meyer saw his chief task was to depict wealth, luxury and leisure. While photographing for *Vogue* he also published in *Vanity Fair*. In 1922, after quitting *Vogue* the previous year, he went on to *Harper's Bazaar* in Paris, where he stayed until returning to New York in 1938 before the outbreak of the Second World War.

In his heyday, de Meyer photographed such celebrities as Lillian Gish, John Barrymore and Irene Castle. Strongly inflected by the early days of film, his photographs retain a theatrical quality that belongs firmly within the terrain of pre-sound cinema, in which gesture and expression played important roles. De Meyer's example was a firm one, since he was a consummate technician, his photographs steeped in lighting that was at turns moody or which sculpted the bodily form and the surrounding objects with super-real crispness. Beaton is said to have called him the 'Debussy of photography', a comment that smacks of a parlour-room patter, although it does connote the scenic and the suggestive. Like Steichen, de Meyer imbibed pictorialist tradition in photography of the end of the previous century and took great pleasure in dressing his sitters up to convey a high level of phantasy and flair. In many respects de Meyer is an important marker in the ethos of fashion photography that climaxes with Newton, inasmuch as it presents images of desire of states of being that are well outside of the constraints of earthly beings. Yet as we will see, Newton drives the camp potential of this visual excess to a limit with self-reflexive candour, while de Meyer's images trade in the transgressive potential dormant in the act of dressing up, and of contrived scenery, for the easier wager of being simply celebrations about what it is to be rich and envied.

George Hoyningen-Huene and Horst

De Meyer was a salient example of the way that the early days of fashion photography were tightly bound to class and social prestige. Bearing a more legitimate title was the Russian-born Baron George Hoyningen-Huene. Fleeing the Russian Revolution, Hoyningen-Huene, like many cultured émigrés, ended up in Paris, where at the age of twenty-five he was running the photographic department of French *Vogue*. Ten years later he moved to New York, where his chief client was *Harper's Bazaar*. Hoyningen-Huene was also a meticulous craftsman, and was well known for his talents with lighting, which also made him a popular society and celebrity portraitist. In 1931, while still in Paris, Hoyningen-Huene met Horst Bohrmann, better known as simply Horst, who served briefly as his model and as his lover. Horst had a solid background in design, having attended the Kunstgewerbschule in Hamburg, and studied under Moholy-Nagy in the Weimar Bauhaus. He moved to Paris to study under Le Corbusier, who himself had had an earlier distinguished career as a painter. Thanks to Hoyningen-Huene, but also to his magnetic imagination, Horst began photographing for *Vogue*, with his first published image in November 1931, and his first exhibition the following year.

This occurred modestly in the basement of a bookstore (La Plume d'Or) in Passy in Paris, but it was reviewed rapturously by Janet Flanner, the French correspondent for *The New Yorker*, shooting him to almost overnight fame. That the exhibition contained a picture of Flanner may have had something to do with it. She writes of Horst's 'linear romance [which] may be taken as descriptive of the Franco-German defection from the standards of abstraction and ugliness which so obsessed Continental photography'.[21] Flanner's phrase 'linear romance' is the best way to begin describing Horst's style, which has a rewarding fullness, a crisp sculptural quality, owing perhaps to his architectural background. Horst had evidently also begun to absorb some of the contemporary experiments by the Surrealists, Bauhaus and the Russian Avant-Garde. One of the characteristics of avant-garde photography was to abstract physical elements in order to amplify formal relationships. Horst preferred this aspect over the tendency to abstract the surface and transform the photographic surface into something more resembling painting and collage (as with, say, photograms). With varying degrees of audacity, Horst was able to set up a dialogue between the figure and the ground that in many cases lifted the image away from real life and into an enclosed, artificial, and uncannily timeless realm. Unlike de Meyer, whose models inhabit a setting and engage in an implied narrative, Horst's models self-consciously pose – in other words, they play at being something different from who they are, acting as dolls or doubles, and therefore something nether-worldly and unreal. It appears that Horst learned a great deal from the baroque painters such as Georges de la Tour, Caravaggio and Rembrandt who used dramatic contrasts in light to sculpt bodies and to give them emphatic presence within time.[22] His crisp and relentless lighting ensured that bodies were often conveyed as waxworks (above and beyond the image entitled *Waxed Beauty* of 1938), the figures teetering between life and idealized petrification.

The celebrities that Horst's photographs hosted comprise another dazzling list, comprising Bette Davis, Noël Coward, Cole Porter and Elsa Schiaparelli. In 1937, shortly after Hoyningen-Huene, Horst also moved to New York, where he met Coco Chanel with whom he would have a lifelong professional relationship. Given that, in Horst's own words, 'Chanel worked closely with Dalì and Cocteau and Balanchineon theatre and ballet costumes',[23] she became the main gate of access to some of the most diverse and brilliant artists and designers of the time. But it was particularly this intertwining of high fashion and Horst's close contact with Dalì and Man Ray that consolidated a style that could best be called elegant avant-gardism. The Surrealists had a particular love of mannequins and dolls, as they symbolized the uncanny other-double, and also parallax, or alternative consciousness. Aside from his personal work, in his own bread-and-butter capacity as fashion photographer for *Vogue*, Horst was able to make ample use of the overlap between fabricated mannequin and the living *mannequin*, both manipulable avatars, agents of the unreal universe whose existence helped to sustain the (misguided) belief that the real world was indeed real. His ability to straddle the stylized oddities of Surrealism with the exigencies of commercial photography is borne out in the cover for New York *Vogue* from 1940 (Figure 8). It features Lisa Fonssagrives – the Swedish-born model frequently referred to as the first supermodel – in various calisthenic poses forming the letters V-O-G-U-E. True to both fashion and Surrealism, the body is used as an objective device. Horst capitalizes on what one commentator would later refer to as her 'lofty sophistication, impossible slimness and radiant physical well-being'.[24] With images like these Horst can be seen to be an exemplary practitioner of female objectification, rife in both Surrealism and fashion photography. But if we choose to look at artists less as perpetrators, Horst's approach may be more charitably observed as objectification of any body, on a par with the stylization of any thing,

Figure 8 Model Lisa Fonssagrives in blue-and-white bathing suit by Brigance, seated in V position and spelling out VOGUE above; Cover of the 1 June 1940 issue of *Vogue*. Photo by Horst. Horst / Vogue © Conde Nast.

in which the *objectif* (the French for photographic lens) plays the disinterested vivisector of form. In this regard Horst's work has an arrestingly aloof air. It is his ability to subdue urgency in the image that helps to dispel the latent anxiety in all fashion that it is already of yesterday. And it was this subtlety of expressing a sense of 'for all time' that made his style so sympathetic to a designer like Chanel.

Horst's time in New York, the 1930s, was part of an enormous period of growth for fashion photography, largely spearheaded by Condé Nast. This period was also when Steichen's authority remained unquestioned, and all fashion photography said to be worth its name was compared to him. Horst's relationship with the company ended when Condé Nast himself said, 'If you can't make a good picture out of this dirty ashtray – a picture that could be hung in a museum – you are no photographer. I realize, of course, that you are no Steichen'. Horst replied that if he didn't think that one day he would be as good as him he would never have embarked on photography, causing the enraged Condé Nast to tell him that Horst's contract would be terminated after the expiration in six months. Horst left for Paris on the next boat.[25] Apart from being juicy, the anecdote not only reflects the supremacy of Steichen and the extent of his influence, but it also reveals the way that fashion photography had come to have its own particular trajectory. Condé Nast's imperative of the 'good picture' has to do with the photograph as the instrument, the tool, with which any object whatsoever was lifted to suggest a potential it did not have in the everyday lived world. The role of the commercial photograph was to make the world appealing, to charge the object with a memorable effect, and to rival works of art through the transcendence of time. In other words, the 'good' commercial photograph must sustain the fashion object beyond its inherent temporality, and aim to lift the image from its transitoriness to the realms of 'classic'.

Horst's career straddled several eras. Owing also to his long life (he died in 1999 aged 93), Horst had a considerable effect on fashion photography and on the slow recognition of photography as an art form in its own right. He had associations with some of the biggest celebrities of the twentieth century, from Marlene Dietrich to Tom Wolfe (both of whom he expressed displeasure in meeting).[26] Influencing photographers such as Richard Avedon and Irving Penn, his presence looms large in the work of Robert Mapplethorpe, whom he also photographed, as Mapplethorpe did him. Mapplethorpe would provocatively amplify on what in Horst remains a veiled homoeroticism, and would continue the depiction of flowers with immaculate and steely intensity.

Cecil Beaton

In 1931 during an earlier stint in Paris, Horst accompanied Hoyningen-Huene on a winter sojourn to England to meet Beaton, who was working for British *Vogue*.

Aesthetically speaking, Cecil Beaton was at that time much the successor of de Meyer, but a far more complex character in more than one respect. Like Steichen, he was a man of wide-ranging talents in which fashion photography played but one part, becoming notable as a writer, and later as a stage and costume designer, which won him an Academy Award. A component of Beaton's success was to be aware of the extent to which status and celebrity had shifted from the previous century due to the persuasive power of photography. Beaton observed that after the First World War, the leisure class had melded with celebrity, naming this new class the 'pleasure class' and also the 'plutography'.[27] The neologism suggests that these people ruled the world of photographic images, just as the photographic image ruled over them, since it projected – and was certainly the kind of idealization that Beaton followed – an aspirational level to a class that, in theory at least, had achieved their aspirations.

In many respects Beaton stood at the crossroads between the reverential photographic icon of the Royals, and commerce. For while photographs, in the form of cartes-de-visite, of Royal personages had been an important propaganda tool since the mid-nineteenth century, it was not until the following century that these images became available in newsprint. As soon as this became possible, in Britain and in Europe, depictions of members of the royal family became staple fare in news media.[28] This was a practice that was so prevalent and popular that in 1939 the Manchester *Daily Sketch* publicized the impending photographs of Queen Elizabeth as an incentive for sales:

> To-morrow the 'Daily Sketch' will publish wonderful pictures of the Queen, taken specially by Cecil Beaton at Buckingham Palace. The pictures will be treasured in hundreds of thousands of homes throughout Britain and the Empire. Make sure of them by ordering your copy of the 'Daily Sketch' from your newsagent to-day.[29]

The photograph in question marked an end point in more than one respect, for during the war the Queen was not depicted in the same jewelled splendour, and Beaton himself turned to more realist and sombre subjects relating to the depredations of wartime Britain. This transition is notable, since one of Beaton's primary aims was to beautify, tasking his retoucher (yes, an independent specialist profession in those days) to go to great lengths to eliminate unwanted wrinkles or discolouration of the skin, and to smooth other surfaces where required. Beaton would continue this in later portraits such as that of 1950, where the cosmetic effects are remarkable. Beaton had arrived at these commissions from his immaculate portraits of celebrities. In the words of Alexis Schwarzenbach:

> Actors needed photographs for personal publicity. In order to satisfy their clients Beaton and [Dorothy] Wilding made them as attractive as possible by

retouching their faces and bodies in the same way in which they later also retouched their royal photographs. Furthermore, Beaton and Wilding frequently worked as fashion photographers, which enabled them to portray their thespian sitters in line with the latest trends and styles. By commissioning the most fashionable and up-to-date stage photographers the royal family therefore tried to capture the imagination of their subjects in the same way as popular actors did. Thus, while in the nineteenth century companies began to use royal portraits to sell a great variety of consumer goods, [. . .] in the twentieth century royal families began to employ professional publicity techniques of consumer society for their own public-relations purposes.

Today's royal families in fact depend on the closely knit nature of celebrity, wealth, perception and fashion. However, after the Second World War, and as we will see in later chapters, the link between royalty and celebrity became increasingly tenuous until it was severed in the 1970s, when fashion photography more widely embraced perversity and the grotesquerie. While beauty for its own sake is exploited and excelled at in contemporary fashion photography, it coexists with darker aesthetic currents that were all but non-existent in the pre-Second World War period.

Richard Avedon

Unlike Steichen, who went from art to fashion photography, Richard Avedon began in commercial photography and gradually transitioned to art, becoming one of the most revered art photographers of the end of the twentieth century. After showing an interest in photography at a young age, Avedon's career was launched early when he became recognized by *Junior Bazaar* then *Harper's Bazaar*. By twenty-three his work was also taken up by *Life* and *Vogue*. By the 1950s, he was an established name in fashion circles and achieved a form of celebrity status by the 1980s, when he had major commissions from the likes of Versace and Revlon.

Avedon's work has a strikingly hyperreal quality, but not in the manner of the blinding crispness of a photographer like Horst. Unlike Horst, in which the bodies have a relative equivalence to objects, shadows and related echoing forms, Avedon placed a premium on the individual, psychological qualities of the sitter. His works manage a rare equilibrium of the staged and the spontaneous; if there is a strong sense of formal intentionality, it is inflected by the indeterminate elements of the lived humanity. It was primarily this responsiveness to the personality and physical presence of the sitter that lent his work to art photography, where it is held up as a standard for the photographer's empathy. Where Cartier-Bresson is remembered for the defining moment, the instant that incorporates all the other instants that it must omit, Avedon's photographic time is patient and penetrating, managing to instil a sense of presence in the photographic image that few photographers have achieved. According to Richard Silberman, Avedon's celebrity portraits

> could be surprisingly grim: a somber Marilyn Monroe gazing off into space; Humphrey Bogart old and tired, without the tough-guy sneer. Where Avedon's fashion work offers glamour, wit, and elegance, his portraits often employ an earnest, clinical directness, as if to make photographs into X-rays and expose the skull beneath the skin.[30]

It is generally recognized that his only rival was Irving Penn with whom, in the view of Bettina Friedl, 'a new fashion aesthetics' came to be invented.[31] This was toward a style that sacrificed the rhetoric of timeless universality to the contingency of human experience and expression (although Penn attempted to rival still-life painting in his photography with arguably less success).[32]

The kinds of photographic truths sought by both Avedon and Penn could only be had by allowing the subject to perform. Avedon confessed that he had learned this through the study of painting, particularly the self-portraits of Egon Schiele and Rembrandt. In his own words:

> The point is that you can't get at any thing itself, the real nature of the sitter, by stripping away the surface. The surface is all you've got. You can only get beyond the surface by working with the surface – gesture, costume, expression – radically and correctly. And I think Schiele understood this in a unique, profound and original way. Rather than attempting to abandon the tradition of the performing portrait (which is probably impossible anyway), it seems to me that Schiele pushed it to extremes, shattered the form by turning the volume up to the screen. And so what we see in Schiele is a kind of recurring push and pull: first toward pure 'performance', gesture and stylized behavior, pursued for its own sake, studied for its own sake. Then these kinds of extreme stylizations are preserved in form, but disoriented, taken out of their familiar place, and used to change the nature of what a portrait is.[33]

Avedon later declares:

> The ultimate expression of this kind of performance – extreme stylized behavior – is of course fashion, where everything – the entire body, hair, makeup, fabric – is all used to create a performance. So many portraits in the history of art are fashion portraits, fashion images, as in so many beautiful Klimts.[34]

This is quite a grand claim, but we'll be content to draw attention to the way in which Avedon gives primacy to fashion imagery as 'the ultimate kind of performance'.

It is perhaps because of this that Avedon in his political work was drawn to the spectacle. By the 1960s Avedon's practice had diversified from high-end fashion and celebrity photography to images of topical political figures, hotel patients, Vietnam protestors and, memorably, victims of war. But although he is well regarded as a fine artist, Avedon is arguably more firmly camped in fashion photography. The psychological sting of his subjects cannot resist the self-conscious smugness of celebrity, and the viewer knows that the fascination is more with the latter. In fact, it is Avedon's genius, if it can be called that, to protect the sham vapidity of celebrity by masking it in a nimbus of sincerity and pathos that is sometimes there, sometimes hanging over the subject like visual muzak.[35] Avedon anoints his celebrity subjects with the 'ordinary', intimate and sincere, while ensuring that this is only a ploy. To take up Avedon's own testimony, they perform at being humble and real, yet their celebrity is precisely what seems to have transcended these qualities to reach a more substantive power. But by pretending at the qualities that are inimical to celebrity, the viewer's appetite for voyeurism is well and truly whetted. Avedon's more politically oriented works, while bearing the mark of a highly gifted photographer, are more like afterthoughts – footnotes in an oeuvre that has played an important role in our celebrity-obsessed age.

Lee Miller

A curious case in the interwar era was that of Lee Miller, who was both model and photographer, often simultaneously. Becoming a fashion model for *Vogue* in 1927 while an art student in New York, Miller very quickly set herself up within the crossroads of art and fashion. In October 1930 she appeared as the lead female role, a draped statuesque figure bedecked in butter and flour, for Jean Cocteau's first film *The Blood of a Poet*. Earlier that year she had participated in the 'Bal Blanc', or white ball, where she was photographed by Man Ray amidst a group of white-clad classical looking figures. Man Ray, who fell in love with her, unhesitatingly took on Miller as an assistant. From there, the imbrication between fashion and art in her world was decisive, since she not only practised commercial photography but immersed herself in experimental non-commercial photographs which had a clear Surrealist bent, with a taste of the denatured and the bizarre. As Becky Conekin explains, a mark of Miller's versatility was the ease with which she moved from one side of the camera to the other. Self-consciously orchestrating her own doubling, her simultaneous position of both seer and seen, as Conekin argues, disrupts the 'active/passive/male/female/photographer/model dichotomies that underlie most narratives of fashion photography'.[36] She continued to consort with artist photographers, including Peters Hans and László Moholy-Nagy, and in May 1934 she was listed together with Beaton as

'The most distinguished living photographers'.[37] Far different from Beaton, however – who in the interwar years was much the court flatterer, the Winterhalter of celluloid – Miller's example not only serves to show the porous boundaries between the growth of fashion and the twentieth-century avant-garde, but also the extent to which fashion photography used art in inventing the language of dreamscapes and artificial worlds that are both remote but deeply within us.

After the Second World War

It was not until the post-Second World War era however that photography became the norm in fashion representation 'reflecting our desires in increasingly tempting and explicitly erotic ways'.[38] The most commonsense reasons can be cited for this, reducible to the pervasiveness of photography and the cheapening of photographic prints in magazines and newspapers. The manual illustrator, while still occupying a place in editorial company, was slowly becoming a niche operator. Besides, there was simply too much fashion and production for illustration to keep up. And with the introduction of television in the 1950s in the United States, people were becoming increasingly used to seeing fashionable and well-attired and appointed bodies in settings, acting out certain roles. By dint of cultural osmosis, the representation of fashion evolved from the discrete, pictorial realm of the autonomous drawing-design to that of an image that pretended to have congress with the so-called real world through suggestions of narratives that in turn reflected a promise of what could be. From the 1950s, fashion photography would continue to tread this inherently contradictory line between what is and what could be. By comparison, in the early days of painterly representation, from Winterhalter to Tissot, the visual dialogue was in the past, soldering the present to a deeper tradition, subverting the suspicion that fashion was transient through sedimentation in traditions that had the authoritative air of permanence. In the early half of the twentieth century, fashion colluded with the utopian aims still alive in architecture and philosophy, in portending a brighter future and a better life. Unlike the other endeavours, though, fashion was materially reducible to the lived body – however, it was the representations in advertising that ensured that this reducibility was only material, since the idea was always elsewhere. The subject wearing fashion both assumed a role but also, paradoxically, was always on the path seeking out a role and concept permanently beyond her grasp.

By the more permissive 1970s, what also becomes noticeable was the extent to which fashion photography maintained a close relationship with film. This manifests on a number of fronts. The first has been covered in the discussion of several photographers above, especially Beaton, where celebrities, from the nobility to film stars, maintained a strong attachment, and interest, in the fashion industry, either directly or on a de facto level. It was also attractive for a film star to enter into commercial photography, as he or she was accompanied by the narratives and identities that were played out and writ large in the cinematic fictions. And as fashion photography evolved, it became more allusive and sophisticated, quoting and troping contemporary events. Thanks to its representation, an important dimension of fashion was telling a story, or being buoyed by a set of assumptions and expectations that were tied to events, fictional or otherwise, it did not matter.

Finally, like film, and as we will see in the chapters that follow, fashion photography would become increasingly intertextual. It would indulge in insider jokes, visual puns, quotations, pastiches, riffs and homages. Unlike art, for which borrowing, stealing and appropriating can be occasionally fraught, just as fashion made its peace with the commodity, so did it with stealing – fashion styling simply used the airily anodyne word 'inspiration'. Similarly, fashion photography, whose goal was to intrigue and lure, operates as a form of conjuring. Its goal is to escape the vulgarities associated with product advertising and to invoke a different world. Unlike the pre- and interwar years, however, this world would not always necessarily be made from the most beautiful substances, and would not always connote the most blissful states. Rather, fashion photography would become imbued by degrees with danger and fear, the two things that distinguish immobile beauty from the dynamism of sex. As we will see in the example of Helmut Newton in Chapter Four, already by the 1970s the spectre of pornography began to hover over the fashion image.

In a special issue of *Fashion Theory, the Journal of Dress, Body and Culture* dedicated to the theme of fashion and pornography, Pamela Church Gibson and Vicki Karaminas examine the role that pornography has played in the construction of the fashion image. If sex sells, it sells particularly well in fashion. Fashion and pornography are connected in various ways. Fashion like pornography chooses the body as a site of desire: both 'expose the body, fragmenting it by cropping and foregrounding the culturally eroticized parts of it, and both use stereotypically gendered and eroticized tropes.'[39] The representation of women in fashion images in the 1970s was the most 'perniciously sexist imagery yet encountered in the very core of sexual stereotyping'.[40] This was aided by the popularization and rise of pornography amongst middle-class adults as a suitable form of consumption. Sex became more glamorous and more threatening; a sense of decadent malaise permeated fashion magazines. There were two dramatic changes in fashion photography: the immense rise in popularity of street photography and the advent of the double-page spread. Fashion photographers, Rebecca Arnold says,

> reveled in images that were an affront to bourgeois morality, blending forties sophistication with an air of sexual deviance. The multi-layered references of

the settings, in crepuscular city streets and opulent hotel rooms, gave an impression of a kind of 'fashion *noir*'. Models exuded the same sense of fatal beauty embodied by the heroines of forties films, viewed as sexualized and dangerous, bringing with them confusion and potential destruction.[41]

It was during this time that Guy Bourdin began photographing fashion images in a style that was sexually provocative and suggestive of violence, often depicting women in scenes of death, mutilation and decapitation – women whose bodies were often brutalized. 'Although this type of photography has frequently been attacked as misogynistic,' comments Valerie Steele, 'some feminists defend it against charges of sexism, on the grounds that it is '"subversive" and "liberating", because it makes explicit the subtexts that are latent in other fashion images: themes like narcissism, lesbianism and the male gaze.'[42] Under the tutelage of Man Ray (who was also a successful fashion photographer for magazines *Vogue* and *Harper's Bazaar* photographing garments by the leading designers of the 1920s and 1930s: Poiret, Worth, Vionnet, Lanvin, Chanel and Schiaparelli), Bourdin went on to become fashion photography's l'enfant terrible. Bourdin's campaigns for shoe designer Charles Jourdan (1967–1981) enforced the pre-eminence of the image over the actual product and often contained a psychological narrative. In the 1975 advertising campaign, a single Charles Jourdan platform shoe in red patent leather is discarded near an electric wall socket. One side of the electric lead is plugged into the wall; the other side lies on the floor next to a wall socket that oozes red blood. The model and the missing shoe are absent from the image, leaving the viewer wondering, could this be a murder or suicide scene, or perhaps even a terrible accident. In another campaign for Charles Jourdan shoes dated 1970, Bourdin creates the archetypal silent-film plot of a young damsel tied to the railway tracks of an oncoming locomotive that will result in her imminent death. In both images, the shoes have become a substitute for the impact of the picture as a whole.

At a time when women were campaigning for equality and asserting their rights, women's magazines like *Vogue* were publishing sexually explicit advertising images and fashion editorials to maintain themselves financially. Whether these images were liberating or objectifying women is open to speculation. Kathy Myers comments on the contradictory messages these images contain:

> The erotic photograph trades on a dubious tradition of sexual libertarianism, which invests that which is censored with the power to disrupt and liberate. Hence the 'erotic' – whether it alludes to sadism, nihilism or whatever – is acclaimed as a sexually liberating force.[43]

It is precisely these undertones of sexual brutality that become increasingly popular in representations of fashion in the following years.

The boundaries between pornography, erotica and the fashion image have been routinely stretched. In the 1980s photographic technology had advanced such that it could confer on its subject an imposing verisimilitude. The fitness movement that emerged out of California in the late 1970s gave rise to bodybuilding among men and women and led to the increased consumption of supplements and products aimed at creating physical strength and muscular bodies – 'super bodies'. According to Marc Stern, it was these 'same people who watched the same movies and TV shows, who saw the same advertising and who consumed the same products and cultural images of beauty, sexuality, masculinity, femininity power and identity'.[44] The popularity of gym culture, the excess of the capitalist boom before the 1987 crash together with the photographic sophistication of photographer Herb Ritts led to the appearance of the super models: Cindy Crawford, Eva Herzigova, Helena Christensen, Christie Brinkley, Naomi Campbell and Linda Evangelista. In 2002, Veronica Horwell wrote in Herb Ritts' obituary for the *Guardian*, 'Ritts suited the emerging taste of the time, the gay-inspired, high-concept Hollywood and fashion culture that venerated the perfect body and the celebritous face.'[45]

The proliferation of gay and feminist critiques and the growth of the retail industries, marketing and advertising paved the way for the 'New Man' phenomenon that shifted the representation of traditional hegemonic male subjectivity that was portrayed as active to passive agents. This shift in discourse and representation that influence images of contemporary masculinity occurred as a result of the wider social movements of the 1970s such as feminism and movements for sexual liberation such as gay and civil rights that disrupted traditionally held views of race, gender and sexuality and promoted a model of democratic equality. The rise of style magazines for men such as *GQ* and *Arena* not only targeted heterosexual men as consumers but also pursued the 'new' gay market coined the 'pink dollar'. Depictions of masculinity contained pornographic visual codes to produce contemporary images of men that appealed to a wider audience. The influence of gay pornography also attributed to key developments in the representation of masculinities in fashion iconography. The active man of the 1960s and 1970s was replaced by the overtly passive, reclining male (a representation afforded only to women), inviting men not only to consume the products but also to look at themselves and other men as objects of desire.

> The body is either draped with garments establishing recognized signs of social and sexual status, or is devoid of garments establishing a new-found strength by representations of the physique. The 'fashion-signifer', is no longer the garment but the male nude.[46]

Photographers Herb Ritts and Bruce Weber were at the forefront in constructing homoerotic images of masculinity that circulated amongst mainstream fashion media from the 1980s. (Ritts' and Weber's major contribution to the reframing of masculinity is discussed further in Chapter Six.) By the end of the 1990s the 'pornification' of fashion imagery and the culture of celebrity were firmly embedded in popular culture.

In the September 2006 issue of *Vogue Italia*, Steven Meisel photographed models portraying terrorists and policemen. The editorial concept *State of Emergency* was of restricted liberties in post-September 11 North America. The images caused an outcry from feminists who argued that the models were portrayed in violent compositions and were represented as victims in opposition to the male models. And again, in the entire July issue of *Vogue Italia* 2008, Meisel only used black models as a response to the racism prevalent in the fashion industry. 'Reaction to Vogue Italia's "black issue",' Sarah Mower wrote in *The Observer*, 'is electrifying the industry, forcing the fashion world to reconsider its resistance to using non-white models.'[47] Other photographers that have made statements in representations of fashion include Steven Klein, whose controlled and hyper-visual imagery challenges socially constructed identities.

In the 1990s photographers played with images of ambiguous gender and sexuality with notions of gritty excess. Shot in sleazy yet glamorous settings such as cheap hotel rooms or back-street laneways, image-makers mixed 'trashy porn' aesthetics with documentary realism. Fashion models are shown in ever more brutal images, argues Rebecca Arnold, 'that both flout and fear the anxieties of decay, disease and physical abuse'.[48] The shift from groomed fashion spreads of the past to a gritty realistic style of photography became a prominent feature of fashion imagery with the likes of photographers Terry Richardson and Juergen Teller.

Benetton hired Richardson to shoot their advertising campaigns for the Sisley Fall/Winter 2010/2011 collections. 'The result was a meeting of soft-porn sleaze and middle market fashion. Photographed in a supermarket, the models are sprawled on the floor of a produce aisle, groping one another and licking cucumbers suggestively.'[49] Juergen Teller has also chosen this 'harsh reality' style of photography to document fashionable garments on 'real people' as opposed to glamorous photoshopped models. His images are often harshly lit, exposing the flaws on mottled or tired skin, bruises and flaws rather than an unattainable 'supermodel' body. Teller's raw aesthetic is a response to the over-styled images so common to fashion photography; 'so retouched, so air-brushed,' says Teller, 'without any human response at all, and, well, you don't really want to fuck a doll.'[50]

This gritty style of photography that rejects the 'perfected' and ideal beauty of the fashion model is becoming an increasingly significant aspect in fashion representation as the myth of the sanitized and ideal body is fast losing currency. 'In its inherent search for the new,' writes Elliott Smedley, 'fashion stumbled upon this particular photographic practice which, while rooted in the avant-garde, went on to penetrate the mainstream. Perhaps the images that proliferated did more than present a challenge to conventional ideals, suggesting that fashion was now more democratic and that anybody could be fashionable.'[51]

Notes

1 Des masques se tendent à nous,/mais on sent en dessous/les visages qui se plissent/et qui, sous prétxte d'abandon,/intiment satisfont/à leur gout d'avarice./Tout es double; à tout une grâce suppposive/prête ce trouble remous/entre desux rives. Rainer Maria Rilke, *The Complete French Poems of Rainer Maria Rilke*, trans. A. Poulin Jnr., New York: Graywolf Press, (1979) 1986, 282–283.

2 Terry Eagleton, *The Event of Literature*, New Haven and London: Yale U.P., 2012, 137; our emphasis.

3 Michael Carter, 'Fashion Photography: The Long, Slow Dissolve', *Photofile*, 4 (4), 1987, 5; the author's emphasis.

4 Ibid., 6.

5 Cit. Valerie Steele, *Paris Fashion: A Cultural History*, Oxford and New York: Berg, (1988) 1998, 224.

6 Cit. Alenka Zupancic, *The Odd One In: On Comedy*, Cambridge MA: MIT Press, 2008, 77.

7 Ibid., 78.

8 Caroline Evans, 'Multiple, Movement, Model, Mode', in Christopher Breward and Caroline Evans, eds., *Fashion and Modernity*, Oxford and New York: Berg, 2005, 130.

9 Nancy Troy, *Couture Culture: A Study in Modern Art and Fashion*, Cambridge, MA: MIT Press, 2003, passim.

10 Cit. Jennifer Craik, *The Face of Fashion Cultural Studies in Fashion*, London and New York: Routledge, 1993, 98. See also 'Introduction', in Eugenie Shinkle, ed., *Fashion and Photograph: Viewing and Reviewing Images of Fashion*, London and New York: I.B. Tauris, 2008, 3.

11 Penelope Niven, *Steichen: A Biography*, New York: Clarkson Potter, 1997, 352.

12 Caroline Evans, *The Mechanical Smile: Modernism and the First Fashion Shows in France and America, 1900–1929*, New Haven and London: Yale U.P., 2013, 186–187.

13 William Innes Homer, 'Edward Steichen as Painter and Photographer 1897–1908', *American Art Journal*, 6 (2), 46.

14 Ibid., passim.

15 Joel Smith, *Edward Steichen: The Early Years*, New York and Princeton: Metropolitan Museum of Art and Princeton U.P., 1999, 15.

16 Edward Steichen, 'A Fashion Photograph', *Vogue* (12 Oct 1929), 99, repr. In Edward Steichen, *Selected Texts and Bibliography*, Ronald Gedrin, ed., Oxford: Clio Press, 1996, 78.

17 Ibid., 79.

18 Christopher Phillips, 'The Judgment Seat of Photography', *October*, 22, Autumn 1982, 30ff.

19 Cit. Phillips, ibid., 40.

20 As Phillips states, 'the next fifteen years were marked by Steichen's inclination not to give a "hoot in hell" for photography conceived as an autonomous fine art'. Ibid., 41.

21 Cit. Valentine Lawford, *Horst: His Work and His World*, New York: Knopf, 1984, 65.

22 See also Martin Kazmeier, 'Horst P. Horst, Photograph', *Horst: Photographien aus sechs Jahrzehnten*, Munich, Paris and London: Schirmer-Mosel, 1991, 16.

23 Horst P. Horst, *Salute to the Thirties*, New York: Studio, 1971, 12.

24 Rosemary Ranck, 'The First Supermodel', *The New York Times*, 9 February, 1997, www.nytimes.com/1997/02/09/books/the-first-supermodel.html.

25 Lawford, *Horst*, 83.

26 M. Kazmeier, *Horst*, 22–23.

27 Martin Francis, 'Cecil Beaton's Romantic Toryism and Symbolic Economy of Wartime Britain', *Journal of British Studies*, 45 (1), January 2006, 90.

28 Alexis Schwarzenbach, 'Royal Photographs: Emotions for the People', *Contemporary European History*, 13 (3), August 2004, 257.

29 Ibid., 257–258.

30 Richard Silberman, 'Richard Avedon: Evidence 1944–1994; New York and Cologne', *The Burlington Magazine*, 136 (1098), September 1994, 641.

31 Bettina Friedl, 'The Hybrid Art of Fashion Photography: American Photographers in Post-World War II Europe', *American Studies*, 52 (1), 2007, 49.

32 For a deconstruction of Penn's pastiche of still-life painting, see Rosalind Krauss, 'On Photography and the Simulacral', *October*, 31, Winter 1984, 49–68.

33 Richard Avedon, 'Borrowed Dogs', *Grand Street*, 7 (1), Autumn 1987, 55–56.

34 Ibid., 57.

35 For an appropriation of this view, see the review by Silberman, 'Richard Avedon: Evidence 1944–1994', 642.

36 Becky Conekin, 'Lee Miller's Simultaneity: Photographer and Model in the Pages of Inter-war *Vogue*', in Eugenie Shinkle, ed., *Fashion and Photograph*, 76. See also Becky Conekin, 'Lee Miller: Model, Photographer and War Correspondent in *Vogue* 1927–1953', *Fashion Theory*, 10 (1–2), March–June 2006, 97–125.

37 Cit. Conekin, 'Lee Miller's Simultaneity', 79.

38 Rebecca Arnold, 'The Brutalised Body', *Fashion Theory: The Journal of Dress, Body and Culture*, 490.

39 Pamela Church Gibson and Vicki Karaminas, 'Letter from the Editors', *Fashion Theory: The Journal of Dress, Body and Culture*, Fashion and Porn Special Issue, 18 (2), April 2014, 118.

40 Rosetta Brookes, 'Fashion Photography: The Double-Page Spread: Helmut Newton, Guy Bourdin and Deborah Turbeville', in Malcolm Barnard, *Fashion Theory: A Reader*, London and New York: Routledge, 2007, 520.

41 Rebecca Arnold, 'The Brutalised Body', *Fashion Theory: The Journal of Dress, Body and Culture*, 3 (4), 493.

42 Valerie Steele, 'Anti-fashion: The 1970s', *Fashion Theory: The Journal of Dress, Body and Culture*, 1 (3), 292.

43 Kathy Myers, 'Fashion 'n' Passion: A Working Paper', in Angela McRobbie, ed., *Zootsuits and Second Hand Dresses: An Anthology of Fashion and Music*, London: Macmillan, 1989, 192.

44 Marc Stern, 2008, *The Fitness Movement and Fitness Center Industry 1960–2000*, Business History Conference, www.thebhc.org/sites/default/files/stern_0.pdf, 5–6.

45 Veronica Horwell, 'Obituary: Herb Ritts. Photographer who Turned the Glamorous Celebrity Lifestyle into Art', *The Guardian*, Sunday, 29 December, 2002, www.theguardian.com/news/2002/dec/28/guardianobituaries.artsobituaries.

46 Teal Triggs, 'Framing Masculinity. Herb Ritts, Bruce Weber and the Body Perfect', in Juliet Ash and Elizabeth Wilson, eds, *Chic Thrills. A Fashion Reader*, Berkeley: University of California Press, 1993, 25.

47 Sarah Mower, 'Fashion World Stunned by Vogue for Black', *The Observer*, Sunday 27 July, 2008. www.theguardian.com/lifeandstyle/2008/jul/27/fashion.pressandpublishing.

48 Rebecca Arnold, 'The Brutalised Body', *Fashion Theory: The Journal of Dress, Body and Culture*, 3 (4), 1999, 489.

49 Pamela Church Gibson and Vicki Karaminas, 'Letter from the Editors', *Fashion Theory: The Journal of Dress, Body and Culture*, Fashion and Porn Special Issue, 18 (2), April 2014, 119.

50 Juergen Teller, in Pamela Church Gibson and Vicki Karaminas, 'Letter from the Editors', *Fashion Theory: The Journal of Dress, Body and Culture*, Fashion and Porn Special Issue, 18 (2), April 2014, 119.

51 Elliott Smedley, 'Escaping to Reality. Fashion Photography in the Nineties', in Stella Bruzzi and Pamela Church Gibson, *Fashion Cultures. Theories, Explorations and Analysis*, London and New York: Routledge, 2000, 152.

3

THE LITTLE BLACK DRESS AND *CAPITOL COUTURE*

In the film *Murder!* (1930) by Alfred Hitchcock, there are several incidences of multiple identity and alias. The story tells of an actress, Diana Baring, who awakens with blood on her clothing next to another actress whom she has assumedly murdered. The actress playing the actress, Norah Baring, bears the same surname, setting up a series of incidences that arise as we reach the film's end. A juror in the murder trial is a stage actor and theatre manager, Sir John, who also, implausibly (as a juror), was the person who recommended that Diana join the acting troupe. Believing in her innocence, Sir John sets about investigating the murder, which he suspects was actually perpetrated by Handel Fane, who, as irony would have it, is known for his roles as women. He casts Fane in one of his productions that also happens to involve murder. In the audition Fane is found out to be 'half-caste' and therefore dissimulating as a white man; Fane believes his identity and his culpability have been uncovered and kills himself on stage. The final scene sees Diana, dressed opulently in a fur, welcomed in a dazzling setting by Sir John. Only then do we realize that this is a scene in a new play. In the former play designed to enact the circumstances of Diana's murder, Sir John discovers that he is in love with her. Earlier indifferent, it is only once he has begun to transpose her story onto stage that he begins to consider her. It is only through her *semblante* or double that he can begin to unite with her.[1]

More famous cases of the double exist within Hitchcock's oeuvre, such as *Shadow of a Doubt* (1943) and most notably *Vertigo* (1958). Yet the sequence of a play within a play, and actors acting as actors, the convolutions that lead to disclosures about the truth about the murder and the truth of Sir John's feelings for Diana, help to direct the tenor for this chapter. Some of this content surfaced in the previous chapter with the discussion of Sargent's *Madame X*, who becomes an object of desire only once re-embodied in paint, and only once enacting a certain role of preening defiance. *Madame X*'s black dress will be remembered, whose only erring from austerity is the generous décolleté supporting model Virginie Gautreau's generous bosom. During the late nineteenth century, many wealthy American women travelled to Paris to purchase garments, and artists like John Singer Sargent were kept busy painting portraits of wealthy men and women. However, Sargent's career was placed at risk with his portrait of the American-born French Creole socialite Virginie Gautreau, identified as Madame X (discussed at length in Chapter One), who was depicted wearing a very-low-cut black dress with a shoulder strap hanging over one arm, suggesting either pre- or post-coital activity. This louche depiction, writes Stephen Gundle in his history of glamour, produced a horrified reaction. 'Not even the capital of sex appeal was ready for a society portrait that presented its female subject as a debauched woman of pleasure.' The black dress etched its way into fashion history becoming synonymous with sex and a sign of sexiness. We are therefore compelled by more than the content; as once we know we have been enticed through something we cannot exactly see and therefore trust, deliciously enticed, or repelled, or both.

As we saw earlier in the confluence of celebrity, nobility and fashion, tendencies in film are inseparable from the shifting expectations and codes of taste that emanated from the fashion world. That is to say that ever since film re-evolution in the United States (since feature film began in Germany) from the 1930s, fashion and film had a symbiotic relationship. While celebrities and other social notables called upon the photographic adepts in fashion, film stars began to insist that they be dressed by couturiers. One citable example of this was when Marlene Dietrich made it a precondition of her contract to Hitchcock that if she were to star in *Stage Fright* (1950), she would be dressed exclusively by Dior. In other cases costume designers played the role of couturiers: as Travis Branton, Edith Head or Adrian Greenberg (better known as just 'Adrian') can all be said to have designed only for the (mostly female) leads in the film.[2] In 1948 Vivien Leigh, before she won fame with *Gone with the Wind* (Fleming, 1939), appeared in British *Vogue* in dresses designed by Cecil Beaton.[3] Or then there is Cary Grant who after the 1950s when had become a superstar insisted on choosing his own suits. After the famous Space Age collection of 1964, André Courrèges, while never entering into film, certainly exerted a strong influence over the sci-fi and retro films of the day. By the 1980s, when corporate sponsorship through product placement became more aggressive and something of a norm in film, it became all but expected for the main stars to be dressed by the most popular fashionable designers. Another notable example in recent years is Keira Knightley, who was dressed by Jacqueline Durran for her role in the adaptation of *Anna Karenina*. To concur with the movie's release, Durran signed a deal with Banana Republic to make an exclusive Karenina range.[4] These are but a small handful of examples. Today the infiltration of fashion design in film is ubiquitous. Giorgio Armani, Miuccia Prada, Valentino (Garavani), Jil Sander, Jean Paul Gaultier, Salvatore Ferragamo and Roberto Cavalli are only a small list of names of designers who have worked in film, or whose designs have been plentifully featured.

Although we might compose an ever-mounting list, in the history of cinema, two films stand out as most central to fashion. The first is an unlikely but, in retrospect, incontestable candidate, *Breakfast at Tiffany's* (1961), starring Audrey Hepburn and directed by Blake Edwards. The other is more self-evidently the film adaptation of *The Hunger Games* trilogy written by Suzanne Collins. In the first, Hepburn plays a character that she is definitely not, a call girl, while the second film is littered with fashion as excess and spectacle. Indeed no other film serves to highlight the importance of fashion and style to class and social control as *The Hunger Games* trilogy (Lionsgate). One has become a classic in the film genre while the other has been placed into sartorial film history as it brings the world of fashion into the mainstream.

The little black dress

As one of the standard classics of fashion, the black dress is imbricated in the phenomenon of the fashion system itself, and increasingly as it became wedded to representation. For the black dress is both a garment and the stand-in for the absence of a garment. This paradox has nothing to do with nudity, rather it has to do with the frontier, or limit of fashionability, in which the garment is the always inadequate replacement for desire itself, of body, figure, identity and image reaching to something to which fashion in itself only portends. By being black and simple in line, the black dress – conventionally now known as 'little' even when it is long – is ipso facto classic and generic. In being black and simple it announces itself as classic prior to being instated as perennial within time. And by denying, or limiting, its stylistic signature, it addresses the wearer's status and identity on one hand and the very promise of fashion, fashion's outside, on the other. It therefore becomes the very site for desire itself, recalling the Lacanian insight that what desire most desires is desire itself. The black dress is therefore at the epicentre of fashion's inter-relation with representation since its very reducibility shifts its meaning into the site of the imaginary – there must be more – which, as we have seen, was how fashion photography evolved in the late twentieth century. From the statements of wealth in painting, photography developed from statements of existence (this is the fashion) to registers of what a person, with fashion, could be and achieve. With the black dress, one dresses up without entirely doing so, thus displacing the meaning away from the garment to hypothetical thought and action.

The provenance of the long black dress designed by Givenchy with which *Breakfast at Tiffany's* is visually synonymous is with the *little black dress* introduced in the 1920s. It was an important component in the broader modernist project of universal styling, epitomized by the Bauhaus, whose objectives were to design articles – furniture, cutlery, clothing, and so on – that were adaptable and versatile. Because it is black, it was more disposed to evening wear and soon became worn as the quintessential cocktail dress, the garment most sympathetic to accessorizing, offsetting hats, scarves, shoes, jewellery and gloves. Although attributing one of its origins in mourning, it was with the black dress that black in womenswear ceased to be solely funereal, and was politically coterminous with the rise of the women's movement, for with the black dress, however eye-catching its details, one looked at the wearer, not the dress.

The black dress has a double origin and, ironically, is complicit in imitation and copying. While mainstream wisdom credits Coco Chanel with its inception, it was in fact Jean Patou, who in the mid-1920s was the most famous and influential designer of his time. Not only did he play a large part in integrating the fashion model to the fashion industry, but he opened up the range of women's clothing. Exceeding the binary between formal and informal wear, with his shop Coin de Sports ['sport's corner'], Jean Patou introduced sport, play and physical activity as concepts within fashion, which have enjoyed a particular resurgence in the last three decades (Ralph Lauren's *RLX* and *Polo Sport*, *Armani Sport*, *Zegna Sport*) even penetrating into fragrance lines. In 1925, the same year as he opened his store, Jean Patou created what was, arguably, the first unisex fragrance, *Le Sien* ['his/hers']. The message from the 'sport' concept is that the garment – or the fragrance – is characterized by a certain lack of encumbrance to allow for a level of exertion exceeding that of everyday social and work activity. What is striking of the entry of fragrances into this field, and of garments like jeans and collared shirts into contemporary fashion lines, is that 'sport' reigns as much, if not more, as an idea than in terms of testable utility. But it was sport, whether as an actual activity or mere allusion, that was the arena by which women entered into modern public life. Accompanying his fragrance Patou announced, 'Sport is the territory where men and women are equal.'[5]

Despite this credit to Patou, his greatest rival, Chanel, was also an unrivalled imitator. She too favoured austere styles of dress, and was herself known for her short hair. Chanel made sure that she was at the centre of the equation where simplicity equalled elegance. Her designs emphasized a woman's silhouette with the emphasis on subtlety, not exaggeration. By 1929 Chanel joined Patou and Lucien Lelong in branching into prêt-à-porter lines. Two years later, in her visit to the United States, Chanel observed the processes of mass production. Understandably the mass production of the little black dress found its parallels with Fordist production, also calling to mind his famous dictum, 'any colour, so long as it's black'. The association was strong enough to prompt American *Vogue* of October 1926 to announce, 'The Chanel "Ford" – the frock that all the world will wear', although by this time Chanel had well and truly cemented the garment as an institution and, rightly or wrongly, her own creation.[6]

As well as being practical, the black dress, which by the 1930s had become available to a much larger market, also tended to break down the division between the middle and upper classes – in look at least – reminding one of Baudelaire's comment almost a century before about the uniformity of black in men's dress.

Making very good use of magazines and newspapers to endear her still-expensive designs to the masses, for Chanel the little black dress was the optimal sartorial alibi to the kinds of narratives used to drive advertisements. These were narratives that revolved around lifestyle, health, leisure – all allies to 'sport' – and wealth. Still in the early 1920s women were dressing in corsets and bustles, the black dress that replaced them was based on the 'less is more' modernist schema in one very important rhetorical respect, and that was that one was supposedly so confident of one's wealth that one did not have to show it. It was also reflective of a woman of action and agency as opposed to a woman as decorative object, or connubial chattel. This being the case, the little black dress was also a convenient vehicle for those who in fact didn't have so much, but who were not in a much easier position to play the part of those that did.

There is no male equivalent for the little black dress – its closest fashion equivalent is perhaps jeans, which is a basic armature able to support an endless series of tweaks and variants. But whereas jeans are rooted to their working-class origins (even in 'dress-up-dress-down' couture versions), the black dress is firmly associated with couture, and is a rite of passage for any aspiring designer, much as a young chef must master a perfect soufflé. This is thanks not only to the legacy of Chanel, but to Hubert de Givenchy, who designed all of Audrey Hepburn's clothing in *Breakfast at Tiffany's* (1961), and would go on to design almost everything she would wear in subsequent films, and in public.

Just as in the way Chanel usurped Patou in the credit-line, it seems that the black dress is a garment with one origin that is succeeded with an overshadowing one in its wake. *Breakfast at Tiffany's* (1961) was not the first significant film to popularize the black dress, for in 1932 Marlene Dietrich in *Shanghai Express* (von Sternberg, 1932) wore a somewhat diabolical black dress designed for her by Travis Banton. Banton continued to work for Paramount Pictures, designing Anna May Wong's dark and elaborate costumes, many of which were far from simple but they were sleek and black. A small time later Rita Hayworth appeared in *Gilda* (Vidor, 1946) wearing a strapless black satin dress designed by Jean Louis. Yet despite this genealogy, as Valerie Steele affirms, the dress worn by Hepburn 'helped permanently imprint an age of the little black dress the world over. Yet popular attention focused more on Audrey Hepburn herself rather than Givenchy',[7] affirming our contention that it is representation's power of conferral – personality, setting, imagination – that acts as an essential driver in a garment's meaning, its dissemination, and its subsequent duplication and adaptation.

Breakfast at Tiffany's

The first encounter the reader has with the unforgettable female protagonist Holly Golightly of Truman Capote's *Breakfast at Tiffany's* (1958) is through a double representation, that of a photograph and that of a sculpture:

> In the envelope were three photographs, more or less the same, though taken from different angles: a tall delicate negro man wearing a calico shirt and with a shy, yet vain smile, displaying in his hands an odd wood sculpture, an elongated carving of a head, a girl's, her hair sleek and short as a young man's, her smooth wood eyes too large and tilted on the tapering face, her mouth wide, overdrawn, not unlike clown lips. On a glance it resembled most primitive carving; and then it didn't, for here was the spit-image of Holly Golightly, at least as much of a likeness as a dark still thing could be.[8]

Not long after the narrator first sets eyes on her late at night trying to enter the apartment block but having lost her key: 'It was a warm evening, nearly summer, and she wore a slim cool black dress, black sandals, a pearl choker.'[9] Subsequently he observes with resignation:

> Of course we'd never meet. Though actually, on the stairs, in the street, we often came face-to-face; but she seemed not quite to see me. She was never without dark glasses, she was always well groomed, there was a consequential good taste in the plainness of her clothes, the blues and grays and lack of luster that made her, herself, shine so. One might have thought her a photographer's model, perhaps a young actress, except that it was obvious, judging from her hours, she hadn't time for either.[10]

Already the narrator is conscious of Holly as posing and acting, and can imagine her as a formal image. Her good taste is thanks to 'the plainness of her clothes', which only piques his imagination all the more. For she exists not only in life, but also as something she could, or might, become.

The film adaptation of *Breakfast at Tiffany's* (Edwards, 1961) has Holly emerge from a taxicab that stops at Tiffany and Co. on fashionable Fifth Avenue. Dressed in the now legendary black dress, she eats a snack as she looks in the shop's windows (Figures 9 and 10). The black dress creates a dramatic silhouette in each scene, marking Holly/Hepburn out from the rest of the characters. Essentially the film is about Holly's machinations to afford herself a better station in life; the black dress is therefore commensurate with her enigma, before her past is revealed, and she finds the error of her ways. Early in the film Holly's former husband Doc Golightly appears, disclosing to Paul that her real name is Lula Mae Barnes. It turns out that the marriage has been annulled, although

Figure 9 Audrey Hepburn looking into the window of Tiffany and Co. *Breakfast at Tiffany's* Dir: Blake Edwards © Paramount Pictures and A Jurow-Shepherd Production, 1961. All rights reserved.

Figure 10 Audrey Hepburn looking into the window of Tiffany and Co. *Breakfast at Tiffany's* Dir: Blake Edwards © Paramount Pictures and A Jurow-Shepherd Production, 1961. All rights reserved.

Doc cherishes the vain belief he can have her back. Holly toys with the idea of marrying first Rusty Trawler, then José da Silva Pereira, both for reasons of money. The happy ending is that she chooses love over avarice, falling finally for the main protagonist, Paul (George Peppard). Typically narratives of the upward mobility involve clothing in some form or another. They are described in fiction – as with the transformation of Lucien de Rubempré in Balzac's *Illusions Perdues* – sometimes very elaborately shown in film, clothing being the most graphic modulator of beauty and status. But in the film *Breakfast at Tiffany's*, the dress for which it is so famous appears at the very beginning, suggesting that it is what is underneath, in the sense of character, that counts. Whereas the conventional transition is from poor and drab to expensive and dazzling, the heroine announces herself as already someone with inestimable gifts and with potential. The dress conveys the message that she need not try too hard to get what she wants. Its rhetoric is that the woman's qualities are innate. The dress functions only to accentuate what is already there, like salt enhancing flavour in food.

Initially it seemed incongruous that Hepburn should play such a character: capricious and sexually manipulative. However, it is the grace for which she was best known that becomes an adequate foil to these traits; a grace that she by all accounts fully assumes once she has sloughed off her undesirable qualities at the end. While the black dress was already positioned firmly within the fashion system, with *Tiffany's* and Hepburn, the association was indelible.

That's entertainment: *The Hunger Games* and *Capitol Couture*

> What do they do all day, these people in the Capitol, besides decorating their bodies and waiting around for a new shipment of tributes to roll in and die for their entertainment?
>
> Suzanne Collins, *The Hunger Games*

The recent spate and popularity of teen novels adapted to film tell us something about the power of consumption that young adults wield in today's retail environment. Dystopian and apocalyptic fiction, and the realization that technology may do more harm than good, have been at the forefront of young adult fiction and film. Such films include the romance fantasy series *The Twilight Saga*[11] centred on a family of vampires and written by Stephanie Meyer, and J.K. Rowling's seven fantasy novels based on the adventures of the young warlock Harry Potter, and his friends Ronald Weasley and Hermione Granger, all of whom are students at 'Hogwarts School of Witchcraft and Wizardry'.[12] No other film adaption, however, serves to highlight the importance of fashion and style to class and social control than the film *The Hunger Games* (Ross, 2012) and the sequels *The Hunger Games: Catching Fire* (Lawrence, 2013), *The Hunger Games: Mockingjay, Part 1* (Lawrence, 2014) and *The Hunger Games: Mockingjay, Part 2* (Lawrence, 2015) produced by Lionsgate films. As Molly Creedon comments apropos of these films, 'fashion, it turns out, factors heavily into this dystopian future'.[13]

Based on the novels by Suzanne Collins, the film adaptation of *The Hunger Games* (directed by Gary Ross, with the screenplay by Ross, Collins and Billy

Ray) is set in a post-apocalyptic distant future in a totalitarian nation called Panem, which is divided into twelve poor districts, and a wealthy Capitol. Situated somewhere in North America and sometime in the future, Panem's post-apocalyptic world is full of fashionable excess, from Effie Trinket's Alexander McQueen garments to the tributes' costumes in the Chariot Rides. 'Cinema, as a potent generator of social imagery,' writes Patrizia Calefato, 'constructs futuristic science-fictional settings, often visualizing eternity and time through signs of luxury.'[14] Each year two young representatives from each district aged between twelve and eighteen known as 'tributes' are selected by lottery at the Reaping Ceremony to participate in the Hunger Games, an annual televised event. The tributes are forced to fight until the death in a process of elimination until the last remaining tribute claims victory. The Games were established by the Capitol as a reminder of its power, and in retribution and punishment for a rebellion that was led by District 13 that resulted in its destruction. The story begins with the 74th Hunger Games, and during the Reaping Katniss Everdeen (Jennifer Lawrence) from District 12 volunteers to take the place of her younger sister Primrose (Willow Shields) who is chosen as a tribute. Peeta Mellark (Josh Hutcherson) is the male tribute chosen from District 12.

The story of sacrifice and power is a familiar one; victorious armies have long demanded tributes of some form or another to cripple conquered peoples and to display their strength as victors. In several interviews, Collins attributes the central plot of *The Hunger Games* to the ancient Greek myth of Theseus and the Minotaur. As retribution for killing his only son at the Pan-Athenian Games, King Minos of Crete demands that every nine years the Athenians send a tribute of seven young maidens and seven youths who are released into a labyrinth then hunted down and devoured by the hybrid half-bull-half-man creature, the Minotaur. Arriving in Athens shortly before the youths are chosen, Theseus volunteers to serve as a male tribute in order to slay the beast. Like Theseus, Katniss Everdeen offers herself as a tribute. When Theseus arrives in the capital of Crete he is paraded (much like the film's tributes) before the citizens. Theseus catches the eye of King Minos's daughter Ariadne who falls in love with him, and offers him a ball of string to find his way out of the labyrinth once he has killed the Minotaur. Plainly the similarities between the Greek myth and *The Hunger Games* are manifold. Theseus is known as a 'founder-hero' in Greek mythology because he battles and overcomes a foe that is part of an archaic order. As the heroine and protagonist of the trilogy, Katniss is aware of the injustices that the Capitol deals out to the twelve districts and rises to lead a rebellion to overthrow the tyrannical leader Coriolanus Snow (Donald Sutherland). And like Theseus, who is helped by Ariadne to escape the labyrinth, Katniss is helped by her mentor and Games champion Haymitch Abernathy (Woody Harrelson), her stylist Cinna (Lenny Kravitz), the tributes' chaperone Effie Trinket (Elizabeth Banks) and the Games' sponsors.

However interesting a comparison between myth and story or a film plot may be, what is of interest and concern to this chapter is the way in which fashion, costume and style play a central role in constructing representations of identities and place in film. Dress (and costume) is a communicative tool and reveals much to do with culture, class, history as well as political affiliation. Dress reveals the way in which identities are managed and contained as a visual reflection of historical and cultural phenomena. Since Charles Eckert wrote the essay 'The Carole Lombard in Macy's Window' (1978), where he argued that the pattern and pace of the modern consumer were shaped by Hollywood, film costume continues to shape fashion and consumption via images of desire and through product tie-ins. For *The Hunger Games* trilogy, American cosmetic brand China Glaze launched a Capitol Colours nail varnish collection, and CoverGirl cosmetics released a line of make-up in colour palettes that evoke the twelve districts, including themes such as agriculture and fishing – District 4 and District 11's primary industries. Each look featured products for nails, lips and face. Samsung Electronics produced *The Hunger Games Movie Pack* application, which gave the user access to exclusive *Hunger Games* products, including scripts, book excerpts and video clips. And then there are the numerous fake copies of the *Mockingjay* pin created for the films by Etsy jewellery designer Dana Schneider that can be purchased on the Internet through Amazon and eBay. In *Fashion and Film: Gender, Costume and Stardom in Contemporary Cinema* (2016), Sarah Gilligan writes that in maximizing brand exposure, the official and unofficial *Hunger Games* products moderate messages of social concern and upheaval into vapid commodities: 'A satirical narrative of rebellion, class conflict and child murder becomes mediated into glossy campaigns for products, which seemingly ignore the tensions that are being explored on-screen.'[15]

Critical scholarship that explores the crossover between fashion, film and consumption is not new – cinema and fashion 'bleed across'[16] different modes of media. This includes digital imaging, the Internet, Facebook, Twitter and Instagram, forming transmedia worlds that exist across multimedia platforms. Gilligan argues that as contemporary popular cinema and television drama shifts, the text–spectator relationship becomes grounded in a participatory convergence culture, and screen costumes become characterized by what she terms 'tactile transmediality'. She writes that mediality elevates screen costume to a level whereby the spatial distance between spectator and text can be crossed via adornment enabling processes of performativity and identity to be played out in everyday life.[17] Gilligan believes that,

in constructing a transmedia universe that commodifies ambivalence, the cross-media tie-ins with *Covergirl*, *Capitol Couture* and Samsung promise the spectator that they can purchase a little bit of a futuristic, fantasy character's identity. On-screen looks, anti-fashion garments, future design fantasies and couture fashion trends become blurred and offered up as a transmedia reality to be consumed seemingly without comment or critique.[18]

Part of the *Hunger Games* marketing and cross-media campaign is the creation of a virtual reality website, thecapitol.pn, where the Capitol relays news and messages to fans who register as virtual residents of Panem. The site, and corresponding Facebook page, are themed as media hubs with headline news running alongside Effie Trinket's *Capitol Couture* magazine, whose tag line '*Oh So Couture*' highlights fashion trends and news from the fashion industry. Constructed as a fashion magazine and written in journalistic style, *Capitol Couture* contains an editor-in-chief and a list of contributors including fashion labels and designers. Virtual residents are invited to '*Be Fabulous. Be Capitol. Be Seen*'[19] as part of the *Capitol Style Challenge*, which is held online every Friday and offers citizens the opportunity to appear on the *Capitol Couture* site as a fashion model. The use of the word 'fabulous' in the tagline acts as an intertextual device that references the British sitcom *Absolutely Fabulous* (1992–2012), starring Jennifer Saunders and Joanna Lumley, which is based on the antics of two fashion-obsessed friends who wear bright and outrageous couture garments and have difficulty pronouncing certain fashion designers' names. In a sense, the subtle reference to a comedy about the 'frivolity' of fashion turns the site into a parody of the fashion industry. The site also highlights current fashion labels and trends that are considered appropriate for Capitol citizens, such as the Miu Miu glitter bootie, or Armani Privé, Chanel Haute Couture and Versace. The digital creation of an alternative reality, or a 'double life', also takes the form of highlighting the work of well-known photographers such as Nick Knight and David LaChapelle, fashion designer Iris van Herpen and fashion 'it girl' Daphne Guinness. The relationship between the online community with the costume and fashion portrayed on *The Hunger Games* and the 'real' fashion industry is as spectators sharing the fragments of a simultaneously experienced event. The simultaneous happening is marked by the sharing of the personal experiences of online residents with that of the film, blurring the division between reality, media and consumption. This double unbinding between 'real' and fictional images of 'fashion' raises implications for the ability of the audience/participant to distinguish between 'real fashion' and 'representational fashion'.

The Hunger Games trilogy is also a critique, or perhaps even a satire, of reality television and the celebrity that is a part of it. The Games follow similar rules, and, like makeover shows, the parading of fashion and the interviews are familiar from shows such as *America's Next Top Model* (UPN, 2002), the reality television series and interactive competition. The series contains nine to thirteen episodes and begins with ten to fourteen contestants. Contestants are given makeovers, and each week contestants are judged on their overall appearance, participation in challenges and the best photo shoot. One contestant is eliminated each episode until the last remaining contestant wins the game. For the tributes, their participation in the Hunger Games means that from the moment that their name is drawn they become celebrities under constant media surveillance. As part of the tributes' new media identity the contestants are 'made over', dressed and styled to the standards of the Capitol – which means removing all blemishes and scars, removing all body hair for the girls, and potentially the use of plastic surgery. Each tribute is assigned a stylist and a team of make-up artists who remodel their appearance and are paraded in front of the audience. The tributes' bodies become commodities to be changed, displayed and controlled according to the wishes of the Capitol. By providing Panem's citizens with entertainment and fashion in the form of a reality television show, the Capitol is able to assert its power and control over the district citizens using surveillance techniques whilst simultaneously 'numbing' the reality of poverty and hunger. Was it not Walter Benjamin who wrote in his great study of consumption and the Parisian arcades at the turn of the twentieth century that '[f]ashion is the medicament that will console for the phenomenon of forgetting on a collective scale'?[20]

Every detail of The Hunger Games from the tributes' garments, the choice of animals, ordering of obstacles, the scenery and the design of the arena is planned and controlled by the Head Gamemakers, Seneca Crane (Wes Bentley, 2012) and Plutarch Heavensbee (Philip Seymour Hoffman, 2013), who are in charge of entertaining the Capitol, including keeping abreast of the death toll, signalling canon fire for the deceased and the twenty-four-hour monitoring of the Games' tributes. The surveillance techniques employed by the Gamemakers act as a disciplinary mechanism and function as an apparatus of power and social control over the residents of the districts by the Capitol. The citizens of Panem have a duel relationship with the systems of surveillance. Whilst the televised game show allows them to follow loved ones and friends every year and aid them by purchasing supplies for the tributes, their involvement in the Games is compulsory and lack of attendance at the annual Reaping Ceremony is punishable by death. Surveillance not only acts as a reminder and tool of the citizens' oppression, but by attending the ceremony and watching and participating in the Games they become active in its functioning.

In the long shadow of the Internet, and the advancements in information technologies Michel Foucault's seminal text, Discipline and Punish: The Birth of the Prison (1991) hovers conspicuously in the background. Foucault takes as his starting point an interpretation of Jeremy Bentham's 'Panopticon', an eighteenth-century design for the ideal reformatory, which consisted of a circular building with an observation tower in the centre surrounded by an outer wall that contained prison cells and was the ideal method of surveillance because the prisoners were visible to the central watchtower. For Foucault, the 'Panopticon' represented the creation of modern subjectivity and a key device, both literally and figuratively speaking, in the determining of the modern subject. The belief that one is under scrutiny and is constantly being watched becomes a driving force in the modernist project. Foucault's concept of biopower, the legislation of people's bodies and their lives through the control of new technologies (Internet, sexual reproduction, birth control, etc.) is exercised and confirmed by today's social order and is a familiar theme that is represented in *The Hunger Games* that we as the audience recognize and identify with, albeit unknowingly. Curiously, in the third instalment of the trilogy, *The Hunger Game: Mockingjay, Part 1* (2014), the surviving rebels in District 13 use the media surveillance techniques in their favour by fabricating and broadcasting their own version of events as propaganda films. (Much in the manner of the way the US military fed the enemy incorrect information by broadcasting misleading and fabricated news stories.)

One departure from Foucault, however is the way that the distribution of power is far more Althusserian. Unlike Foucault, who maintained that the locus of power was a false decoy for what is unlocatable, and for whom power's relationship to knowledge means that it is always a matter of relations and exchanges, Althusser divides social and subjective relations into two camps. One he calls Ideological State Apparatuses (ISA), the other the Repressive State Apparatus (RPA). It would be tempting to form a longer digression on how these are applicable to this film, but we must confine ourselves to how these manifest in terms of dress and appearance. The RSA is the state itself and those who run it and the means by which they maintain their power. These are embodied in the despot, the king, the religious leader, and so on. ISAs are far more diverse and more nuanced and are the foundation by which ideology is reproduced, and the ways in which personal and social norms are regulated. These are institutions, or subjective systems with their rules and protocols, from the schools, to family structure, to police and the legal system. It can also apply to the communication systems such as the decisions that determine what is seen and what is not. The RSA belongs to the public domain and ISAs to the private.[21] When we apply these schemata to *The Hunger Games*, from a symbolic point of view ISAs are the districts, while the RSA is the nefarious urban elite running the Games. The districts are dressed in various shades of pale colours, while the elite are individualized and flamboyant to the point of eccentricity.

The Hunger Games begins with the Reaping Ceremony as the district citizens gather in the town square as tributes are chosen by a lottery system. The audience is introduced to the tributes' escort Effie Trinket who acts as the lotteries host who chaperones the protagonists Katniss Everdeen and Peeta Mellark to the Capitol to prepare them for the Games (Figure 11).

Clothing and styling play a major role in representing the contrasts and disparities between the wealthy Capitol and the District's poverty. Colour and choice of fabrics are used to highlight the differences between class status and social position. Katniss Everdeen and the district citizens are dressed in simple cotton garments in various shades of blue, and their hair is pulled back in

Figure 11 Peeta Mellark, Effie Trinket and Katniss Everdeen at the Reaping Ceremony.
The Hunger Games Dir: Gary Ross © Lionsgate, Color Force 2012.

plaits or simply tied back in either a bun or a loose ponytail. 'We looked at a lot of photographs of coal mining districts from the turn of the century to the 1950s, because we wanted it to have a very American feel,' costume designer Judianna Makovsky says of the costume design for the citizens of District 12.

> We wanted to make a very serious impact, and color was very important – to keep it mostly gray or blue . . . very cold because coal leaves a black dust everywhere. But we didn't want it so overly stylized that it wasn't a real place – it is a real place – it could be Appalachia, you know, a hundred or fifty years ago.[22]

By contrast, Effie Trinket's costume is ornate and constructed of plush fabric with excessive ruching and voluminous shoulders. The silhouette is almost theatrical and chosen to highlight the luxury and excess of the citizens of the Capitol by contrasting Trinket's bright fuchsia suit (Schiaparelli pink) with that of Katniss's drably muted blue dress. Trinket is heavily made up with a powdered face, bright-red lipstick and matching fuchsia-coloured eyeshadow to accentuate the evil under the artifice. 'These are people who like to watch children beat each other to death in an arena,'[23] says Makovsky, referring to the 74th Hunger Games. The effect gives the characters a ghostly, haunted look that is intended to evoke seventeenth- and eighteenth-century French court culture whose style and manners were determined by a small circle of the wealthy and privileged. Trinket's heavily made-up face and excessive hair is analogous to caricatures of pre-Revolutionary eighteenth-century courtly decadence. No single character embodies the role of the fashion muse or 'it girl' than Effie Trinket, whose glamour and ostentatiousness often verge on the outrageous and the kitsch. Dressed in haute couture Alexander McQueen, Trinket signals the woman of fashion and by implication the woman of high status. In the televised Victory Tour of Panem, Effie wears a Monarch Butterfly Alexander McQueen dress with Iris Van Herpen thorn soled boots from the Spring 2012 collection, and at the beginning of the Victory Tour Trinket wears a black-and-white fur-collared couture garment from the Fall 2012 McQueen Collection.

Portrayed as a fashion stylist, there is an element of the showgirl in Trinket that hints of sexual appeal, a key attribute for the performer. As the embodiment of fashion glamour, Trinket's character is the sartorial representation of status, wealth and style. 'Her costumes are characterized by excess,' writes Gilligan, 'her looks are too much: heels are too high, colours too gaudy, waists too tight, skirts too short and frills too large. She teeters uncomfortably, sacrificing being able to walk, bend or move properly, in favour of constructing herself as a slave to sartorial spectacle.'[24] 'Cosmetics, fine clothing, rich foods, gold, erotic dissoluteness spicy perfumes, heavy brocades: the mind is crowded with symbols and images that evoke splendor and profusion. An almost nauseous sensation accompanies these kinds of excess.'[25] Stella Bruzzi proposes that some film costumes function as 'iconic clothes': 'spectacular interventions that interfere with the scenes in which they appear and impose themselves onto the character they adorn'.[26] She makes the point that couturier designs in particular exercise this function, disrupting the narrative by creating an authorial statement by the designer for the specular gaze. Effie Trinket's garments by Alexander McQueen are therefore pure spectacle. The visual demonstration of noble status and rank determined fashionable dress and maintained conceptions of taste, which were driven by luxury and excess.

In *Théorie du luxe* (1771), Georges-Marie Butel-Dumont explains, 'Things are either necessary or superfluous; and that which is superfluous is luxury.'[27] Dumont's intention is not to depict luxury in the light of ostentation, but to portray the qualities of convenience, promoting the upper-class privilege of living a more comfortable life. In *Fashion in the French Revolution* (1988), Ribeiro writes that,

> with the French Revolution came for the first time, intrusive politics, a greater awareness of class differences, and a restless need for change and for self-expression – all ideas which were to be reflected in dress, that most sensitive of social barometers.[28]

In *The Theory of the Leisure Class* ([1888], 2007) Thorstein Veblen coins the term 'conspicuous waste' and proceeds to give the reader an explanation of the behaviour exercised by the affluent class and their habits of production and waste linked to the economy and social behaviour. The consumption and exploitation of fashion goods and beauty for example by institutions for their own personal gain denotes 'wealth' and is classified as 'waste'. 'Throughout the entire revolution of conspicuous expenditure,' writes Veblen, 'whether of goods or of services or human life, runs the obvious implication that in order to effectively mend the consumer's good fame, it must be an expenditure of superfluities. In order to be reputable, it must be wasteful.'[29] Veblen likens conspicuous waste to that of the middle class that he refers to as the 'leisure class' and identifies tastes and lifestyles rooted in historical periods. By leisure class, Veblen meant those who had the power to exploit and the commitment to idleness and lack of productive economic activity. There was a difference between those who made their way via exploitation and those who made their way via industry and labour. Veblen uses the ideas of conspicuous leisure, consumption and waste to explain the idea of fashions. As Veblen explains, 'no line of consumption affords a more apt illustration than expenditure on dress'[30] and offers three principals as a means to explain the changing of fashions. He notes that the 'great and dominant norm of dress' is the 'principle of conspicuous waste'. The second principle is 'the principle of conspicuous leisure', and the third is that the principle of dress must be 'up to date'.[31] Wasteful expenditure is greatly increased, he says, if each garment is to be worn for a short period of time.[32] The ability to replace a garment for another before it is worn out is characterized as waste and is evidence of wealth, or 'pecuniary strength' as Veblen puts it.

In the twenty-first century, conspicuous consumption is the demonstration and display of wealth and status akin to luxury, excess and waste. In *The Hunger Games* films conspicuous consumption is exercised through dress and the abundance (or lack) of food. The wealthy residents of the Capitol gorge on rich and exotic foods such as bread rolls shaped like flowers and oranges served with a sauce, 'a world where food appears at a press of a button' (Lionsgate) whilst the poorer residents of the districts are starving and whose labour is spent gathering food to feed the wealthy Capitol. In the words of Katniss Everdeen, 'In District 12 a plump person is envied because they are not scraping by like the majority of us.' The concept of excess consumption and luxury and the disparities between wealth and poverty are introduced to the audience after the Reaping Ceremony, when Katniss and Peeta, escorted by Effie, board the fast train bound for the Capitol in preparation for the Games. The high-speed Capitol train is suggestive of the *Shinkansen* network of high-speed bullet trains that connect Tokyo with the country's major cities and acts as a sign of capital, excess and 'quirkiness' that is stereotypically attributed to Japanese cultural production. In the film, the train becomes a metonym for modernity and the speed in which capital (including ideas) is produced and manufactured. The Capitol trains are used to transport tributes, government officials, food, produce and manufactured goods throughout Panem and connect the Capitol with the twelve districts. The citizens of Panem are prohibited from travelling by train unless they are a chosen tribute or on officially sanctioned duties. Ostentatious wealth is displayed in the design of the interior of the train with its luxurious polished panelled walls and fitted compartments, including a bedroom, a bathroom, a bar and a dressing room. This idea of luxury produced in the train's aesthetic spatial design can work as a cultural strategy that produces the idea of luxuriousness itself. As Patrizia Calefato has argued in *Luxury: Fashion, Lifestyle and Excess* (but in a different context), 'the strategy of the amplification, hyperbole, and sumptuousness of forms, characteristic of the baroque, returns today in synergy with new technologies, sometimes verging on the kitsch, in architecture, fashion, interior design and tourism'.[33] Much like the extravagant styling and set design of the film, which borders on the kitsch and the outrageous. The train's mahogany tables are laid out with sumptuous culinary delights and refreshments, 'eggs, ham and piles of fried potatoes' (Lionsgate), and the audience is introduced to Haymitch Abernathy (Woody Harrelson), a past victor of the Hunger Games who is represented as a drunkard. The textual reading here is made quite explicit, Harrelson's character partakes in excessive drinking as a means of escape from the horrors of his experience of the Games (represented with all the character traits of a returned war veteran), whilst simultaneously alluding to the Capitol's excessive consumption. The train scene where Haymitch, Peeta and Katniss sit at the abundant table of food is quite Dickensian and draws almost intertextually on *Great Expectations* (1861). In Charles Dickens' novel, the young protagonist Pip meets the wealthy old spinster Miss Havisham, who, abandoned by her groom on her wedding day, is sitting at the head of a wedding banquet covered with rotting food waiting for his eventual return. The novel's themes are comparable to those of *The Hunger Games*: wealth and poverty, love and rejection (Katniss falls in love with Peeta and rejects Gale Hawthorne's love (Liam Hemsworth)) and the eventual triumph of good over evil.

Katniss's and Peeta's fashion make-over process for the pre-Games begins when the high-speed train arrives in the Capitol and they meet their stylists Cinna (Lenny Kravitz) and Portia (Lartasha Rose) whose task it is to prepare complimentary garments for the Tribute Parade, also known as the Chariot Rides, that create an image of unity between Katniss and Peeta. The Chariot Rides form an important component of the film, especially in terms of costume and spectacle. The tributes arrive in numerical order into the arena on chariots, like gladiators parading in the Coliseum, dressed in costumes representing their districts' colours and industry. As a public event, the parade creates a symbolic link between the citizens of the districts and the Capitol and distracts them from their dreary lives of poverty and hard labour. In *Rabelais and his World*, Mikhail Bakhtin discusses carnivalesque, a speech genre, which occurs at particular cultural sites, such as the carnival, or in this case, the Chariot Rides. It is a moment when everything is permitted and is marked by excess and grotesqueness. It is a type of communal performance with no boundary between the audience and the performer and creates a type of alternative space that is characterized by freedom and abundance. Like the Chariot Rides, the carnival creates a whole collective body rather than a single individual voice. 'All were considered equal during the carnival, here in the town square a special form of free and familiar contact reigned among people who were usually divided by the barriers of caste, property, profession and age.'[34] The self is transgressed through practices such as masking, or in this case, costume. The Tribute Parade takes the form of a pageant in this brief moment the reality of the social and economic divide between the citizens of the Capitol and the citizens of the districts is erased, the violence and death of the Games escapes its official channels and enacts a utopian vision of freedom.

The parades also double as a fashion runway, a stage for the appreciation of the spectacle provided by the tributes' costumes. 'Fashion goes hand in hand with the pleasure of seeing, but also with the pleasure of being seen of exhibiting oneself to the gaze of others.'[35] Following Guy Debord's critique in *The Society of the Spectacle* (1967), where he argues that modern life was dominated by the commodity and the false desires that it engenders, Caroline Evans writes that 'the fashion show is self-absorbed, or narcissistic, "spectacle onto itself", locked into its own world, self regarding, sealed in the show space of the runway, with its attendant protocols and hierarchies'.[36]

Representing District 12's coal-mining industry, Katniss and Peeta wear matching black garments with flaming fire and capes that look like wings and mimic burning coals (see Figure 12). Made from a synthetic stretch material with embossed plastic and patent leather, the garments capture the spectacle of the Games. In real life the dress and suit are unwearable, but they exist in the realm of the symbolic as a display of wealth, dreams and desires that suggests conspicuous waste. 'The realm of consumption is here transposed to the visual, for there is no other way in which we can consume it.'[37] 'The spectacle,

Figure 12 Katniss and Peeta wear matching black garments with flaming fire and capes for The Chariot Rides. *The Hunger Games* Dir: Gary Ross © Lionsgate, Color Force 2012. All rights reserved.

according to Debord, is 'capital become an image', the theatrical presentation of the Tribute Parade transforms the excesses of the Capitol into a dazzling display, aestheticizing and transforming the signs of capital (the primary industries of the twelve districts such as coal mining, masonry, agriculture, etc.) into an image of everyday wealth produced into commodity form.

Like the garments in the Tribute Parade, the conceptual theme of fire is also translated in the dress that Katniss wears in the interview with the Games host Caesar Flickerman (Stanley Tucci) the night before the start of the Games. The spectacle of the unwearable dress is made visible when Katniss twirls and the Swarovski crystals on the dress's hemline light on fire seducing the audience with its spectacular glamour. Makovsky says 'that [by] having this dress covered in flame-like jewels, it's no longer about Katniss. It's about the dress. First of all, [with] all those jewels [the dress] is going to be so heavy [and] it won't twirl. She won't be able to move or walk. People don't realize that.'[38] Much like fashion designer Julien Macdonald's Spring/Summer 2001 black knitted mini dress with a corsage on the shoulder that contained more than a thousand hand-cut De Beers diamonds, Katniss's dress begs the question of who or what exactly was commodified in fashion's spectacular excesses, Katniss or the dress. Writing on London-based designer Maria Grachvogel's diamond dress and Antonio d'Amico's wedding dress encrusted with 350 diamonds, Evans tells us how these garments 'evoked the showgirl's costume whose enormous feathered, wired and jewelled extensions spread many centimetres beyond her body, both framing and drawing attention to its near nudity like a jewel in its elaborate setting.'[39] Combining fashion's ability to create a world of surface and illusion with that of show business heightens the glamour of the Games. 'The creation of clothes as spectacle,' writes Bruzzi in her seminal book *Undressing Cinema: Clothing and Identity in the Movies*, 'is the prerogative of the couturier; the overriding ethos of the costume designer is conversely to fabricate clothes which serve the purpose of the narrative.'[40] Tom Gunning aptly writes that 'fashion in film serves as a transfer point between issues of great importance to the medium, visuality and the body. In film, fashion – modes of costume and clothing – reveals character traits and displays the bodies of stars'.[41] Character traits are representations that lie in cultural forms and their relations to production and reception. The Tribute Parade and the making of Katniss and Peeta as celebrities takes place in the Training Centre, a skyscraper located in the centre of the Capitol where the tributes live and train in preparation for the Hunger Games. Their escort, mentor, stylist and prep team stay with them during this period. The making and representation of Katniss and Peeta works as a 'doubling', whilst Katniss and Peeta are constructed as Game victors and fashion celebrities in the film they are also simultaneously portrayed as celebrities in 'real time' via product tie-ins, marketing and promotional strategies. *The Hunger Games* uses costume that doubles as fashion as a focus of the plot, character and identity. Fashion is a key element not only for suggesting wealth and social class but also in exploring a character's pursuit of identity through appearance.

Notes

1 Alenka Zupancic, 'A Perfect Place to Die: Theatre in Hitchcock's Films', in Slavoj Zizek, ed., *Everything You Always Wanted to Know About Lacan (But Were Afraid to Ask Hitchcock)*, London and New York: Verso, (1992) 2010, 77.

2 See Jonathan Faiers, *Dressing Dangerously: Dysfunctional Fashion in Film*, New Haven and London: Yale U.P., 2013, 13.

3 See also Pamela Church Gibson, 'Fashioning Adaptations: Anna Karenina on Screen', keynote presentation, 'Fashion in Fiction: Style Stories and Transglobal Narratives', City University Hong Kong, 2014.

4 Ibid.

5 Cit. Amy Homan Edelman, *The Little Black Dress*, New York: Simon and Schuster, 1997, 15.

6 Cit. Valerie Steele, *The Black Dress*, New York: Harper Collins, 2007, n.p.

7 Ibid.

8 Truman Capote, *Breakfast at Tiffany's*, (1958) e-book 2008, 6.

9 Ibid., 15.

10 Ibid., 19.

11 *The Twilight Saga* consists of five films adapted from Stephanie Meyer's novels for young adult readers. *Twilight* (2008), directed by Catherine Hardwicke, *The Twilight Saga: New Moon* (2009), directed by Chris Weitz, *The Twilight Saga: Eclipse* (2010), directed by David Slade, and the two-part film *The Twilight Saga: Breaking Dawn* (2011/12), Part 1 and 2, directed by Bill Condon.

12 The seven novels penned by J.K. Rowling were adapted into eight films. The first two films *Harry Potter and the Philosopher's Stone* (2001) and *Harry Potter and the Chamber of Secrets* (2002) were directed by Chris Columbus, *Harry Potter and the Prisoner of Azkaban* (2004) was directed by Alphonso Cuarón and *Harry Potter and the Goblet of Fire* (2005) was directed by Mark Newell. The four remaining films, *Harry Potter and the Order of the Phoenix* (2007), *Harry Potter and the Half-Blood Prince* (2009), *Harry Potter and the Deathly Hallows – Part 1* (2010) *and Part 2* (2011), were directed by David Yates.

13 Molly Creeden, 'Dressing The Hunger Games: Costume Designer Judianna Makovsky', www.vogue.com/873551/dressing-the-hunger-games-costume-designer-judianna-makovsky/. Accessed 1 January 2015.

14 Patrizia Calefato, *Luxury: Fashion, Lifestyle and Excess*, London: Bloomsbury, 2014, 50.

15 Sarah Gilligan, *Fashion and Film: Gender, Costume and Stardom in Contemporary Cinema*, Bloomsbury: London, 2016 (forthcoming).

16 See Pamela Church Gibson, *Fashion and Celebrity Culture*, London: Bloomsbury, 2012, 11.

17 www.academia.edu/223638/Fashion_and_Film_Gender_Costume_and_Stardom_in_Contemporary_Cinema. Accessed 2 January 2015.

18 www.academia.edu/9336182/Capitol_Couture_Fashion_Spectacle_and_Struggle_in_The_Hunger_Games._Invited_speaker. Accessed 5 January 2015.

19 http://capitolcouture.pn/post/58453399997/capitolstyle-challenge-every-friday-our-editors. Accessed 5 January 2015.

20 Walter Benjamin, *The Arcades Project*, ed. Rolf Tiedemann. Trans. Howard Eiland and Kevin McLaughlin, New York: Belknap Press, 2002.

21 See Louis Althusser, 'Ideology and Ideological State Apparatuses (Notes towards an Investigation)', trans. B. Brewster and G. Lock, in Slavoj Zizek, ed., *Mapping Ideology*, London and New York: Verso, 1994, 100–140.

22 Creeden, 'Dressing The Hunger Games'.

23 Ibid.

24 Sarah Gilligan, *Fashion and Film: Gender, Costume and Stardom in Contemporary Cinema*, Bloomsbury: London, 2016 (forthcoming).

25 Patrizia Calefato, *Luxury: Fashion, Lifestyle and Excess*, London: Bloomsbury, 2014, 52.

26 Stella Bruzzi, *Undressing Cinema: Clothing and Identity in the Movies*, London and New York: Routledge, 1997, xv.

27 Michael Kwass, 'Ordering the World of Goods: Consumer Revolution and the Classification of Objects in Eighteenth-Century France', *Representations* 82, 2003, 93.

28 Aileen Ribeiro, *Fashion in the French Revolution*, BT London: Batsford, 1988, 19.

29 Thorstein Veblen, *The Theory of the Leisure Class*, London: Teddington, [1899], 2007, 49.

30 Thorstein Veblen, *The Theory of the Leisure Class*. New Brunswick and London: Penguin, 1992, 118.

31 Ibid, 1992, 121–122.

32 Ibid, 1992, 122.

33 Patrizia Calefato, *Luxury: Fashion, Lifestyle and Excess*, London: Bloomsbury, 2014, 11.

34 Mikhail Bakhtin, *Rabelais and His World*, Indiana U.P.: Bloomington, 1984, 10.

35 Gilles Lipovetsky, *The Empire of Fashion: Dressing Modern Democracy*, trans. Catherine Porter, with a Foreword by Richard Sennet, Princeton, NJ: Princeton U.P., 1994, 29.

36 Caroline Evans, *Fashion at the Edge: Spectacle, Modernity, Deathliness*, Yale U.P.: New Haven and London, 2003, 67.

37 Ibid., 68.

38 Amy Wilkinson, 'Hunger Games Costume Designer Reveals Biggest Wardrobe Challenge' www.mtv.com/news/1681295/hunger-games-costumes/. Accessed 10 January 2015.

39 Evans, *Fashion at the Edge*, 113.

40 Stella Bruzzi, *Undressing Cinema: Clothing and Identity in the Movies*, London and New York: Routledge, 1997, 3.

41 Tom Gunning, 'Making Fashion Out of Nothing. The Invisible Criminal', Marketa Uhlirova, ed., *If Looks Could Kill*, London: Koenig, 2008, 22.

4

PERVERSE UTOPIAS

Helmut Newton

I am a voyeur! I think every photographer, whether he does pictures that are erotic or he does something else, is a voyeur. Your life goes by looking through a little hole. If a photographer says he is not a voyeur, he is an idiot! I think he can't be much of a photographer. It has nothing to do with sex. With the advent of AIDS I wonder if there's going to be a new renaissance of interest in pornography, in voyeurism.

HELMUT NEWTON[1]

There is a photograph that Helmut Newton shot for Yves Saint Laurent (YSL) and French *Vogue* in 1979 of two women in a hotel lobby near the lifts in a stylized amorous encounter (Figure 13). One wears a suit with short, slicked-back hair, while the other is in a small tank-top covering her breasts, a short white bolero-style jacket with lapels, her dress split to the hips, leading to a generous bow, and revealing her gartered stocking. The dragging female assumes the dominant pose as the womanly dressed woman arches her back in a mixture of coquettishness and abandon, her long fingers fending off the other's advances with coy ambivalence. Instead of kissing, the space between their lips is occupied with two cigarettes that are joined at each end, in an affectedly ironic act of lighting each other up. The column supporting them hums with a lustrous glow. In Newton's own words about this particular shoot:

> I've had this idea in my head for some time: Pictures of men and women together, only the men are women dressed up as men. But the illusion must be as perfect as possible, to try to confuse the reader. This man/woman ambiguity has always fascinated me, so I submitted the idea to Kargère, the art director of French *Vogue*, and he liked it. So, here we are in the basement of the George V, the men/women look wonderful, their waists nipped-in so tight in their elegant suits that they can hardly breathe, their short hair pomaded and the only truly feminine part of them that is revealed are their

Figure 13 Retro-Verseau, YSL, *Vogue* France, Paris 1979. © The Helmut Newton Estate / Maconochie Photography.

beautiful hands. I have a great time taking these pictures, but the pleasure is not shared. As the sitting progresses, through the second day, the girls become more and more depressed, they hate the role they are playing.[2]

Evidently Newton could inspire ambivalence on more than one level.

Up until Newton, fashion photography was a business dominated by men who produced immaculate images that glorified the female form, ensuring that their clients' designs were placed in places of immaculate, but ultimately sterile beauty. Even the mercurial Cecil Beaton was a master of respectability whose playground of status and consumption were gilded with the most decorous values. The *Vogue* photographer Chris von Wangenheim said that 'fashion photography is a way to sell clothes. The way to sell clothes or anything else connected with it, is through seduction'.[3] It is ironic that the photography so closely associated, at least in popular public opinion, with the male gaze should introduce a number of shifting co-ordinates of sexuality and seeing. Before Newton's images, cross-dressing was best left to ribald Surrealists and other bohemian queers. To have women kissing, or effectively so, was anathema, and liable to court considerable reprisal. It appeared antithetical to what the representation of fashion was all about, as it sullied clothing with perversity. And in a sense, images of perversity in fashion hinted at fashion's ruin, since the image suggested eventual undress. It said that fashion existed to be discarded. It was worn to be removed.

Precisely. Fashion exists in the moment, and the moment of its manifestation is linked to its imminent abolition. 'Its close relationship to an industry dependent on fast turn over,' Rosetta Brookes wrote, 'makes the fashion photograph the transitory image par excellence.'[4] The model and the garment are present for the purpose of their disappearance. But to lend a narrative that fashion was but one integer in a broader purpose of social and sexual congress was not altogether new – as we have seen in previous chapters – but it was only with the post-1968 era, the protest era and the sexual revolution, that fashion photography became more risqué, allowed to escape the straight jacket of decorum and safe good taste.

It was in the 1970s when Newton was working for French *Vogue* under the adventurous editorship of Francine Crescent, who on occasion placed her job in jeopardy because of decisions that showed a taste for the extreme and unconventional. As Newton himself commented of this time, 'The seventies was a very exciting and wonderful period in fashion photography. We broke a lot of ground. We really whacked it down the throats of the readers at the time. We had a lot of battles – it wasn't easy going.'[5] Newton had far greater latitude in Paris than he would have, and had, in Australia, Britain and America, where he also worked contractually. In Paris, Newton was able to stretch the limits of the representation of flesh, but also, as we see in the picture above, of gender. He not only made provocative use of drag, but also what is now termed BDSM.[6] In 1977 he shot a series of photographs of models in orthopaedic corsets, a clever manoeuvre since it was, after all, a remedial device, which made it harder to censor – but everyone gets the intended meaning of the image. One of Newton's great talents was to set a scene, to generate an atmosphere, which frequently meant that more was asked of models; in his work models are seldom indifferent and certainly not mindless ciphers. All of them have an inner emotional life, and what is so alluring is that it is given with one hand and taken away with another. Newton presented the viewer with a possibility that was, in the next movement, thwarted by coquettish coolness, thereby creating a zone, or circuit of desire. With Newton the fashion image is not just a hypothetical offering, it teases the viewer's desire with the opposite: the tacit refrain of 'you cannot have this', the inexorable theatre of the unattainable only makes the scenario more desirable. To do this Newton frequently sacrificed clothing for pose; the garment may be obscured, out of shape, blown or hiked up in order to enable a tableau of implausible extravagance.

If Newton tinged his models with experience and subjectivity it was not in the interests of empathy, but more in the way in which pornography, as it had begun to evolve, assigned bogus names and bogus stories to the nude models. While *Playboy* (founded in 1953) then *Penthouse* (1969) had already begun to do this, pornography witnessed a new level of permissiveness and broadening of its visual syntax with *Hustler* in 1974. It was in the mid-1970s that pornography came of age, showing women's genitalia with an explicit ribaldry that not only sparked controversy, but made its competitors look coy, and indeed even more stylish. It was after the release of Gerard Damiano's controversial pornographic film *Deep Throat* (1972) that pornography became fashionable. According to Church Gibson and Karaminas, the French 'soft-core' film *Emmanuelle* (1974) became a global phenomenon that engendered a wave of European explicit features intended for mainstream screening, thus establishing 'the early 1970s as the most pornographic period in film history'.[7] Referred to as the 'golden age of porn', these early pornographic films were rendered suitable for adult entertainment and consumption. It was then that the term 'porn chic' began circulating in mainstream media and was used to describe a genre of fashion photography made popular by Helmut Newton (and Guy Bourdin) that was sexually explicit and suggestive of violence. 'Newton's characteristic mix of masochistic heroines and sadistic mistresses,' write Church Gibson and Karaminas, 'and Bourdin's graphic depictions of mutilated bodies explored the connections between death, sex and power.'[8] In the article 'The Beautiful and the Damned', by art critic Barbara Rose published in American *Vogue* (November, 1978), Rose writes that, Newton's 'photographs of beautiful women trapped or constricted accentuate the interface between liberation and bondage. . . . An anonymous hotel room evokes fantasies of potential erotic adventure. Glittering surfaces catch and reflect light in images that couple elegance with pain, fin-de-siècle opulence with contemporary alienation.'[9]

It was during this period that Newton confessed to an interest in pornography and to have made some forays into it, but in only a limited way, since he feared for his career should he have gone too far.[10] As it was, Newton had a reputation in the 1970s for perversity that has changed to veneration in our time. It is perhaps to everyone's benefit that Newton censored his pornographic images from his public oeuvre because it exists in his work in a more powerful way, as suggestion, as the repressed limit or blind spot. In what it withholds the viewer yields to a train of other suppositions and associations to which the Newtonian image is a catalyst. As Karl Lagerfeld comments, 'Helmut is certainly the photographer of women, but the pictures he takes of them are not necessarily what men expect. In his way he has changed, or at least profoundly influenced, the erotic fantasies of our time.'[11] In his commentary Lagerfeld is at pains to defend Newton's attitude to women: 'In his photographs he never makes fun of women. . . . And yet the feminists detest him.'[12] What is confronting about Newton's image is that the viewer is made self-consciously aware of his or her desire. The feminists that Lagerfeld was referring to would have been feminists from the 1970s Women's Liberation movement, but the opinion amongst women has since changed. There is no other photograph that best captures the seduction and allure of fashion more than Newton's iconic image of YSL's *Le Smoking* Tuxedo shot for French *Vogue* in 1975 at the height of the Women's Liberation Movement (Figure 14).

Figure 14 *Le Smoking* (nude), Yves Saint Laurent, Rue Aubriot, *Vogue* France, Paris, 1975. © The Helmut Newton Estate / Maconochie Photography.

The monochromatic image features an androgynous woman standing in a dimly lit alley in the Marais in Paris, crisp white cravat, hair slicked back, cigarette, entwined with a nude model dressed only in black stilettos. The tuxedo was part of YSL's Pop Art collection of 1966 and made a controversial statement about women's sexuality tapping into a generation of women who were fighting against patriarchal control of their bodies. Androgyny became a mode of dress that challenged restrictive gendered dress codes and dominant constructions of femininity. Newton's work is remarkable for the way it places a mirror up to the wanting, searching viewer. 'Great fashion images,' writes Margaret Maynard, 'engage the viewer aesthetically (or by overt grittiness, voyeurism, sensationalism, or even excess ordinariness), but they also play with our minds.'[13] And Newton's images do that precisely.

Even though Newton was not especially fussed about being called an artist, what makes his work art is precisely that it formalizes the particular gaze that is deployed in a fashion magazine, or in the fashion industry generally. (Lagerfeld: 'Although Helmut Newton made his name as a fashion photographer, his pictures have survived better than the fashions they were meant to represent or illustrate.'[14]) In so doing his work also disclosed a repression within art photography. In an essay on photography and simulacra, Rosalind Krauss argues persuasively about photography's reliance on painting, since it is painting that supplies the visual syntax that is either subconsciously invoked by the photographer, or by which we read the photograph. She invokes the photography of Irving Penn which is divided into commercial work and artistic work, citing a meticulous still life that is lifted directly from the centuries' old tradition.[15] But Newton never aimed at two arms of his practice, but rather by seeking out the limits of what fashion photography could do opened a space that was no longer dependent on painting in the same way. Throughout his career Newton was very clear about his position. While it can be read as anti-intellectual, it is perhaps better to see him as relaxed with his profession and uneasy about what could be extraneous complications.

It is again pornography – that is, pornography in a stretched, metaphoric sense, where in his work it is connoted and never fully delivered – that allowed him to do this. For painting has a limited tradition with pornography. Pornography in painting (as famously disclosed by Manet with *Olympia* in 1863) is covert, sanitized, or metaphoric through the safe tropes of mythology and allegory. Any paintings of bondage or perversion come after the pornification that photography instigates. As with Surrealism and artists influenced by it, images with pornographic content, or hints of it, were almost exclusively photographic.[16]

Formalism in photography

We might even go so far as to make bigger claims of Newton. Although he was far from solely responsible, he played a large part in the closest thing to approach formalism in photography. Formalism in painting began in Russia at the beginning of the twentieth century and reached a climax with the writings of the powerful New York critic Clement Greenberg. In a series of influential essays, Greenberg argued that painting had reached a significant limit with the painters in New York (now known collectively as the Abstract Expressionists or alternatively as the New York School) who were able to create works of deep humanitarian affect through identifying the formal conditions of painting, namely the physicality of the paint and the flatness of the picture plain. By eschewing illusion and letting paint be paint as opposed to say flesh, painting, according to Greenberg, steered a closer course to deeper abstract truths. Now to apply these ideas to photography may seem misguided, for photography's material conditions are multiple. Taking analogue photography (which was of course Newton's medium) it is the celluloid and the silver emulsion as well as the paper. Photography is also representational, indexical of its subject matter through light. (And to present a series of entirely black or white surfaces is only to stretch the viewers' indulgence.)

Rather, it is precisely in photography's status as a representational medium that aligns it to a different set of conditions. And Greenberg was, after all, highly selective (never reading Pollock's work for example as partly performative) in the criteria he used, revealing that formalism was a more unbounded concept than it would like to be. As it emerged at the same time when Greenberg was most influential, from the late 1930s to the 1960s, the greatest public currency for photography was in advertising and propaganda. It was at the service of directing and shaping desire. Even today, when the use of photography has now been outstripped by social media and image transaction on electronic devices, the purpose has not altered much, only shifted. The formal qualities of photography are therefore to be abstracted from its material qualities, and directed to how it functions. For photography is always about lack, be it registering the moment never to exist again, a representation of something I have and you don't, where I am and you're not, or to something that you are supposed to need. Art photography ponders the possibility of transcending this condition by being in and for itself. However, we would argue that art photography exists as a foil to commercial photography, and therefore must always accept its magnitude, if not ubiquity. Given both the length of the history of painting on the one hand, and the sheer profusion of commercial photography on the other, art photography teeters (with agility or with fatality), always a minority, between the two. Newton himself stated, as early as 1970, well before the surge of photography theory a decade or more later, that

> [w]ith the intellectual questioning that has been going on in recent years about photography, many photographers hesitate so long before they take a picture that they seem never to trip the shutter. A kind of constipation has set in: maybe the day will come when the only photographers left will be the press, the others will just philosophize.[17]

Although this has not exactly eventuated, it emphasizes that Newton's sensibility was positively attuned elsewhere from art, pinning his attentions on photography's immediacy and its collusion with the material world of commodities and the physical and psychic realm of sex. Moreover, it is also curious to observe the extent, as in this very essay, people have begun to 'philosophize' over *him*.

What makes Newton so important is the way in which his work is inscribed with a fundamental gap. This gap is proper to all photography, as suggested in the theoretical term 'photo-death' in which we register what will never be again. It is also an image of a truth and evidence – even if it is false and non-evidential these conditions are rhetorically in place – of something else or somewhere else. But we choose to disavow the unsettling consequences of this gap, much as, on a related but slightly larger scale we avoid psychoses in choosing not to contemplate at every living moment the absolute imminence of our death since it would lapse us into vertiginous psychosis. Advertising makes optimal use of the photographic gap through the way we are prompted to engage in a paradox: we identify with the image while at the same time distinguishing ourselves from it. One imagines one as having as well as lacking. Thus the collusion within advertising is that you don't have 'it' but you could. However, with Newton this possibility is made far more remote, insinuating an *insurmountable* gap between the life-world and the world of fashion that exists within the imaginary prism of the photograph. Among Newton's favourite venues for photographic shoots was the Riviera, from Monaco to Saint Tropez, places associated with wealth, luxury and salubriousness. Beside pools or in hotel rooms, his models engage in strange encounters, or register a tension of suspense or aloofness. In his meditation on fashion photography, Michael Carter states:

> The fascination of Newton or Goude with certain marginalized visual conventions of a pre or ante modernist bias (Academic painting – erotica – Balthus – Singer Sargent) may not necessarily be in the desire to shock, which is far too modernist, but with the fixing of a set of conventions of the delineation of an imaginary topography. The lobbies of Grand Hotels, pornographic boudoirs, formal gardens, or figures journeying to and from balls, each of them provide examples of situations where the organization of appearances is at its most intense and where there is a possibility for that ideal coalescence of line and matter.[18]

To put this differently, body and setting merge to become one; the unattainable event of the instant of photography quickly gives way to tableau and to prolepsis, what will eventuate. But what will eventuate is left permanently open. And what is central to these images that, even for those denizens of the places where the images were shot, this world is both familiar but also elsewhere, unattainable, forbidden. What is therefore so compelling is that, analogous to the temporal reality of photo death, we are presented not with what we could have but what we would never have.

In this respect Newton 'comes clean'; no advertising image, let alone fashion image, is realizable, and its integers are constructs like a made-up language, a visual Esperanto. But also, and strikingly, Newton's conceptual formalism, if it can be called that, is to make the viewer self-conscious of the extent of his or her desire; placing a mirror before their desire. This is achieved by constructing a guilefully provocative theatre of sexuality, but it is sexuality whose content is always incomplete. It is here that we see the extent to which Newton is a photographer as opposed to a film-maker, for his narratives are played out in a state of suspension. There are many images of semi-dressed and nude models sitting on sofas or standing around. The repressed narrative force of these images is in the simple question as to why they are nude. Nudity is easy to justify in classical painting, with its residues of classical tradition, and in pornography, which is linked to gratuitous sexual desire. But Newton's female figures hover precariously between naked and nude. Often producing images in pairs, one with clothes on, another in the same pose, with clothes off. What makes these works so intriguing is that in the traditional act of unmasking the mask is reinstated all the more since nothing deeper than the representation of flesh is revealed. Moreover, why, as a commercial fashion photographer, does Newton take pictures of women without clothes? This can be said to have to do with fairly standard ideas about the way in which, in the object of desire, dress functions as something to be undressed, as the first stage from inscrutability to disclosure.

But it is precisely this transition, which hangs as a promise in conventional fashion photography, that Newton abruptly disavows. The model functions alternatively as object-to-be-had, or person-I-could-be, yet the paradox of our desire is that we take pleasure in the way that we know that the promise will never be realized. Newton's work makes this very plain. Instead of 'you could have this', we are given 'you cannot have this'. The imminent vanity of the fetish is there with us from the beginning, that is, within the photographic image. But it is this truth being known to us from the outset that has the very opposite effect of stopping us from indulging commodity fetishism. For the truth about the fetish – that it will only end in another replacement to make up for an unfillable void – exists in the *representation*. However in our own lived *actions* (however enframed by imagination) we believe that we have recourse to something more, something different. By the photograph representing something not real and decisively out of reach we register that it is not our world, however in our world we might possibly have something else; we might make something, perhaps better, for ourselves by perhaps building our own illusion that rivals that of the fashion image. If we fail, which we always do, our fall is softened by the ability to return to the fact that we knew all along that the fashion image is permanently barred from us. Even the person in real life looks different (note the obsession of gossip magazines of spotting stars in the street in their everyday mufti and without make-up).

Woman doesn't exist

Much is made of Newton's attitude to women. Lagerfeld (whether it matters or not in this analysis, who also happens to be gay), for example, defends the way Newton preserves the dignity of women.[19] Newton himself even claimed to be a feminist.[20] That's maybe drawing a pretty long bow but it is also a mistake to dismiss Newton too glibly with charges of male voyeurism and female manipulation. For that, in truth, would be to condemn the fashion industry as a whole. But in light of the extreme nature of Newton's photographs, in themselves or still better what they lead to in the viewer's mind, makes it worth pausing to ponder feminist revisionism's attitudes to fashion itself.

In her classic *Fashion and Eroticism* (1985), Valerie Steele discusses some feminist onslaughts on fashion, particularly women's fashion and conventions of feminine beauty:

Recent works, such as Lois Banner's *American Beauty* and Susan Brownmiller's *Femininity*, have attacked fashion and ideals of feminine beauty as deeply oppressive to women – not only in the past, but today as well. According to the neo-feminist critique, fashion is bad because it is sexually exploitative and artificial. It is also conducive to self-absorption, and it is a waste of time. In fact, fashion and beauty culture form the *basis* for all other inequalities that women face. Fashion and feminism have always been at war. . . That these books have been, on the whole, well received, indicates that many presumably more-or-less fashionable people are nevertheless inclined to think badly about feminine fashion.[21]

In light of this analysis of Newton's work, two words jump out: 'artificial' and 'self-absorption'. As we have observed already, Newton's world is abundantly artificial. Not only as other-worlds – perverse utopias ('non-places') – but in their celebration of contrivance, from pose to drag to devices that gesture to sado-masochism. His images are places of contrivance where sexuality is always a matter of invention, converting utopias into dystopias. The purported dignity that Lagerfeld attributes to Newton's women ('he never makes fun of women, never sneers at them nor tries to make them look ridiculous'[22]) can be boiled down to the self-absorptive aplomb of so many of his models. It is their air of nonchalance, of being happy in their skin that is attractive. In some cases they sneer at us, act as if we don't matter, or simply ignore us (again, note, 'you can't have this/me'). This is the vanity of the *femme fatale*, where we are attracted to the very things we are told we cannot have.

Steele's sober defence is: 'Certainly fashion is erotic and artificial, but are these necessarily negative features? It is apparently a difficult concept for most people to accept that there is no "natural" way for men and women to look.' She proceeds to dismantle the view that there is somehow a natural way of dressing, or a naturally irreducible model of femininity or masculinity. There is also no way of drawing a line between what is acceptable grooming before it lapses into 'vanity' and 'narcissism'.[23] She presages later queer theory when she reproaches the feminist stance to relegate feminine fashion to a conspiracy of the male gaze:

Few argue today that both male and female attitudes toward adornment should change, but rather that women should adopt a more 'utilitarian' male standard. Thus homosexual men are also criticized for their attention to their appearance; only lesbians and heterosexual men are supposedly free from the need to be sexually attractive to men. Clearly, practicality is not really the issue.[24]

The years when Steele was writing this witnessed the birth of new kinds of queer identities, from 'muscle Marys and clones' (muscular gay men) to lipstick lesbians. In fact the muscular gay man was immortalized earlier by Touko Laaksonen, aka Tom of Finland, whose images of muscle-clad men indulging in lascivious acts to one another began to appear as early as the 1950s, but gained mainstream popularity after Stonewall in 1969 when censorship rules were either relaxed or defiantly tested. Such gay men were thus 'more men than men', thereby turning the stereotype of male homosexuality as pre-eminently feminine on its head. While the proud and increasing visibility in the 1970s of sexual difference with its attendant subcultural styles made it increasingly uncertain to impute a correct or natural way of dressing, or of sexuality for that matter – although heteronormativity is maintained, construct of the natural is a locus of power for state and religion.

This digression serves to illustrate the importance of the Helmut artificial universe and its relationship to personal and sexual identity. For as we have established in this chapter, Newton's work is unmistakably heterosexual yet it does not seek to defend a socially circumscribed and sanctioned version of this idea. Rather, he does the opposite, not limited to getting women to dress in drag. The alluringly mysterious atmosphere of some possible threat, that something else will eventuate from what the photographic scene describes, or that the image is the residue of something far more dramatic and exciting is frequently helped along by an unconventional act (a man biting a girl's ear)[25] or of what has now come to be known as 'pornochic', to be discussed in the following chapter. In some cases bodies are all but trussed up, women wear gimp masks, or are placed in poses that are far removed from the spry elegance of what is associated with high fashion.

The representation of a certain kind of woman, that is the desirable women associated with fashion, wealth and privilege will always court criticism. Yet Newton cannot be singled out for the objectification, for rather we would need to bring most if not all of the fashion industry into account. Rather, what we need to emphasize here is the disconnectedness between the fashion image and everyday reality. The closed and nonchalant air of Newton's models for the most part hints at self-possession, power, confidence. On the other hand, what is also noticeable in his work is disquiet, disjuncture, and imperfection. Or rather, Newton reveals to our consciousness what is there, latent within the equation of high fashion and wealth, namely that beauty and wealth always come at some kind of price. In his *Domestic Nudes* (1992) series he takes no measures to hide the scars in the bottom fold of the breasts, in other cases hotel lobbies or suites become the theatre of confrontation, the threat of violence, with a veiled menace that may mean that this is a special event, or perhaps it just happens all the time for these nameless people. But unlike the people in, say, the paintings of Edward Hopper steeped in their ordinariness, Newton's models are never like us, and we are made sure to know it.

The Helmut Newton model is one of a type, wrote Rosetta Brookes in her seminal essay 'On Fashion Photography,'

Presented with the cold distance of a fleshy automaton, an extension of the technology, which manipulates her and converts her into an object. Her veneer, which is one with the gloss of the image, to be flicked past and consumed in a moment. When the models strike up stereotyped poses, it is their deathliness and frozen quality that strikes the viewer most strongly.[26]

What is unclear in Newton's work is whether the aplomb and the inscrutability of his models is inherent or affectation, or whether this is because of them or the photography. In the essay for which she is best known, 'Womanliness as a Masquerade', Joan Riviere explains that womanliness must be understood as a representation, as both a compensatory measure and a means to prevent the possibility of any confrontation that she might be lacking something:

> Womanliness can therefore be assumed and worn as a mask, both to hide the possession of masculinity and to avert the reprisals expected if she was found to possess it [. . .] The reader may now ask how I define womanliness or where I draw the line between genuine womanliness and the 'masquerade'. My suggestion is not, however, that there is any such difference; whether radical or superficial, they are the same thing.[27]

Riviere identifies womanliness outside of the supposedly rational confines of reproduction, which have mythically bound her to the metaphoric and semantic terrain of nature. She reverses the venerable and tenacious binaries of woman/nature vs man/culture and woman/*soma* and man/*psyche* to argue that womanliness is not anything natural but rather a series of subversive and perverse illusions.

In several case studies Riviere cites a savvy housewife who downplays her knowledge when a tradesman pays a visit, 'making her suggestions in an innocent and artless manner'.[28] Then there is the example of a university lecturer, an 'abstruse subject that seldom attracts women'. When she lectures to colleagues as opposed to students, 'she chooses particularly feminine clothes. Her behavior on these occasions is also marked by an inappropriate feature: she becomes flippant and joking, so much so that it has caused comment and rebuke.' Since her topic area is untypical to women and more the province of the masculine, she treats the symbolic masculinity she is forced to wear because of her discipline as 'a "game", as something *not real*, as a "joke" . . . moreover, the flippant attitude enables some of her sadism to escape, hence the offence it causes'.[29] Her sadism is in undermining the situation with her masquerade; for in playing to the weak expectations of her male audience, the evidence of this play exposes the weakness, relocating it from latent to central to the psychosexual dynamic of their interaction.

Although the essay is verging on a century old, it still holds currency, and does much to shed light on Newton's work and the representation of woman in fashion imagery in general. Indeed the fashion industry is apt to incur the accusation that it participates in propagating this condition. This is the subject of a great deal of feminist literature, which also includes recent forays into the 'lesbian gaze', as Reina Lewis and Katrina Rolley have forcefully argued, where lesbians are found to take pleasure in imagery of women as much as men.[30] But what makes these matters more complicated is that with the phenomenon of the lipstick lesbian, and the fact that high heels and lipstick continue to enjoy prime position in the fashion world, it is no longer so easy to ascribe the acquired attributes and accoutrements of femininity to a male conspiracy. For more in the manner of Steele's analysis, the dispensable and excessive within feminine dress, from stilettos to decorative lingerie, long nails to suspenders, also provide women with the possibility of autoerotic phantasy. What is harder to deny is that in the processes of self-beautification women engage in an intricate web of representations in which the fashion image plays an integral part.

Thus underlying our conceit of the notion of Newton and conceptual formalism in photography is the self-conscious knowledge of the seamlessness of the representation (photographic, filmic), self-representation (posing, playing the part, masquerade), socialization, and, more broadly, gender identity. With the latter we are brought back full circle. For if womanliness does not exist, it is arbitrated according to a series of both stable and mobile stereotypes propagated by ideology on the one hand (bourgeois, heteronormative 'traditional' values) and popular, commercial representation (magazines, media, film, television) on the other. According to Kathy Myers, 'the ability of the media to continually recreate new meanings gives a certain instability to the image which constantly threatens to escape the analytical categories or stereotypes within which we seek to contain it'.[31] The contrivances within Newton's oeuvre are insistent reminders of the constructedness of femininity. The persistence of a certain female type can therefore be read as first, that the women are by and large beautiful, and beauty is, simply put, pleasing; second, that his photographs are commercial or related to commercial interests.

But it is also the female stereotype as persistent within fashion and other commercial photography for over a century that something well beyond the purview of fashion or photography, and that is that socialized identity requires the imaginary avatar of a stereotype for its coherence. It is only the redoubling of this fact in photographic representation that makes this fact seem less real and more constructed. For the term 'female stereotype' is used with as much abandon as its definition is scarce. One only needs to survey fashion imagery from Poiret or Patou onward to see that this stereotype is constantly shifting. However the persistence of one stereotype of woman in one era or another can be viewed as oppressive, or it is the symbolic image that compensates for a primary lack, the lack of a definition.

Brookes convincingly argues that Newton manipulates existing stereotypes of female image to the extent that she ceases to connote any reality apart from the images that constitute her. The alienness of the models, she writes, 'is accentuated, and yet they are almost archetypes in their own sexual dramas'.[32] She continues, 'The passive reclining woman offers no threat; she is completely malleable, a dummy made of flesh. The object of gratuitous sexual violence and violation, she offers no resistance, but because of this she becomes unreal, like de Sade's libertines.'[33]

However, Brookes also argues that Newton has applied the same conventions of the erotic photograph to challenge existing stereotypes that inform the dominant conventions of fashion photography. Brookes suggests that this stylistic subversion is facilitated by making the photographer's mediation on this image apparent. In doing so, the image distances the spectator from the image, rending any identification impossible. She continues,

> Many of Newton's more successful photographs hold a distant engagement with the manipulative devices of fashion photography and with the process of mediation. Those alien features present in suppressed form in fashion photography and current images of women are exposed and made explicit. The image is presented as alien, as a threat rather than an invitation. Stereotypes are presented as falsity.[34]

In all of Newton's images the female figure is defined strongly either by her surroundings (odd or sumptuous setting), her company (man staring, a dog), her clothing (high heels, or more fantastic BDSM trappings), or by some surreal aberration (such as a photo appended to a forehead). 'Woman' is never allowed just 'to be herself', and yet it is because of these extraneous influences that 'she' is given a certain ineffable autonomy. The autonomy is that she exists outside not only the boundaries of desire, possession and commodity, as suggested above, but that she is fundamentally unknowable by the eye (and hence the lens) that paradoxically defines her.

In 'Otto Weininger, or, Woman Doesn't Exist', a brilliant unpacking of one of the most misogynistic theses ever to have been penned, Slavoj Zizek exposes a fundamental disturbance in the way women are understood and theorized by men.[35] The text in question is 'Sex and Character' (Geschlecht und Charakter, which is actually 'Gender and Character'), a passionate and caustic text which Weininger published in Vienna at the age of twenty-three. His was not the first of its kind, already a professor in Leipzig, Paul Julius Möbius had published On the Physiological Deficiency of Women from which Weininger was accused of plagiarizing (which was one of the factors that precipitated his suicide shortly after his book's release). At the beginning of the essay Zizek quotes Weininger in a passage, which in light of this chapter, deserves reiteration: 'Woman is only and thoroughly sexual, since her sexuality extends to her entire body and is in certain places, to put in physical terms, only more dense than others.'[36] For Weininger, Woman is incapable of a simple, or disinterested, apprehension of beauty because she is bounded, defined, by coitus. Genital desire relates to her as an organ of human reproduction. In Zizek's words, 'Coitus is therefore the only case apropos of which woman is capable of formulating her own version of the universal and ethical imperative, "Act so that your activity will contribute to the realization of the infinite ideal of general pairing".'

At first we may seem to be in the general realm of Newton's visual-sexual politics, or perhaps rather the politics left behind in the residue of his reluctance to be part of any ethical or ideological debate. On the face of it, women are presented as desirable objects *tout court*, even if they cannot be possessed; after all that only increases the desire and the scrutiny of the gaze. A further definition advanced by Weininger lends credence to open criticism: women's beauty is apparently 'performative', it is a reflection of man's love. Women therefore exist entirely as a reflective duplication of what men wish for. It is therefore the case, Zizek argues, that according to this conception, male love is a 'thoroughly *narcissistic* phenomenon', for in seeking out what he wants in woman, man ends only in loving himself.[37] This is what makes of love both a mystery and a sham, suspending the shattering truth that 'it utterly disregards the object's (woman's) true nature, and uses it only as a kind of empty projection screen'.[38] 'Woman' therefore doesn't exist insofar as she is man's creation; man has no access to some noumenal thing in itself over which there is some aesthetic sheath, rather 'woman' is entirely his aesthetic construct. Ethically speaking, she is an empty vessel, or as Schopenhauer would put it, a veil of Maya, which exists only as representation and where the illusion plays itself ad infinitum. For when man seeks out the enigma of the sphinx, its riddle eludes him unless he is willing to identify that the enigma is based on a basic misapprehension.

Zizek boldly equates Weininger's theory to the famous dictum of Jacques Lacan, 'la femme n'existe pas' (woman doesn't exist). In a way closely analogous to the ideas about female subject formation outlined above, Lacan asserts that woman is a 'symptom' of man. Lacan states that woman does not fit in a satisfactory way into the symbolic order, which is due to her status as symptom of a series of efforts to shape her into a coherent entity. However, it is this very need and effort to shape and mould and project that *exposes* the deficiencies in such processes. Hence Zizek's remark that

'Woman does not exist' does not in any way refer to an ineffable female Essence beyond the domain of discursive existence: *What does not exist is this very unattainable Beyond*. In short . . . the 'enigma of woman' ultimately conceals the fact that there is nothing to conceal.[39]

She is a male fabrication. Paradoxically, the male position is at once one who renders woman visible while trying to resolve 'her' under different conditions from those that constituted 'her'. As Zizek concludes,

The ultimate result of our reading of Weininger is thus a paradoxical yet inevitable inversion of the anti-feminist ideological apparatus espoused by Weininger himself, according to which women are wholly submitted to phallic enjoyment, whereas men have access to the desexualized domain of ethical goals beyond the Phallus: it is man who is wholly submitted to the Phallus ... whereas woman, through the inconsistency of her desire, attains the domain 'beyond the Phallus'. Only woman has access to the Other (non-phallic) enjoyment.[40]

Enter again Helmut Newton: the 'performative' women that pervade his work exemplify the constitution of woman according to the constructs and expectations of male desire in a way that is almost self-reflexive – 'You want this so I'll give you this', 'Admit, you like it and you want it' – thereby granting access to this desire. Yet this access is foreclosed from the beginning. You are offered the all of what you cannot have. This exposes the artificiality of the scene and the convolutedness of desire and desired object. Hence the inscrutability of the women, so often commented upon: this is both a sign of the void behind, the enigmaless enigma, while simultaneously a sublime expression – that threshold of sense perception and intellection which conveys that there is something there that can neither be apprehended or understood – of a universe where non-phallic enjoyment holds sway. So if Newton is a feminist, it is a statement that is only defensible according to a similar deconstructive inversion, which Zizek submits to Weininger. But on the other hand this argument in no way implies that Newton's attitudes to women are cut from the same cloth as Weininger. Rather, the industry of fashion photography up until now had been, by and large, an industry, a macrocosm of the theatre of male projection and of female performance. Newton only scrapes away a few layers and takes us to places where desire and disgust rub shoulders, thereby hinting at the terrifying beyond of the construction of femininity that braces itself in the knowledge that the more pervasive and abundant, the greater the certainty that non-phallic enjoyment can be known, or shared.

An image that demonstrates this in the most rudimentary or perhaps even literal sense depicts the photographer's reflection, stooped over his Hasselblad, studiously composing a photograph of a naked woman (+stilettos of course), whose behind is in the foreground and whose front is exposed because of the reflection. Another pair of unidentified legs (+stilettos) jut from the left (Figure 15). This work can be read according to the tradition of self-reflexivity; from the artist's studio to the Vertovian eye of the camera in which the gaze of the photographer, or other maker of images, is crossed with our own. This could be so, except for the presence of another woman, definitely not a model, to the far right of the image. This is Newton's wife June, her legs crossed, supporting a patient, if not bored, head with her left hand. Her gaze is neither that of the photographer, nor us, nor does she exhibit the stylized performative brio of the model. Is she the sign of the inexpressible remainder, the unfathomable excess, to this image and

Figure 15 'Self Portrait' with wife and models, Paris, 1981. © The Helmut Newton Estate / Maconochie Photography.

to Newton's work in general? Her attitude is neither enthusiasm nor opprobrium, it is just something else, to the side of the image, but somehow more alive and conscious than the rest of the image put together. More brutally perhaps, there is his series of works of suited men ministrating to women, before we realize that they are lifeless mannequins.

Excess and Eros

The relationship that most of us have with the fashion image is that, just as with commercial cinema, we like to suspend our disbelief. It is desirable for us to do so. It is indeed the remit of commercial photography to undermine the viewer's critical capacity and make him or her waver between desire and resistance, much as the woman in this picture. For as soon as the fashion image introduces hesitation, then it has achieved its goal, for it means that the door of critical distance, and/or resistance, is not hermetically sealed. Newton offers us another place: shady gardens, melancholy chateaux, seamy auberges, sumptuous hotels, dilapidated hotels – but also different bodily places; the possibility of alternative experiences. Danger.

Since Newton's characters are not of the everyday type, there is always the suggestion that therefore their sexual inclinations are not 'normal' either. If these are the privileged few, they have a much wider latitude, in what they receive and what they wish for. In this respect Newton's images express the inevitable excess associated with high fashion. The excess of consumption, and the excess of ornamentation implied in haute couture, finds its equivalent in sexual excess. In his important study of sensuality, death and sacrifice, *Erotism* (1957), Georges

Bataille remarks, 'Physical eroticism has in any case a sinister quality. It holds on to the separateness of the individual in a rather selfish and cynical fashion.'[41] Bataille offers us yet another co-ordinate to explain the apparent inscrutable wholeness of Newton's models. By and large, the models enact the excess that is fashion itself, that is, what separates fashion from clothing. For any discussion of excess inevitably devolves into the erotic, and as Bataille's work shows in great detail, the erotic is inextricably linked to excess, ritual and death.

If the woman in the image had not been wearing gloves we would have had to subject it to an entirely different reading. For it is the presence of these gloves that tips this image into a realm of sexual worldliness and experimentation. She is not the good woman being visited by a foreign spirit with sinister desires (Rumpelstiltskin) or ulterior motives (as Zeus impregnated Danaë). Nor is this a scene of agape, benign love. It is a visitation whose essence is in the power dynamic within the sexual encounter. We already sense a conflict and are intrigued by the tension the image sets up. The woman in the frame is at once indifferent but aroused, in control yet haunted by the possibility of violation, which may be forced upon her, or to which she may invite. The excess lies in that part of the sexual activity that is done for its own sake, which is to say most of sexual activity, and the way that the fetish writes sex over the body. The rawness of the commodity fetish, and its rootedness in sexual desire, is here played out in the most explicit terms, but never brash or insistent. The two women, or rather their hands, appear to give flesh to the struggle of the viewer to resist or submit to the commercial image, and to try to separate the image from the object itself, the state of mind, the place, the look from the thing, as if we delude ourselves into thinking that there is a separation between the image and what it sells. There is no separation, yet we sacrifice ourselves to the delusion that there is, and that we are free agents able to negotiate ourselves around it. At least Newton's imagery makes this lie available to us in some kind of jarring semantic nudity, yet it is for this very reason that we run back more with even greater rapidity to the illusion of it all.

Notes

1 Helmut Newton in conversation with Carol Squiers, *Helmut Newton: Portraits*, Munich: Schirmer Art Books, (1987) 1993, 14–15.

2 Helmut Newton, 'Paris, France, Summer 1979', *Helmut Newton: World Without Men*, Cologne: Taschen, 2013, 128.

3 Chris Von Wangenheim, quoted by Malcolm Barnard, 'Fashion and the Image', in *Fashion Theory: A Reader*, London and New York: Routledge, 2007, 513.

4 Rosetta Brookes, 'Fashion Photography: The Double-Page Spread: Helmut Newton, Guy Bourdin and Deborah Turbeville', in Malcolm Barnard, *Fashion Theory: A Reader*, London and New York: Routledge, 2007, 520.

5 Ibid., 18.

6 See Adam Geczy and Vicki Karaminas, *Queer Style*, London: Bloomsbury, 2013.

7 Pamela Church Gibson and Vicki Karaminas, 'Letter from the Editors', *Fashion Theory: The Journal of Dress, Body and Culture*, Fashion and Porn Special Issue, 18 (2), April 2014, 116.

8 Ibid., 118.

9 Barbara Rose, quoted by Valerie Steele, 'Anti-fashion: the 1970s', *Fashion Theory: The Journal of Dress, Body and Culture*, 1 (3), 291.

10 'I've never published them, obviously, and I'm not going to because it would close too many doors for me – especially in America, but in Europe, too. I can't afford it.' Helmut Newton in *Helmut Newton: Portraits*, 14.

11 Karl Lagerfeld, 'Nordfleisch', *Helmut Newton: 47 Nudes*, London: Thames and Hudson, 1981, 14.

12 Ibid., 8.

13 Margaret Maynard, 'The Mystery of the Fashion Photograph', in Peter McNeil, Vicki Karaminas and Catherine Cole, *Fashion in Fiction*, Oxford: Berg, 2007, 55.

14 Ibid., 10.

15 Rosalind Krauss, 'A Note on Photography and the Simulacral', in Carol Squiers, ed., *The Critical Image: Essays on Contemporary Photography*, Seattle: Bay Press, 1990, 25–27.

16 We are ruling out the overt eroticism of Surrealist painters such as Paul Delvaux who draws heavily on traditional painting since the Renaissance, and shrouds his bodies in the fantastic and the allegorical.

17 Helmut Newton, 'Rome, Italy, Summer 1970', *Helmut Newton: World Without Men*, 24.

18 Carter, 'Fashion Photography', 7.

19 Lagerfeld, *Helmut Newton: 47 Nudes*, 8.

20 'Helmut Newton: Sexist Fetish to Magazine Mainstream', at the Museum of Fine Arts, Budapest, *Artdrum*, 17 April 2013, http://artdrum.wordpress.com/2013/04/17/helmut-newton-sexist-fetish-to-magazine-mainstream/.

21 Valerie Steele, *Fashion and Eroticism*, Oxford and New York: Oxford U.P., 1985, 243–244.

22 Lagerfeld, *Helmut Newton: 47 Nudes*, 8.

23 Steele, *Fashion and Eroticism*, 245.

24 Ibid., 245–246.

25 See also Michelle Harvey, 'Sex. Desire. No Romance', *Blanche Magazine*, n.d. 2011, www.blanche-magazine.com/sex-desire-no-romance/.

26 Rosetta Brookes, 'Fashion Photography. The Double-Page Spread: Helmut Newton, Guy Bourdin & Deborah Turbeville', in Malcolm Barnard, *Fashion Theory: A Reader*, London and New York: Routledge, 2007, 522.

27 Joan Riviere, 'Womanliness as Masquerade', *International Journal of Psychoanalysis*, 10, 1929, 306.

28 Ibid., 307.

29 Ibid., 308.

30 See Reina Lewis and Katrina Rolley, 'Ad(dressing) the Dyke: Lesbian Looks and Lesbian Looking', in Peter Horne and Reina Lewis, eds, *Outlooks: Lesbian and Gay Sexualities and Visual Cultures*, London: Routledge, 1996, passim.

31 Kathy Myers, 'Fashion 'n' Passion: A Working Paper', in Angela McRobbie, ed., *Zootsuits and Second Hand Dresses: An Anthology of Fashion and Music*, London: Macmillan, 1989.

32 Rosetta Brookes, 'Fashion Photography: The Double-Page Spread: Helmut Newton, Guy Bourdin & Deborah Turbeville', in Malcolm Barnard, *Fashion Theory: A Reader*, London and New York: Routledge, 2007, 522.

33 Ibid., 522.

34 Ibid., 522.

35 Slavoj Zizek, 'Otto Weininger, or, Woman Doesn't Exist', *The Metastases of Enjoyment*, London and New York: Verso, (1994) 2005, 137–164.

36 Ibid., 137.

37 Ibid., 139.

38 Ibid., 140.

39 Ibid., 143.

40 Ibid., 160–161.

41 Georges Bataille, *Erotism*, trans. not cited, New York: City Lights, 1986, 19.

5

MUSIC VIDEO, PORNOCHIC AND RETRO-ELEGANCE

*Our preponderant, spontaneous idea of identification is that of
imitating models, ideas, image-makers: it is noted (usually from
the condescending 'male' perspective) how young people identify
with popular heroes, pop singers, film stars, sportsmen . . . This
spontaneous notion is doubly misleading. First, the feature, the trait
on the basis of which we identify with someone, is usually hidden – it
is by no means necessarily a glamorous feature.*

SLAVOJ ZIZEK[1]

As we found in the previous chapter, after the 1970s the fashion image
transmogrified into something that was far more than presenting clothing, face,
body and lifestyle for the purpose of inciting consumption. In other words, it had
transcended 'mere' beauty and took recourse to darker places, and it gestured
to some excess beyond the confines of the commodity. Since then, fashion
photography has decisively become dynamically suggestive, metatextual, multi-
layered, allusive and, therefore, highly psychological. One indicator of this is that
it became clear to advertisers by the 1980s that for an advertisement to be
successful it need not always be desirable. The sexual permissiveness of the
1970s, and the relaxing of censorship in the West in the 1980s, meant that
nudity was far more available in both photography and film. The risqué could
penetrate into the deeper recesses of desire, in which beauty and ugliness,
certainty and doubt comingle. But what fashion photography osmotically
discovered in the last decades of the twentieth century was that to mine this
doubt was to expose a weakness that would make the viewer more receptive,
since it took her to the threshold of desire, and therefore to realms of possibility
in excess of the fashion object itself.

To some degree this position can still claim a painting like Sargent's *Madame X* as part of its genealogy. But while such an image is part of the history of the representations of fashion, it did not have any commercial intent. What we have seen, however, is that fashion photography was far more responsive to this kind of picture as opposed to works of art with more explicit sexual content for commonsense reasons relating to social propriety. With the sexual revolution of the 1970s coyness was no longer such a necessity. While Hugh Hefner had founded *Playboy* as early as 1953, it was not until the appearance of *Hustler* in 1974 that pornography had begun to nudge into the public sphere. With this, fashion photography's lexicon of allusions shifted to other realms, since it could avail itself, covertly and suggestively, of imagery and visual tropes about which the public had become more literate. With the advent of the Internet, this literacy reaches new realms altogether. But before the Internet penetrated into the mainstream in the late 1990s, other media, principally music video which began a decade before, began to exert their influence. MTV ('music television') was launched in August 1981 and proved to have an indelible and complex influence on subcultural style, fashion, youth and the medium of film more generally, from mainstream to the then still emergent genre of the art video. Out of it grew a set of distinctive looks: chic and slick on the one hand (from David Sylvian to Roxy Music) to decidedly grungy and Goth on the other. The latter style of 'rock chic' came to be embodied in the fashion model Kate Moss. As Janice Miller in her study of fashion and music observes, while this style originated in figures such as Marianne Faithfull, this style evolved with people living vicariously – fans and the like. 'In all cases, black garments, leather, studs, just-out-of-bed hair and smoky eyes are de rigueur.'[2] We will discuss a contemporary day re-imagining of this, and in many ways a merging of the two poles of classy and trashy, an example which will be discussed later in the chapter with an analysis of Madonna's stage performances and her video-cum-short-film 'Justify My Love' (1990) and 'Girl Panic' (2011) from the quintessential New Romantic 1980s band Duran Duran.

Taking 1969, the year of the Stonewall riots, as a convenient ethico-sexual marker, values of family, sexuality and self became increasingly unstable and more diversified. Women vied for greater independence and recognition, polarizing society in what was acceptable and appropriate. The next major watershed comes in the new millennium when the Internet made pornography more commonplace than the exception. This is not the place to delve into the debates as to what the tsunami of pornography from the Internet has done to women's rights – there are arguments for and against – since the emphasis here is on its effect on body and dress. Given that it is freely available to anyone with a computer, it can be said to have entered into everyday life, or to put it another way, as everyone's worst-kept secret. The legacy of the distrust or reorientation of earlier conceptions of beauty, followed by the appropriation of sadomasochism and pornography in the mainstream by the late 1990s, signalled a new phenomenon in fashion: pornochic and its variant SM chic.

Pornochic is not porn, but the representation of porn in a non-pornographic context, in this case through fashion imagery. The use of stylistic and visual codes appropriated from porn and embedded in a fashion context serves to heighten fashion's transgressiveness but at the same time serves to numb and sanitize the 'shock value' through mainstreaming and commodification. A prime example is the entry of bondage and sadomasochism (BDSM) as a stylistic form into mainstream fashion, which also suggests a certain muting of motives which do little more than annul sadomasochism's transgressive power. Susan Cook argues that the commodification of this style turns it into just another cultural chattel: 'S/M fetish paraphernalia is one more sign of S/M's appropriation, in this sense economic, into the very dominant culture it sets itself in opposition to.' The sense of deviance that is the modus operandi of this style is thereby 'always controlled, always deferred'. Thus 'S/M's mainstream commodification reveals that by playing the normative against itself – by operating forever at the borders – S/M risks appropriation by the very social structure it sets itself against'.[3] As much as this makes sense, a countervailing position is that we are in an era (post-human, post-democracy, etc.) in which the very notion of subversion is different from the age of revolution and the avant-garde. Moreover, we would also assert that porn-chic and its related styling 'infects' the world of mainstream 'straight' styling; it is a salutary form of queering fashion, dress and identity.

This chapter will examine the porn-chic phenomenon and its variant 'S/M chic' within a fashion context by critically analysing its impact on the contemporary fashion image through its dissemination in music videos. The transformation of porn and its conventions into cultural artefacts such as music clips and garments for the purpose of consumption has provoked much criticism and debate concerning the construction of desirable bodies and the objectification of women. As Brian McNair writes, 'pornography has to be *outside* and *beyond* the mainstream in order to perform its function to retain its value as a commodity. It must present a visible violation of moral values and sexual taboos, or it loses its transgressive, erotic power'.[4] Excuse the pun, but music, fashion and porn make good bedfellows.

Pornostyle and the pornification of fashion

In April 2014, Pamela Church Gibson coined the term 'pornostyle' to describe the way in which pornographic cues, tropes and visual styling had entered the representation of mainstream fashion. Gibson had come far from the publication of the weighty tomes *Dirty Looks: Women, Pornography, Power* (1993) and *More Dirty Looks: Gender, Pornography and Power* (2008), where she argued that the transformation of the politics of pornography into mainstream culture has had great importance and impact in understanding issues of power, gender and cultural identity. According to Gibson, the amalgamation of pornographic styling codes by the fashion industry, what she calls 'pornostyle', has produced an unacknowledged system of fashion promotion that has emerged in the last decade. As Gibson explains:

> This new fashion system has its own leaders in young female celebrities, its own magazines to chronicle their activities and showcase their style, its own internet presence and its own retailing patterns. These young women often resemble in their self representation the 'glamour models' or pin-up girls of popular men's magazines, whose 'look' is a muted version of the styling associated by many with that of hardcore pornography.[5]

Unlike any other fashion phenomenon, pornochic (and SM chic) is born from representation, beginning with photography (helped along by Newton and his imitators) and accelerated by the domestication of the Internet. The black dress undoubtedly owed a large part of its imaginative resonance to films, actors and other celebrities who were captured wearing it, but the relationship to representation is still grounded, if mythically and rhetorically, in life, that is, it existed as a fashion item before representation. Pornochic, on the other hand, is more a stylistic idiom that tropes pornography, skirting the borderlines of acceptability. Fashion's use of porn 'codes' has established new norms and viewing positions, whilst increasing the sexually explicit material portrayed in fashion films, editorials and advertising. Fashion imagery and pornography expose the body, fragmenting it by cropping and foregrounding the culturally eroticized parts of it, and both use stereotypically gendered, eroticized tropes. In fashion media, pornographic bodies appear as *ideal* bodies placed in *ideal* and desirable lifestyles. This mutually exclusive relationship between fashion, the body and pornography which is being played out in popular culture and the mass media has been described by Brian McNair and Annette Lynch as 'porn-chic' and by Ariel Levy as *raunch culture* or 'raunch eroticism'. The definition of 'porn-chic' includes, 'fashion and related trend based behaviors linked to the porn industry that have now become mainstreamed into the dress of women and girls'.[6]

Pornochic might be new to fashion, but it has been around since the 1970s when viewing pornography amongst adults was considered *risqué* and fashionable. Nostalgically referred to as the 'golden age of pornography', the 1970s was a decade that was marked by the sexual revolution whose slogan of free love anticipated gay and lesbian love rights and the women's liberation movement which called for sexual equality and bodily autonomy. The success of hardcore pornographic films *Deep Throat* (1972), *Behind the Green Door* (1972) and *The Devil in Miss Jones* (1973) transcended the clandestine nature of the genre and it became acceptable for mainstream viewing and public consumption. 'These films were pornography,' writes McNair, 'as defined by the censorial taste regimes within which they circulated, which at [this] particular moment had been given space in mainstream culture.'[7] Pornography found its way into fashion via photographers who worked across the two mediums, taking stylistic elements of pornography into the domain of fashion. As discussed at length in Chapter Four, Newton's and Bourdin's photographic oeuvre contained sexually explicit material and was quite often suggestive of violence against women. Newton's characteristic mix of masochistic heroines and sadistic mistresses and Bourdin's graphic depictions of mutilated bodies explored the connections between sex, death and power. Similarly, Just Jaeckin, who directed the French soft-core film *Emmanuelle* (1974), was a fashion photographer who occasionally worked for French *Vogue*. The proliferations of overtly erotic hard-core images in fashion media texts have not been limited to the representation of women. Depictions of masculinity have also deployed pornographic codes, creating contemporary homoerotic images of men that appeal to a wider audience, though based in and appropriated from conventions of representation and structures of looking that are characteristic of twentieth-century gay male culture. The influence of gay pornography, especially from the 1980s onwards, through the work of photographers Herb Ritts and Bruce Weber for Calvin Klein and Abercrombie and Fitch, was a key development in the representation of masculinities within fashion iconography that explicitly invited the viewer to enjoy eroticized images of men. This homoerotic style of photography takes its materiality of sex and desire from the language of gay pornography and is reworked via postures and images that also evoke classical Greco-Roman sculpture. This style, most notable in the images created by Robert Mapplethorpe, also found expression in the work of the fashion photographer Nick Knight and stylist Ray Petri, and subsequently in the images created by other photographers – Mert and Marcus, Alasdair McLellan, David Sims and Steven Klein. The overtly passive and reclining male, previously a role only offered to women, replaced the active man of the 1960s and 1970s; now men were invited not only to consume fashionable products, but also to *look* at themselves and other men as objects of desire. [8]

Unwieldy fashion in representation

Before we turn to a few examples of pornochic in music video clips it is first helpful to wind back a bit and to look at the representation of fashion in light of the extreme and dysfunctional, for after all pornochic is everything that sensible utilitarian dress is not. If it weren't a little too perverse, one is tempted to assert that pornochic is where represented fashion was bound to end up, first because the representation is of a fathomable yet exterior world, and second because this world is one that is desired. In the more decorous age of fashion photography before and between the world wars, fashion was represented within the ambit of impeccable grooming; it was spotless and immaculately pressed. This can be strongly contrasted with images after the 1970s in which it has not been uncommon for models to be dishevelled, sometimes *en demi-déshabillé*, and sometimes even soiled to betray a suggestion of interaction in purported real life. But the dramatic integer of real life in fashion imagery is only a rhetorical distraction for the truth, which is the very obverse – it is far from real.

Although the 1970s was a period of sartorial looseness and liberation, with its hippie dress of sandals and flowing thin Indian cottons, it was also ironically the beginning of unwieldy fashion. Signs of this were already in the sci-fi collections of Courrèges after 1964, but 1964 was also the year that Kenzo Takada decided to settle in Paris, initiating the so-called 'Japanese revolution' in fashion in 1970. Although the Japanese fashions placed a premium in flow and movement, the movement could be stylized and slowed due to the encumbrance of the mass of cloth.[9] Issey Miyake, who also worked in Paris in the late 1960s, and later Yohji Yamamoto, created garments that were strikingly architectonic and sculptural. Japanese fashions from the late 1970s onward had a tendency to repudiate the bodily form and instead use the body as an armature for the angular and implausible sartorial carapace. The sympathy of these garments to exhibition is clear testament of their substantive sculptural qualities; substantive here meaning they can have a parallel but equally valid life when disembodied. In 1988 Issey Miyake had his first major exhibition at the Musée des Arts Décoratifs, not, note, at the Musée de la Mode. Subsequent exhibitions, and those of his Japanese-Parisian peers, reveal how adept these designers are in innovating forms of display and blurring the line between clothing, sculpture and architecture.

While these designers branched into more wearable prêt-à-porter lines, they began a trend for haute couture to be outrageous, extreme and defiant of versatility. It became harder and harder to imagine wearing these garments. Instead, they existed more in the manner of what we now call conceptual fashion, fashion that exists more as an idea from which workable sub-solutions may emanate, much in the manner of the experimental models of the deconstructivist architects like Piano and Rogers, Venturi, Eisenman or Libeskind existed virtually for the sake of generating ideas, or of supplying an extreme image of which the workable version was a dilution. The example of architecture is a suitable analogy for what had begun to emerge as very discrete lines of fashion practice, with the highest end existing in a realm that straddled both the real and the imaginary (and more recently it occupies the virtual sphere as well). After the Japanese designers in Paris, designers such as Christian Lacroix would become known for outrageously baroque designs whose actual public wearability beggared belief – a tension that was satirized in the comedy series that began in 1992, *Absolutely*

Fabulous. These garments were real in the respect that they had a physical incarnation and were worn by living models, but became known only through film and photographic imagery after the release of the collection. In short, by dint of their extremity, these garments were made to be exhibited and to be photographed. The concepts of the embodiment and interaction in social relations so important to fashion still exist, but as preponderantly theoretical. Paradoxically, such garments have a strong performative quality, for although they are resistant to physical wear, they are highly theatrical and place the body within quite graphic roles, as with the provocatively vicious Highland Rape collection of 1995 by Alexander McQueen which featured armour-like tops and others with breasts fully bare, hardly something that anyone other than the most confident exhibitionist is likely to wear in the everyday world. Miyake and McQueen's breastplates for example – a pseudo-Hellenism for women since the Greco-Roman breastplate suddenly spawned breasts – and the variety of references to violence are all components of pornochic. Like pornochic which gestures to pornography and the semantics of theatricalized eroticism without actually carrying it out, from the late 1980s couture itself was made increasingly less for the lived world, and joined hands with the rich imaginaries evoked through fashion imagery. Both pornochic and haute couture share the same tripartite structure with the image: they begin with an image (which is usually part of a hypothetical narrative), are worn and end in an image again (the representation in film and/or photography). They reveal a condition of fashion that had always been present but conveniently repressed.

Anti-social and impracticable, pornochic is an extreme and eroticized incidence of what Jonathan Faiers has termed 'dysfunctional fashion' and 'dressing dangerously'.[10] Examining narrative cinema from 1940s noir to the near present, Faiers' exhaustive and original study looks at the role of clothing and dress when it is either overblown, supplemental, diverting, pointless or inadequate. As Faiers observes:

'Dysfunctional' as a term is understandably construed as negative, suggesting that the object to which it is applied has ceased 'working' or become 'unstable' and, although many of the garments considered in this book fail to deliver their original purpose at the most fundamental level, the disproportionate or unexpected emphasis placed on them triggers an automatic and complex series of additional emotional responses in the viewer. This may include references to other film moments where similar examples exist and that are contingent with our own experiences and situations such as wearing inappropriate clothing, clothing that does not fit, gets dirty or mislaid. The catalogue of dysfunctional clothing is both endless and universally experienced and so when a similar scenario is played out on film we feel an empathetic response.[11]

Faiers is dealing with some quite specific variables here, such as kitsch suits, overcoats that do not keep out the rain, hats whose brims are too small, the eternal overcoat over the arm that is never worn, overdressing, or uncomfortable fabrics (vinyl). According to this assessment, dysfunctionality is what is inadequate or impedes manoeuvre within natural or social environments. However it seems that if scrutiny can be diverted away from the verisimilitude of film to the hypertrophied universe of the fashion image in recent decades, dysfunctionality is altogether desirable precisely because, to use Faiers' words, it triggers 'an automatic and complex series of additional emotional responses in the viewer'. Unfathomable haute couture and the garish lubricity of pornochic are of a piece in this regard, since their importance lies in their evocative power over their utilitarian capacity as dress. If we are impressed by such garments, it is differently from the most conventional, default modalities we expect from fashion, which boils down to elegance. The *je ne sais quoi* of sartorial eloquence is replaced with *Je sais, mais je n'ose pas* (I know, but I dare not).

Another point of reference for unmanageable fashions refers back to some extent to the eighteenth century, but more so to the late nineteenth, before the dress reforms that allowed for greater physical mobility and more relaxed demeanour. Examining the fashions of this era, Gina Dorré makes the astonishing assertions that the corseted torso and the 'backward-sweeping bustle' created 'a posture, movement and silhouette that . . . is conspicuously horse-like'. For 'these extravagant fashions presented the body as an "unnatural" and overdetermined artifact'.[12] This period witnessed what Dorré calls 'moral panic' due to the unwieldiness of women's dress. Increasingly, feminist voices spoke out against the severity and control of corsets, which disfigured and slowed down women's bodies to the brink of immobility.[13] She draws attention to the many analogies between harnessed horses and perturbed 'tight-laced' women; both are 'reined in' and in almost perpetual discomfort, even pain.[14] Dress reformers of this time made much of what they viewed as the more salutary 'healthy', 'beautiful' and 'natural' body as opposed to one inconvenienced and misshapen.[15] 'Aesthetic costume' as it was called in late Victorian England obeyed the form of the body without adverse contradiction which, it was implied, had deeper ramifications to one's psychological well being. Hence when the corset and its attendant ensemble like the stiletto return in the 1980s, this appearance is in no small part a reaction to the version of 'aesthetic dress' of the late modern age, the quasi-Orientalist free-flowing fashions of the 1970s. While the fashion corset metonymically references pain through knowledge of its history, pain is very much a physical reality with especially high heels. Both are the retro-elegance of the impracticable.

Let us return to the assertion we made about Newton in the previous chapter, namely that rather than goading the viewer into believing that they might or could have what is in the image, it goes a step beyond to the cold truth that the viewer indeed cannot. In doing so it ostensibly contravenes the assumption of the fashion photograph that it creates a fictive opening between image and viewer. But in setting up the metaphoric bar between the two and suggesting to the viewer 'that is why you are only the viewer', the image sets up a masochistic fantasy of two levels of disavowal. The first is to disavow the raison d'être of the fashion (and commercial) image that it sets up the illusion of the some entry portal for the viewer, the potential consumer. The second is infinitely more complex, but goes to the very heart of the chaotic phantasmic order within commodity fetishism. It is in being told that you definitely cannot have something that opens up a much greater desire to have it. By going to the heart of the void that spawns the process of fetishization, this process becomes more refined, and more ardent. In pre-Second World War photography fashion photography largely partook of a discourse that worked on the presumption that the fashion image was the graphic intermediary between the disembodied product and the public. By presenting the product in the best possible light, the consumer could then imagine the best that she could be and what she might be if she tried harder (more money, weight loss, make-up, and so on). These are roughly causal, analogue presumptions which work on emotions like empathy and aspiration.

But pornochic, in representation, is the embodiment of the perverse and decentred core of the fashion image. For pornochic is the *condition* of the fetish given shape. This is not to say that it is a material resolution, rather one of perpetual instability and *Unheimlichkeit*. The state of uncanniness is borne from the unease of, literally, not feeling at 'home' (*Heim*). For pornochic and its variant S/M chic is pre-eminently impractical – this was always the nature of bondage wear, in which the rhetoric of threat is built into the garment, and where it is a precondition of the garment that it fall outside the realms of feasible utility, and with it, feasible acceptability. The manifestation of the seepage of bondage wear into the public realm, pornochic also exists within a highly coded set of representations, from the private realm to that of mainstream popular culture. The first major manifestation of which was the close collaboration between Jean Paul Gaultier and Madonna.

Madonna's Blond Ambition

A major watershed for the evolution of pornochic arrived with performer and style icon Madonna in the late 1980s. Although Madonna was already known for her highly sexualized performances, The Blond Ambition Tour, launched in 1990, catapulted Madonna to superstardom and solidified pornochic in popular culture. Madonna's performances were transgressive enough to be *outré* rather than being a representation of pornography packaged as fashion. What sets pornochic (and S/M chic) apart from pornography is that pornochic is led by celebrities and arbiters of style whose aim is to shock and scandalize by transferring the taboo and transgressive qualities of pornography into mainstream cultural production. Pornographic narrative sequences and visual cues are watered down and repackaged as 'erotic' rather than porn, a strategy that Madonna used to promote her oeuvre and The Blond Ambition Tour. The use of fetish garments such as leather, corsets, studs and dog collars was not new to fashion; Vivienne Westwood had dabbled in bondage wear in the 1970s with her interest in punk and it was still a peripheral interest to designers in the 1980s. Madonna morphed into a dominatrix when Jean Paul Gaultier designed her corset cone-bra for the tour. The pink corset over a stylized version of a man's suit made reference to the breasts and the phallus. Madonna was the masculine aggressive woman, the phallic-woman, with a voracious sexual appetite that transmogrifies her into a dominatrix and an *überfrau*. The message was clear; this woman gets what she wants. The costume design by Jean Paul Gaultier was to have an indelible effect on both performer and designer, since both would continue to make use of fetishistic, pseudo-BDSM styling. Madonna's bad-girl repertoire and corset with cone-bra would etch itself into fashion history and Gaultier would secure his place as the *l'enfant terrible* in fashion's hall of fame.

As an arbiter of style, Madonna constantly reinvented herself with pornographic codes and signifiers. Her performances on stage and on video were highly sexualized and homoerotic, often transgressing taboos. 'Justify My Love', recorded by Sire Studios in 1990, is explicitly pornographic, but marketed as erotica. Steven Meisel, who collaborated with Madonna on the book *Sex* and would later photograph her as a raging bull and a wild horse for *W Magazine*, placed Madonna in an *ménage à trois* scenario with its performers dressed in fetish gear. Populated by a cast of characters playing various sexual roles, the song and accompanying music video is a celebration of polymorphous sexuality. Banned by MTV because of its sexual explicitness, the music video was filmed in grainy black and white in the style of 1940s film noir, the European auteurs in the 1960s, but also – with the gesticulating impish character that crops up here and there – harkening back to German Expressionism. The male love object in the video, Madonna's then boyfriend and model Tony Ward, confirms that the video was inspired by multilayered pastiche and from a cinematic history of taboo:

> When Madonna and I started dating, we watched a lot of old Italian movies – Fellini, Rossellini, the Pasolini movie that's got the shit eating [*Salò*]. I don't know if she would agree, but I would say that the idea for *Justify my Love* came from me. She was editing *Truth or Dare*, and we talked about sexual scenarios, being voyeuristic. Seeing two girls make out, that made her excited.[16]

It is the mark of any successful cultural object (should we demur from using the word 'art' here?) that it can draw so many overlapping lines of reference and interpretation. For as well as the references already mentioned, much of the imagery evokes Christopher Isherwood's *Goodbye to Berlin* (1939), which includes a similar cast of characters. The action takes place in an elegant hotel that caters to alternative lifestyles. Madonna's character enters looking tired and distressed as she walks down the hallway toward her room where her sexual fantasies are lived out with a mysterious man and with various couples cavorting in fetish outfits: leather, latex bodysuits and corsets. In many respects it was a coming of age for Madonna, and many defended it for the way it also subverted the desiring gaze. As the video's director, Jean-Baptiste Mondino, explains, 'the idea was simply that a woman is to be loved emotionally and sexually, at the same time. Most of the time, we think sex is something that is for the man. If a woman admits that she likes sex, we think she's not a respectable person, which is completely stupid.'[17] What is incontestable is that Madonna played a central role in the sexualization of woman and her MTV presence ushered in a sexualization of fashion and dress that no longer elicited scorn or fear.

The stage performance of 'Justify My Love' as part of The Girlie Show Tour (1993) contained visual themes and props reminiscent of the big-top circus, but, in this case, a sex circus with burlesque performers dressed in costumes designed by Dolce & Gabbana (D&G). On stage, Madonna is partially cross-dressed as a Victorian dandy with monocle, silk cape, cravat, cuffed shirt and waistcoat teamed up with a black satin skirt and leather lace-up boots. Dressed as a mythological half-man/half-woman demi-god, Madonna's costume once again alludes to the power invested in the sexually aggressive phallic woman. The costume also draws on the legends of nineteenth-century circus and so-called 'freak' shows as a visual device to comment on alternative sexualities.

Madonna released her concept album *Erotica* (Maverick Records, 1992) simultaneously with the companion photo book *Sex*, photographed by Steven Meisel. Released the day before the music video clip, the book features Madonna simulating sex acts with models, pornstars and celebrities. In *Erotica* Madonna plays her alter ego Mistress Dita, a riding-crop-wielding dominatrix dressed in a latex corset that invites her lover to explore the threshold of pleasure and pain. *Erotica* was shocking, sexy and arousing, depicting naked women cavorting together with Madonna dressed in sadomasochistic accessories; a harness, studs, dog collar and leather military captain's hat flogging her lover.

'*Justify My Love*, *Erotica* and *Sex* were by any standards transgressive, explicit and sexy,' notes McNair.

> Their *mises en scène* were quite intentionally those of the pornographer – masturbation, group sex, sadomasochism, lesbianism and even simulated rape, all framed as the product of the star's sexual fantasies. Though marketed

as erotica rather than porn – i.e. art rather than trash; beautiful rather than 'ugly'; true rather than 'faked' – this body of work stands as one of the first attempts by a popular artist, working in any medium, to appropriate the transgressive qualities of porn in a mass market context.[18]

Madonna was not the only musician challenging boundaries of sexual representation; the New Romantic pop band Duran Duran had produced 'adult' music promos since the 1980s to accompany songs like 'Girls on Film' (1981) and 'Rio' (1982) that depicted near-naked women. But it was not until 'Girl Panic' was produced in 2011, that fashion supermodels were united with SM styling and pornochic.

'Girl Panic'

A cityscape in black and white; the beginnings of a voice over: a man is interviewing a woman who is evidently a member of a band talking over her longevity: 'People don't teach you how to be famous,' she preens. The camera enters the sumptuous Savoy Hotel in London, then cuts to a grid of four surveillance cameras in the corridor to one of the floors. There is some motion and maybe something is amiss. Next is a close-up of the face of Naomi Campbell, who has just awoken. The faces and body parts of other women, some in awkward positions, appear to us at oblique angles to the opening chords of the song; a hand having released a champagne glass; a skimpy, belted body suit. One woman in black lace is sleeping on the bed on the stomach of another in thick make-up wearing a studded leather dog collar. Another, asleep on the floor, wears studded lingerie and long black vinyl boots with platform heels. As Campbell rises there is a cut to the close-up of a woman's hand with long silver nails in sawn-off black gloves with a skull ring on her forefinger supporting a half full, now flat glass of champagne. She too wears leather lingerie with extra belt details near the neck. Campbell rises and is shown to be wearing a corset-style black body suit with black fur shoulder stole and fur sleeves, and high platform stilettos.

The combination of rough trade and the high end of town, luxury and squalor, sophistication and trash lies at the heart of pornochic. The video to 'Girl Panic' (2011) was directed by Jonas Åkerlund, who also directed the videos of Lady Gaga's 'Paparazzi' and 'Telephone'. As with pornochic, it is imagination that rules, and the thrill of connotations of bodily and existential limits. With all this in mind, the girls in the opening shots of 'Girl Panic' lolling about in the lavish hotel room recall the beauties conquered by the ruling vampire, if not the orgies of sex and flesh celebrated in retro-cult classics typified by the dreamy delicious ero-kitsch of *Vampyros Lesbos* (1971).

To return to the video for 'Girl Panic', the following scenes show more models assembling, presumably to join Campbell. They are all star supermodels of the late 1980s and early 1990s: Naomi Campbell, Cindy Crawford, Eva Herzigova, Helena Christensen and Yasmin Le Bon. In a mock documentary 'making-of' style – hence a film about a film – the women introduce themselves, but not as their female selves but as members of the band, thus Herzigova as keyboardist and band co-founder Nick Rhodes, Christensen as drummer Roger Taylor, Campbell as Le Bon and Crawford as John Taylor. Christensen's opening words are, 'Hi I'm Roger and I play drums in one of the coolest bands in the world.'

To see such a recognizable female model introduce herself as Roger is preposterous, but it is done with such laconic aplomb as to suggest that something more artful is afoot. Crawford, in a close-fitting leather jacket, pre-empts the entry of Yasmin Le Bon as the extra guitar player, who arrives to a rapt entourage of paparazzi from Hyde Park. Campbell, sitting in a lavish white fur and wearing a thick batch of jewellery is asked by a male voice about 'Girl Panic'. As she answers the camera moves to the man's profile and it is that of the lead singer himself, Simon Le Bon. '"Girl Panic",' she replies, 'is about a girl who is trying to drive a man crazy like the dance of temptation – does he get the girl in the end? Probably not.' (This is interrupted by Herzigova-Rhodes telling us that she wrote the song and takes 'full credit for it'.) The guiding narrative Campbell-Le Bon in which love and its pursuit remain unrequited fits plainly within the topology of thwarted desire prevalent in the fashion image in film and photography from Newton onward. The man fetishizes the woman, but the woman, or woman in general, vanishes from male view. This is all fairly standard love-story stuff, but what is curious is that by the end of the video, if one happens to remember this at all, it is left uncertain whether this scenario ever took place, because it is not part of any narrative arc.

Figure 16 Cindy Crawford, Helena Christensen, Naomi Campbell, Eva Herzigova and Yasmin Le Bon. Photographer Stephanie Pistel. Courtesy of Sharon Cho for Duran Duran.

Figure 17 Nick Rhodes and Eva Herzigova. Photographer Stephanie Pistel. Courtesy of Sharon Cho for Duran Duran.

As the song begins its momentum, the models are represented in parts of central London, alone or in pairs, being photographed by fashion photographers, who, together with their assistants, are themselves also models. In between snap footage of Yasmin Le Bon and Herzigova embracing for the camera, Crawford appears in a sumptuously hairy green coat in the back of a Rolls Royce driven by her alter ego John Taylor. Cut to Campbell-Le Bon saying that there is still more work to do as a band. Then to Nick Rhodes interviewing Herzigova-Rhodes: 'You have had some truly shocking reviews over your career,' whereupon she replies with a broad smile, 'Damn! Love to read all of those!' Rhodes was founder of the band, which grew out of glam rock and punk. Always fashion conscious, Rhodes was known for his effeminacy in early years. The band were quick to pick up the cue from Bowie and Roxy Music by wearing suits and outfits designed by Antony Price, especially in their enactments for music video which in the early 1980s was in its very nascent stages.

Duran Duran's commitment to the fashion and the visual medium of video from the very beginning of their career meant that they were always in different looks and, in effect, playing roles. As homage to this, in between footage of models of sundry races and looks preening before the camera, an off-camera voice asks Campbell-Le Bon, 'You must be playing some kind of role when you go on stage.' She says, 'For me that's part of the art of being Simon Le Bon.' In her essay 'Carnival of Mirrors: The Hermetic World of Music Video', Kathryn Shields makes the comparison of the figures within music video and the commedia dell'arte, the stylized theatre that used masks originating in Italy in the sixteenth century. Paradoxically, this becomes more evident the more famous the star: 'Iconic performers like Madonna, Prince, Mick Jagger of the Rolling Stones, and U2's Bono become identifiable due to their stage presence. They seem to have a timeless, masklike quality that transcends the subtle changes in appearance that occur over the course of their careers.'[19] This is also the paradox in celebrity, the hypertrophied character type who becomes a super-self through playing that self. Not only that, but masks, as Shields explains, have an emblematic visual quality that can stir the imagination and are easily identifiable.[20] She cites examples (such as Panic at the Disco's 'But It's Better if You Do') which use 'masks to disguise an identity and scenario of intrigue and unexpected reversal'. But in 'Girl Panic', such a reversal is dramatically and overtly enacted.

The mask-like character that emerges from music videos is also a product of the prioritizing of the main singer with a degree of close-ups not found on feature film. It is given a primacy that is often extreme and saturating, leading Carol Vernallis, in her extensive analysis of music video, to admit she wishes 'the star's appearance were not so rigorously enforced'.[21] In a video such as 'Girl Panic' she appears to have had this wish granted since the identities of the stars are so theatrically displaced. Even the practice of lip-synching that has bedevilled music video, especially when the singers cannot 'be their voice', is self-consciously referenced at the end when the ersatz-band perform the song, and Campbell-Le Bon proficiently synchs to the male voice.[22]

The aesthetic enclosure of the video is enforced by reflexive devices that are only possible in a virtual realm. As Vernallis explains, the intimacy of a music video is enhanced by the way 'the viewer can break the viewing plane or, as is said in the theater, the fourth wall'. This occurs when the star or other band members acknowledge the camera, kiss it, play up to it, and so on, or where the set of the clip-in-the-making is made abundantly clear.[23] Yet in 'Girl Panic', the intricacy of its multiple and interlocking frames is also estranging. (Intimacy is also explicit in various enactments of lesbian desire.) Another way of thinking of this 'fourth wall' is the *mise en abyme*, which in 'Girl Panic' is deeply resonant. Literally meaning conferred or placed into the abyss, the term was first used in heraldry for a heraldic symbol that was layered over another set of symbols. It is likened to the 'droste effect', which is that of being stationed between two facing mirrors. In film this term is used for the film within the film and other conceits such as the making of the film that has just been seen, or a character partaking in two parallel sequences. In linguistics, the term, especially prided by deconstruction, is used to designate the infinitely referential nature of language; the way linguistic designations will go in multiple directions as opposed to some ideal atomic core. Thus the *mise en abyme* is at the heart of the intertextual nature of both language and film. In Åkerlund's 'Girl Panic' we have recognizable people being interviewed by other recognizable people whom the former also play. The song is both already made, yet the film is a stylized 'making of'. And the characters, all of whom are both themselves but playing at being someone else, are set within the frame of not one, but at least four narrative structures: the making of the song, the fashion shoot, the goings on between these, and finally the video itself that seals these into a closed circuit. One scene has Herzigova leaving the Savoy hotel and being set upon by models all dressed in black playing fans and paparazzi. As she leaves she stops to kiss a woman in a frizzy blond wig on the lips. Later, another paparazzi scene has the band members incorporated amongst the photographers. Another scene has Rhodes dressed as a bellboy who wheels a slumped Christensen-Taylor on a luggage trolley. This is followed by another model slamming down a clapper board.

Around the middle of the film Campbell-Le Bon boasts that 'we [Duran Duran] were one of the first to put models in our videos'. As if to offer proof, the video is interrupted again, this time with a set of excerpts from earlier videos: 'Girls on Film', 'I Won't Cry for Yesterday', 'Notorious', 'Rio' and back to 'Girls on Film', which at the time (1981) scandalized and attracted audiences in equal measure with its strong (for then) sexual content. These clips provide support for the next albeit fragmentary scene where all four women appear lined up posing against a red background being styled by Dolce & Gabbana (D&G), who also smile and pose for the camera. It will transpire that this *mise en scene* will wind up in reality, or if that is not a world that creditable in fashion, then the material world. For the image of the five models posing in sheer black outfits will grace the December 2011 cover of *Harper's Bazaar* bearing the title, 'The Supers vs Duran Duran'. The product placement – which is somehow pardonable because again it is so reflexively woven into the double-helix structure of the video – is not limited to cameos by D&G and *Harper's*, for an undaunted Campbell brandishes a Swarovski 'Dead or Alive' skull designed by Fabien Baron. The crystals of this skull are then applied to her microphone. While the presence of D&G seems decisive, the use of the Savoy hotel also references Marc Jacobs' post-show interviews, and the pornochic BDSM styling throughout bears a close reference to the Louis Vuitton autumn/winter collection of that year (2011).[24] While the cover shoot is being made, there are several flashes to three models dressed in suggestive BDSM-style clothes sitting outside on the steps. One smokes and looks contemptuously at the camera; the sound is muted as if coming from inside; the camera zooms in to her foot cradled in a thin black strap pump – the cigarette and the attitude say sleaze, and the foot says fetish.

Whether the reference to Vuitton is intended or not, it is certainly relevant to recent developments in the way that luxury fashion houses have sought to penetrate, to inhabit, a range of practices and genres, from art to music video. Vuitton, which is known for its signature logo stamped across its very expensive luggage, has made considerable use of references to gritty and grimy associated with BDSM styling. In one notable instance, in 2008 Vuitton had Annie Leibovitz photograph the lead guitarist for the Rolling Stones, Keith Richards, in a hotel room with a customized guitar case, the lamps on each side of the picture draped with scarves that bare an unmistakable skull motif. The image oozes luxury but the important component of grit and gristle is, rhetorically, preserved.[25] A more complex hijacking of genres takes place in the advertisement for Blason jewellery and Louis Vuitton, where Pharrell Williams, with his unmistakable hip-hop credentials, appears to be performing a version of his song with band N.E.R.D., 'Everyone Nose'. Resembling a music video at first, within seconds it becomes evident that this is a jewellery commercial – so with a hip-hop star, the jewellery, associated with (white) affluence, immediately takes on the street-cred cachet of 'bling', while keeping the status as a high-end commodity. In reference to this advertisement, Janice Miller suggests, 'Music video is always advertising in that its function is the promotion of an artist and a song. Accordingly, the distinctions between music video and moving advertisements may not be as great as they first seem.' What proves unusual about this advertisement, according to Miller, is that it exposes the way advertising has encroached into entertainment.[26] The association between brand and star is more than endorsement, in which the star steps out of his performative role to endorse a product, rather the product is internal to what the star himself produces. He thereby 'imbue[s] the product with the creative and authentic characteristics of music expression and the simple glamour of a star body'. This makes it 'increasingly difficult to separate different kinds of visual material'.[27] While this is an instance of advertising ventriloquizing music video, the obverse is also prevalent, as evidenced in the video for Gwen Stefani's 'Rich Girl' (2009), whose title and content are complemented by references to advertising campaigns from Westwood and Galliano.[28]

The 'Girl Panic' video, thick with product placement, is feasibly a blending of the two, and also a kind of meta-commentary on the complex connections that exist between music video, advertising, fashion, sexuality and identity. For the many intercessions, quotations, allusions, and the very heaping on of content in 'Girl Panic' create an arresting weave of references that tend to destabilize the video's genre – indeed we use the word 'video' more for convenience than anything else. Campbell's lip-synching to the male singing is a reference to decades of music video, in which the performer synched his or her own pre-recorded singing to greater or lesser degrees of success. The final performance, for want of a better word, occurs in the middle of a large room (the function or ball room of the Savoy hotel) with the women standing in the middle of a circular track used to support cameras. These are operated by models in black pornochic gear previously featured in earlier photo-shoots and in other sequences, such as the party-cum-lesbian orgy.

As a prelude to this, Christensen, dressed in a dress that is a dark travesty of a ballerina's outfit, and heavily studded platform high heels, photographs a number of girls, all in scantily clad (dark) pornochic outfits and lingerie who lie asleep about the elegantly disordered hotel suite. This shortly transforms into a gathering with the women, now well awake, gyrating, preening, languishing, rubbing against each other and kissing in and around the four-poster bed. While this scene now appears to have been presaged earlier in the video, its dislocation of the male gaze is all too evident. Women photograph other women; women play men – while at the same time keeping their femininity – who subserviently interview them; a woman covertly photographs sleeping women; women play with other women. There is always the countervailing position that sees all of this still regulated by the male gaze, beginning with the commonplace fact that the video is directed by a man, and that the video was commissioned by and ultimately serves men, namely the band members of Duran Duran. These elaborate filmic configurations can conceivably be understood as presiding within a male ambit, much as early pornography such as eighteenth-century engravings of female sex was ultimately there for male delectation.

But the presence of pornochic, which is the fetish worn all over the body, at the sartorial epicentre of this piece doesn't allow for such a pat ideological view. In his rereading of Freudian fetishism, Lacan states that the fetish, in its efforts at the preservation of the maternal phallus (which, remember, is different from the penis), will manifest in different ways for men or women: 'this desire [for the phallus] has a different fate in the perversions which she presents'.[29] It is instructive that Lacan uses the word 'perversion' here, since Freud had originally relegated perversion to the domain of men, while women were possessed of neurosis. Curiously enough, with Lacan the perverse desires emanate from 'homosexual women'. It is the lesbian who is proficient in courtly love as she 'excels in relation to what is lacking in her'. The use of 'excels' is intriguing, rendering the relationship to desire ardent, intentional and perhaps even transgressive as it also implies a certain joy – for Lacan *jouissance* – that is more celebratory than ridden with anxiety. Hence she makes the transition from (mere) feminine sexuality to the broader reaches of desire. The lesbian, for Lacan, is one who does not have the penis but possesses the phallus through the very avowal of the lack. More ambiguously, Lacan states that this kind of woman has the '*envy* of desire'.[30] As Marjorie Garber in her incisive reading of this passage explains, this is the 'desire for desire'. Thus, '"Having" the phallus, having the fetish, becomes therefore of one's position in the symbolic register and in the economy of desire. "Men" have the phallus; "men" have the fetish. What is at stake is the economy of desire.'[31] Lesbian desire reorients desire through exposing its circular logic. With men, there is a habitual presumption, which is a forced but mistaken corollary, that he has the phallus. But with lesbian desire the fetish is always 'out there' somewhere. In Garber's words, 'Thus Freud's "penis", the anatomical object, though understood through Lacan's "phallus", the structuring mark of desire, becomes reliteralized as a stage prop, a detachable object. No one has the phallus.'[32]

This tension is not only evident in the sexual suggestion and play of the models in both key and anonymous roles, but in the band members themselves.

For not only does Rhodes play a bell boy, and John Taylor Crawford's chauffer, but all of the band members play less dominant, service roles, with Roger Taylor also as a bell hop and Le Bon as a waiter whose tray bearing champagne and a pair of glasses is destabilized by a drunken Christensen. In the latter case, his entry marks the beginnings of the girls' goings-on; they have now awoken and appear to be partaking in a pagan orgy in distinctive BDSM styling. While again it may be argued that the subservience of the male band members is only a subterfuge that masks that the video product ultimately belongs to them, this may be countered with the suggestion that their subservience is only registered through the clear recognition of them. In the context of the analysis above, they are a subsidiary 'subaltern' gaze on the more self-sufficient girl throng, for whom the men are of no great consequence. In another important analysis of female fetishism, Naomi Schor draws on the work of Jacques Derrida's friend Sarah Kofman, drawing attention to the way it introduces a 'paradigm of undecidability'. Schor emphasizes the way the fetish introduces an active 'oscillation between denial and recognition of castration'. As she explains, 'In Kofman's Derridean reading of Freud, female fetishism is not so much, if at all, a perversion, rather a *strategy* designed to turn the so-called "riddle of femininity" to women's account.'[33]

This sense of a strategy used for the sake of 'women's account' is later developed by Frenchy Lunning in her book *Fetish Style* where she explores the status of the postmodern fetish. Again, the fetish is in the first instance perceptibly 'owned' by the male, yet this is a support for a more covert state of affairs. The fashionable female, 'in dressing "for success" as it were . . . can serve as the hanger upon which her masked identity – among her many choices – hangs'. This is a form of masquerade in which the fetish plays a leading role. The 'female masquerader' uses the 'highly fetishized mask of the popular construction of the desirable woman as a commodity form (for there are other possible roles of the wardrobe of the feminine) for the purchase of power through desire'.[34] Lunning's analysis is assisted partly by Laura Mulvey's important comparative analysis of Marxist and Freudian fetishism and its relation to recent culture. Significantly, Mulvey suggests that the postmodern condition – of looking, believing, desiring and being – is to a greater degree locatable in the way in which we locate ourselves in mass media. Mulvey thrice uses the phrase, 'I know very well, but all the same . . .' from Octave Mannoni – the expression that Christian Metz uses to characterize the film viewer's suspension of disbelief.[35] This, she states,

creates an oscillation between what is seen and what threatens to erupt in knowledge. What is disavowed is felt to be dangerous to the psyche, either the black void of castration anxiety or some other threat that sets up a split between knowledge and belief. In the same way, the threat to an autonomous self-sufficiency of the image, that is, value located in the image and not its production processes, threatened the cohesion of Hollywood cinema. But danger and risk are exciting, on a formal as well as narrative level, and Hollywood cinema has made use of a greater degree of oscillation in its system of disavowal than has often been acknowledged.[36]

The filmic image enacts a disavowal which viewers are only too happy to emulate; inserting themselves into narratives, characterizations, and economic and social frameworks that they would have no possibility of inhabiting, no one would.

Gendering pornochic and SM style

We find ourselves back in the world that Newton explicitly established and which we explored in the previous chapter, namely to lay bare the 'truth' of this disavowal that only instigates a greater desire for what only effectively exists as a fabricated image. While pornochic and BDSM styling is exploited by Newton, it is in full flight in Madonna's performances and video clips and in Duran Duran's 'Girl Panic', and may be interpreted both as the 'danger and risk' – panic – of *knowledge*, to use Mulvey's terminology, but also plays on *belief*, because of its very improbability and its limited usefulness. It needs warm rooms for the scantily clad, and flat floors for the preposterously high-heeled; in a word, it exists in fantasy. Improbability in 'Girl Panic' gives way to impossibility but still allowing for belief through the direct in-situ sanction of the band: 'yes she's me'. In salvaging Mulvey's more pessimistic position, Lunning observes that the fetish is a means of 'acknowledgment', where 'fetish becomes a celebration of the gap of what is known and what is believed and forms a performance of desire through its debatable ontological status'.[37] In a video such as 'Girl Panic' this gap is all the more evident precisely because of its stylized, to the point of mannered, performativity. Its sheer unreality on so many levels – the assembly of models in the Savoy, girls being men while being girls, and so on – serves to highlight the reality of the void that the fetish registers through its effort to cover it up and compensate for it. The video is so compensatory and excessive that the condition of the fetish and of fashion representation itself is all but laid bare. On a more worldly level, the kind of restitution of fetish style that Lunning engages with is of a piece with Rosalind Gill's argument that the sexualization of women's bodies, in which states of dress and undress are inextricable, has shifted in the new millennium. From the twentieth century where women were 'passive, mute objects of the female gaze', in the new millennium women have noticeably shifted to become 'actively desiring sexual subjects'.[38] To this Annette Lynch pertinently adds:

The question that follows is who is creating the story, and does this apparently empowering guise of female sexuality cover up escalated levels of misogyny and related white heterosexual privilege? Or, in rebuttal, do these changes constitute a move forward for women, giving them permission to express their own sexual needs and desires?[39]

The answer, as Lynch shows in her book *Porn Chic*, is never simple. Madonna is an important figure in this transition, but one who, in earlier music videos at least, went too far. She suggested that slutty assertiveness is the pathway to what any girl wants. Lynch argues, 'A second important message of Madonna as an icon is that the route to power is through representation – that you need to get your image out, it needs to be provocative, it needs to grab attention – and if you do that success will follow.'[40] In 2010 Madonna together with her daughter Lourdes launched an exclusive line at Macy's department store, *Material Girl*. Its allusions were distinctively nostalgic of the beads, lace, studs and all round cutsie-punk look of the earliest years of her career.[41] Lynch claims that Madonna created 'a branded image that captures the beginning of the co-opting of the 1960s and 1970s [sic] struggle for empowerment by commercial interests at the end of the twentieth century'.[42] Here female desire was directed at various forms of conspicuous consumption that did not necessarily benefit women in the longer term. Lynch concludes, 'The sexy empowerment is a charade in terms of authentic power.'[43]

Can the same be said of 'Girl Panic'? An answer might be ventured through the way fashion and representation is placed at its epicentre. The kind of false empowerment that Lynch warns of can certainly be related to the aggressive women in 'Girls on Film', a video that in many ways is the coda for all the other videos in its wake that drew on soft pornography. But there is a strong suggestion in 'Girl Panic' that it was fashion that was one of the main drivers of the success of Duran Duran's videos in the earliest days, using the fashion industry to drive an image of opulence and panache. At one point Cindy Crawford says she is 'nostalgic for the fashion of the old days, the shoulder pads, the big hair'. She and her other 'band members' are in many ways the physical custodians of the fashion industry that the band so liberally drew from. It is also the complex way in which the video engages with queer and lesbian fetishism that makes it more than a ploy for facile exhibitionism that is ultimately for the sake of the male gaze, for the degree to which males occupy the periphery – even accounting for the bar scene toward the end where the male band members mix with all and sundry – of the video, either as physical presence or disembodied gaze, is striking.

An enlightening counterpoint to this video can be found in Man Ray's deservedly famous *Noire et blanche* (1926), the stark black-and-white photograph of a model (Alice Prin, aka Kiki of Montparnasse) whose face rests as if asleep on a table while she holds upright an African mask. First appearing in Paris *Vogue*, the work immediately sets up analogies between the fetish of African ritual and the fetishism driving fashion photography. The accompanying caption to the image, which we presume is from the magazine as opposed to the artist, included the lines: 'It is through women that the evolution of the species to a place full of mystery will be accomplished. Sometimes plaintive, she returns with a feeling of curiosity and dread'. To this, in his analysis of the works and those associated with it, Whitney Chadwick observes:

> The aesthetic discourse of the fashion photograph and the colonialist discourse of early modernism meet in this image, brought together under the sign of woman's doubling. By 1926, these discourses also shared concepts of the fetish capable of investing formal relations with highly charged sexual and/or racial meanings. . . . The play of signifiers that positions woman, her sexuality, and her image at the intersection of desire and fear, and that [sic] conflates the perfectly constructed surface and the 'primitive' unconscious, underlies representations of femininity within vanguard art practice and consumer culture in the first decades of the twentieth century.[44]

In many respects, 'Girl Panic' can be read as a developmental riposte to the conditions of race and sexuality that occurred together with the birth of fashion photography and the fashion shoot. For seen against Man Ray's image, we are unerringly drawn to the fact that the only woman band 'member' is a black woman who plays the 'front-man', which she is sure to emphasize. It is as if the fascination for the 'primitive' in earlier fashion imagery has been reprocessed in which the fascination is no longer latent but on the very surface, self-consciously played out. By playing Le Bon, Naomi Campbell renders him dangerous, for she is the figure to be feared, who incites panic. If earlier videos by Duran Duran have been criticized for sexism and racial typecasting (as in 'Hungry Like the Wolf', 1982),[45] the same reproach cannot be made so easily with 'Girl Panic'. Chadwick joins a chorus of art historians in reading Man Ray's photograph

> in terms of word and picture play (black/white) [Man Ray also did a negative version of the photograph], or the fragmenting of form that destroys unitary meaning, or as emblematic of the doublings and substitutions that site the Surrealist image/object within an oscillating visual field in which meaning cannot be fixed.[46]

In 'Girl Panic' this oscillation resurfaces, or is remobilized in terms of the lesbian fetish. Moreover, unlike the earlier fashion image in which there is a doubling of the feminine as subject and sign, here the models *play out* this doubling at the expense of the male counterparts while safeguarding and re-enunciating their doubled identity as professional models.

'Girl Panic' draws attention to music video's extraordinary indebtedness to the fashion industry. In many ways it is a paean, if quirky, to this inheritance. As if coming full circle, fashion is now drawing from music video and other filmic genres. The moving image threatens the static image in a way that places fashion not as a component or attribute, as with feature films, but as a driver of the film's very structure and meaning.

Notes

1 Slavoj Zizek, *The Sublime Object of Ideology*, London and New York: Verso, 1989, 117.

2 Janice Miller, *Fashion and Music*, Oxford and New York: Berg, 2011, 1.

3 Susan Cook, 'Subversion Without Limits: From *Secretary*'s Transgressive S/M to "Exquisite Corpse's" Subversive Sadomasochism', *Discourse*, 28 (1), Winter 2006, 125. For a discussion that argues against S/M in reference to lesbians, see Lorena Leigh Saxe, 'Sadomasochism and Exclusion', *Hypatia*, 7 (4), Lesbian Philosophy, Autumn 1992, 59–72.

4 Brian McNair, *Striptease Culture: Sex, Media and the Democratisation of Desire*, New York: Routledge, 2002.

5 Pamela Church Gibson, 'Pornostyle: Sexualized Dress and the Fracturing of Feminism', *Fashion Theory: The Journal of Dress, Body and Culture*, Fashion and Porn, Special Issue, Pamela Church Gibson and Vicki Karaminas (eds), 18 (2), 2014, 189–190.

6 Annette Lynch, *Porn Chic: Exploring the Contours of Raunch Eroticism*, London: Berg, 2012, 3.

7 McNair, *Striptease Culture*, 62.

8 See Pamela Church Gibson and Vicki Karaminas, 'Letter from the Editors', *Fashion Theory: The Journal of Dress Body and Culture*, Fashion and Porn, Special Issue, 18 (2), 2014, 117–122.

9 See Yuniya Kawamura, *The Japanese Revolution in Paris Fashion*, Oxford and New York: Berg, 2004, and Adam Geczy, *Fashion and Orientalism: Dress, Textiles and Culture from the 17th to the 21st Century*, London and New York: Bloomsbury, 2013, 168–174.

10 Jonathan Faiers, *Dressing Dangerously: Dysfunctional Fashion in Film*, New Haven and London: Yale U.P., 2013.

11 Ibid., 8.

12 Gina Dorré, 'Horses and Corsets: "Black Beauty", Dress Reform and the Fashioning of the Victorian Woman', *Victorian Literature and Culture*, 30 (1), 2002, 158.

13 Ibid., 165.

14 Ibid., 166, 168–171, and passim.

15 For an illuminating and thorough examination of this subject, see Ken Montague, 'The Aesthetics of Hygiene: Aesthetic Dress, Modernity, and the Body as Sign', *Journal of Design History*, 7 (2), 1994, 91–112.

16 Tony Ward cit. Craig Marks and Rob Tannenbaum, eds, *I Want my MTV: The Uncensored History of the Music Video Revolution,* New York: Dutton, 2011, 488.

17 Ibid., 489.

18 McNair, *Striptease Culture*, 66.

19 Kathryn Shields, 'Carnival of Mirrors: The Hermetic World of Music Video', in Jane Kromm and Susan Benforado Bakewell, eds, *A History of Visual Culture: Western Civilization from the 18th to the 21st Century*, Oxford and New York: Berg, 2010, 349.

20 Ibid., 350.

21 Carol Vernallis, *Experiencing Music Video: Aesthetics and Cultural Context*, New York: Columbia U.P., 2004, 63.

22 See also ibid., 49, 55, 64, 97.

23 Ibid., 57.

24 'Duran Duran and Supermodels Spark Girl Panic', *Telegraph*, 8 November 2011, http://fashion.telegraph.co.uk/videos/TMG8877048/Duran-Duran-and-supermodels-spark-Girl-Panic.html.

25 See also Miller, *Fashion and Music*, 15–16.

26 Ibid., 21–22.

27 Ibid., 22.

28 Ibid., 23.

29 Jacques Lacan, 'Guiding Remarks for a Congress on Feminine Sexuality', in Juliet Mitchell and Jacqueline Rose, eds, *Feminine Sexuality: Jacques Lacan and the école freudienne*, trans. Jacqueline Rose, New York: Norton, 1982, 96. See also Marjorie Garber, 'Fetish Envy', *October*, 54, Autumn 1990, 46–47.

30 Ibid., 97.

31 Garber, 'Fetish Envy', 47.

32 Ibid. For a discussion of the male playing the fetish, see Laura Hinton, '(G)Aping Women; Or, When a Man Plays the Fetish', *The Journal of Cinema and Media*, 48 (2), Fall 2007, 174–200.

33 Naomi Schor, 'Female Fetishism: The Case of George Sand', in Susan Rubin Suleiman, ed., *The Female Body in Western Culture*, Cambridge, MA: Harvard U.P., 1985, 368–369. See also Sarah Kofman, *L'Énigme de femme: La Femme dans les textes de Freud*, Paris: Galilée, 1980.

34 Frenchy Lunning, *Fetish Style*, New York and London: Bloomsbury, 2013, 73.

35 Laura Mulvey, 'Some Thoughts on Theories of Fetishism in Contemporary Culture', *October*, 65, Summer 1993, 7, 12, 19.

36 Ibid., 19–20.

37 Lunning, *Fetish Stye*, 74.

38 Rosalind Gill, 'Empowerment/Sexism: Figuring Female Sexual Agency in Contemporary Advertising', *Feminism and Psychology*, 18 (35), 42. See also Annette Lynch, *Porn Chic: Exploring the Contours of Raunch Eroticism*, London and New York: Bloomsbury, 2012, 3.

39 Ibid., Lynch.

40 Ibid., 43.

41 Ibid. (See also Monica Sklar, *Punk Style*, London and New York: Bloomsbury, 2013.)

42 Ibid., 44.

43 Ibid., 183.

44 Whitney Chadwick, 'Fetishizing Fashion/Fetishizing Culture: Man Ray's "Noire et blanche"', *Oxford Art Journal*, 18 (2), 1995, 11–12.

45 See for example Denise Kulp, 'Music Videos: Friday Night Sexism', *Off Our Backs*, 14 (4), 1984, 21.

46 Ibid., 3. The other commentators that she cites are Rosalind Krauss, Sidra Stich and Jane Livingston.

6

FASHION FILM, OR THE DISAPPEARING CATWALK

Guaranteed to have all the ingredients of a great performance – high emotion, dramatic encounters, unexpected spontaneity, and the transformative power of glamor – backstage is where the real magic happens. Here is where the image makers – the hairdressers, stylists, makeup artists, and models – gather to animate a designer's collection. Without this team of highly skilled professionals, the collection would remain no more than sketches on a page.

NILGIN YUSUF[1]

After forty years in the fashion industry, Yves Saint Laurent announced his retirement in 2002 declaring, 'I have nothing in common with this new world of fashion.'[2] As we move through the twenty-first century, fashion is rapidly changing to meet the demands of a fast-paced, mediated consumer. Designers are thinking beyond the catwalk show as a means of generating publicity and sales and using the Internet, e-commerce and other three dimensional (3D) technological and digital formats such as fashion film to communicate and stimulate interest. No longer does fashion rely on seasonal catwalk shows and conventional media such as magazines and newspapers to highlight and communicate couturiers' ranges. Fashion and the fashion system as we have understood it to be in the nineteenth and twentieth century have changed. Mass mediation and digitalization have increased the way that contemporary fashion is now perceived. 'This is an era dominated by search engine culture,' writes Gary Needham, 'inhabited by "netizen" with their increasing fluency in digital convergences, where successful online retailers and teenage bloggers collude unabashed'.[3] Almost all couture collections are now live-streamed enabling observers to watch pre-taped runway shows with detailed images and backstage footage available online and on social media applications, such as Twitter, Facebook and Instagram. Where once the runway show was the domain of press elites, journalists and catwalk photographers, now the public can access 'front row' seats to major couture collections. In 2009, Alexander McQueen streamed his summer collection Plato's Atlantis on the web at the same time as he paraded his range on the catwalk in Paris. Since McQueen, other designers such as Diane von Fürstenberg, Marc Jacobs and Chloé have followed suit. Digital media platforms have afforded a new accessibility to the fashion product and given rise to new voices, fashion bloggers that emerged on the Internet in 2002. In February 2011, Swedish fashion retailer H&M launched a line designed by leading fashion blogger Elin Kling. Kling's collection, which launched in ten select stores in Sweden, comprised nine pieces and two accessories. Other bloggers that have influenced fashion products are Bryanboy for Marc Jacobs and Rumi Neely for Forever 21. The importance of fashion bloggers as cultural intermediaries (not designers) who influence today's fashion market by *their ideas* of style and fashion cannot be underestimated. Marc Jacobs was one of the first designers who understood the power of bloggers when in 2008 he named a bag after Bryanboy.

In today's global markets, bloggers have equal status, influence and power as fashion buyers and the mass media. 'Bloggers start a critical conversation that can spread virally'[4] in seconds, what Agnes Rocamora calls 'fast fashion' to describe temporality and the idea of speed in which fashion websites and blogs circulate fashion discourse. 'The rapid turnover of information,' notes Rocamora,

> has become a trait . . . of online fashion media. Not only have they responded to the popularity of the blogosphere through the launch of their own blogs, but they have also embraced speed and immediacy through the creation of sections that clearly feed into the trend of fast news.[5]

The bloggers' emergence as a fashion elite in recent years has shifted the terrain of the traditional fashion system and dramatically changed the fashion industry and the ways in which fashion is disseminated. Commerce and media have united and created new ways of experiencing runway shows and events that differ dramatically from the inaugural days of fashion in the early twentieth century, when fashion was paraded in salons in private shows for wealthy clients.

In her controversial article 'The Circus of Fashion', printed in *The New York Times*, fashion journalist Suzy Menkes criticizes bloggers for ignoring journalistic codes whilst styling themselves as critics. 'Ah, fame!' laments Menkes,

> or, more accurately in the fashion world, the celebrity circus of people who are famous for being famous. They are known mainly by their Facebook pages, their blogs and the fact that the street photographer Scott Schuman has

immortalized them on his Sartorialist web site. This photographer of 'real people' has spawned legions of imitators, just as the editors who dress for attention are now challenged by bloggers who dress for attention.[6]

There has also been a sizeable change in fashion photography, or two-dimensional (2D) formats in which the visual presence has became more evident. Apart from the use of computer applications such as Photoshop to enhance and change body shape and ideals of beauty, the temporality of the photograph has become tipped more toward filmic time and reminiscent of film stills. It is as though the photographer is more of an interloper, who chances on the scene, or, in a more risqué way, as if the photographer was never there at all, or a spy. From the 1970s onward, the fashion image had a greater narrative element, as if the scene were wrested from a larger continuity.[7] We can observe this more with the benefit of hindsight, since fashion representation has moved steadily since then into the realm of film, such that film is now integral to the manner in which fashion is read and understood. As we saw in Chapter Five, fashion has always had a stake in music video since the genre appeared through Music Television (MTV) at the beginning of the 1980s; and music video has itself evolved to become short films which not only emulate short films, but a much newer phenomenon: fashion film.

The growing accessibility of the Internet, observes Marketa Uhlirova, 'combined with its increasing capacity to store and play audio visual content, that made fashion film finally enter the public consciousness as a distinct category of both the fashion image and the moving image'.[8] Fashion film arrived at a time when the technologies of film and cinema were being transformed by the digital experience, a time that Steven Shapiro describes as 'witnessing the emergence of a different media regime'.[9] Originally the brainchild of the British photographer Nick Knight and Peter Saville through his fashion media company SHOWstudio[10] launched in 2000, fashion film has been critical in the evolution of film as a platform for the display of fashion and for creating the embellished scenarios that make us want to buy the product. Rather than inviting the consumer to purchase a product via a showcase of seductive imagery, fashion film *immerses* the audience into a lifestyle environment via three-dimensional (3D) applications. In Chapter Three we examined fashion in film and the meaning of costume and fashion in cinema. In this chapter we explore the emergence of fashion film as a new media genre. Although commercial in intent, like the great photographs of the previous century, these films are aesthetically pleasing objects in their own right.

Early days of fashion film

While fashion film is undeniably something that was facilitated by the Internet, it cannot be said to have had an immaculate and sudden conception. To begin with, contemporary fashion photography, which grew out of the 1970s, was characterized by its knowing cannibalizing of film. The celebrity portraits of Avedon and Penn have a fleeting quality – often studiously achieved – that lends to their immediacy and intimacy, while a good deal of the work of Helmut Newton, as we have seen, seems prized from a story whose larger contours remain unknown to us. More recently, designers such as Hussein Chalayan and Martin Margiela have created garments whose very form and meaning seem to invite, anticipate movement – they are in a state of virtual animation even when they are static. Just from this brief synopsis, fashion film is an inevitable consequence of a series of implicit demands laid out by photographers and designers alike.

The body-in-motion has a much longer lineage than this, however, dating back to the beginning of the twentieth century with the chronophotographs of Étienne-Jules Marey and Eadweard Muybridge, and the considerable influence of Italian Futurism. In her essay on the historical antecedents to the fashion film – now primarily synonymous with SHOWstudio – Marketa Uhlirova cites numerous photographers of this ilk, such as Jacques-Henri Lartigue, Martin Munkacsi, Herman Landshoff, John Cowan and Bruce Weber. Others 'explored the fluidity of body and gesture against transitory urban environments', such as William Klein and David Bailey, while Guy Bourdin, Philip-Lorca diCorcia, and Ellen von Unwerth are others who deployed the fictive film still look.[11] Scholars agree that the first examples of what we now call fashion film were made by the great eccentric and experimental George Méliès between 1898 and 1900, commercials of women wearing Mystère corsets and Delion hats manipulated into reverse motion, which were projected on the exterior of the Théâtre Robert-Houdin in Paris.[12] In the same year as the first fashion shoot, 1911, Poiret undertook a film of his *The Thousand and Second Night*, and a year after he executed another, which was to serve as a stand-in for a fashion parade.[13]

In *The Fashion Film Effect*, Marketa Uhlirova argues that although fashion film existed in some form or other throughout the twentieth century, its emergence as a phenomenon has been delayed. What differentiates fashion film from film itself is that it is 'owned by the fashion industry – fulfilling almost exclusively its creative and business needs'.[14] Fashion film also grew in a more de facto form as a result of the rising popularity of newsreels and documentary footage and exploded as a form of product promotion with digital technologies. Fashion was also an important modulator in the rising demand for tinted films that grew out of the pre-sound era.[15] Film was used to stage and dramatize the fashion item, for enticing both consumers and prospective store stockists. A notable development took place with a film by Humphrey Jennings in 1939, *Making Fashion* (formerly titled *Design for Spring*), a prolonged advertisement for Norman Hartnell, who acted as both couturier and co-producer.[16] In Uhlirova's words:

It is an intimate yet highly idealized portrayal of the behind-the-scenes of one of England's grandest and most successful fashion salons, showing a perfectly co-ordinated team of busy skilled workers demonstrating a range of design processes, from draping on a dummy to the execution of a sample, to a fitting on a model and encrusting with sequins and jewels.[17]

In this regard, it was of a piece with one of Knight's intentions with SHOWstudio's fashion films, to show fashion items being made, and to reveal the process and *mise-en-scène* of the fashion shoot. As he noted about his first film *Sweet*, he wanted to

show how much effort and even pain, goes into making a single dress. I wanted each garment to seem precious, like an art form. . . . I am aware of the fact that fashion is entirely disposable – but I am lucky enough to be able to work with people who prove there's more to it than that.[18]

In the same year the French government funded Marcel L'Herbier to do a film for the New York World Fair to promote French couture. Here models emerge from a painting in the style of Watteau wearing garments from Nina Ricci, Lucien Lelong and Elsa Schiaparelli.[19]

As we know, the interwar period was an important transitional period for fashion as much else. Before it was decimated by the advent of National Socialism, the burgeoning German film industry witnessed many different forays of genre and spectacle. The hedonism of the Weimar period, its love of show, gave way to a new filmic sub-genre, the *Konfektionskomödie*, or 'fashion farce', which was influenced by the live fashion shows, the *Modenschau*. Mila Ganeva in her study of the films of this period cites the example of Richard Eichberg's 1927 film *Der Fürst von Pappenheim* (*The Prince of Pappenheim*), a light-hearted drama of a princess who has fled home and now works as a fashion model, and a former model who marries a count who is able to indulge all her fashion whims. There is nothing profound about the film, but, as Ganeva observes, the 'film belongs to a group of works from the Weimar era in which fashion is not only part of a spectacular *mise-en-scène* but served as the raw material for the narrative'.[20] She argues that fashion was an essential integer to the way audiences experienced images of modern life and provided a material and vicarious link to the way in which people engaged with one another. Such films were of particular interest to the modern-day working woman who, with limited time and resources, could avail herself of the up-to-date images of contemporary fashions, hairstyles, make-up and the like.[21] As such, the *Konfektionskomödie* was not only valued for its ability to divert and entertain, but also as a vehicle for commodities, serving as an early example of what we today know as product placement. And there are curious factual details that lend themselves to the genesis of this form, such as the fact that in earlier years Ernst Lubitsch worked in a Berlin clothing store, at the behest of his father, himself a clothing store owner.[22] Ganeva concludes:

> The fashion shows within the films constituted significant breaks in the narrative flow, during which spectators were offered glimpses of the earlier cinema of attraction preserved fragmentarily in the fabric of Weimar's popular story-based cinema. This disruption associated with the fashion show in early Weimar cinema reflected (even in the most straightforward and trivial narratives) the experience of modernity, which was in essence the experience of an environment becoming increasingly distracting, disjunctive, and fragmented.[23]

No doubt stirred by such instances, from the late 1920s and early 1930s fashion's relationship with the moving image burgeoned with growing intensity. For example Horst's mentor and lover Hoyningen-Huene made a series of short films containing very little narrative of Horst and Natalia Paley, wife of Lucien Lelong, as well as a now lost documentary for *Vogue* in 1933. In more recent memory, Serge Lutens, Richard Avedon and Helmut Newton all made promotional films for the Japanese brand Jun Rupé.[24] For new-wave designers like Hussein Chalayan, who made several notable films in the early 2000s (e.g. *Place of Passage*, 2003, *Anaesthetics*, 2004, *Absent Presence*, 2005), film was an obvious choice, since it is his project, as with contemporaries like Margiela and Viktor and Rolf, to extend the conceptual, affective and physical potential of garments to their fullest.

Although part of a feature film, Jean Paul Gaultier's designs for Peter Greenaway's *The Cook, The Thief, His Wife and Her Lover* (1990) deserve special mention for the way the clothing plays a vital part in the film's composition and meaning. Nita Rollins describes how Gaultier's costumes actively complemented the film's withering criticism of class and social pretention. Gaultier assists in the myriad historical references that Greenaway immerses himself in through garments that are at once complementary and dissonant. As Rollins states:

> The *corporeal*, integrally related to Greenaway's narrative, has a dynamic relationship to the costume designs and increasingly seems to overtake them, to attenuate their integrity in a way that supersedes class motivations and manifests Greenaway's avowed interests in the physicality of vices and virtues.[25]

She argues however that while Gaultier's clothes appear in the first instance to partake in the critical 'outrage' at consumerism and excesses of mass consumption, references such as those to punk do less to transgress and do far more to show how fashion emulates and absorbs styles and languages to its own benefit.[26] But what this film unwittingly demonstrates is the active tussle that can exist between narrative intent and the meaning inherent within garments themselves. The story, as Knight would later claim in relation to fashion film, is already in the garment itself. Knight's own musings on fashion film begin with the commonsense observation that film lends itself to fashion because it is made to be worn, which implies movement. Fashion film is different from film, he says, in the same way fashion photography is different from photography. To the question,

> what makes a great fashion film? It's very easy to answer: great fashion makes a great fashion film. The narrative is already *in that piece of clothing*. So the narrative is already, if you want, inside the dress or the suit or the skirt . . . the designer has already created that vision, so the narrative's all there; every bit of clothing speaks. It's always got an intention behind it, it's always got a desire behind it.[27]

He goes on to assert that to add an 'event sequence', that is, a narrative, to the garment is 'totally superfluous'.[28]

Knight returns to the distinction between fashion photography and fashion film, claiming that photography is defined by a 'certain set of parameters', and that it 'stopped when the digital world came along. And that's when we should "let it be what it was"'. The potential of what photography could become in the digital age, he suggests, was not supported by fashion magazines who, rather, trivialized and 'dumbed down' what fashion photography could potentially become. Photography is no longer the Zeitgeist medium that it was. The new medium of fashion film, Knight observes, tends to break down the barrier that had formerly existed between artist and audience, as it also provides the possibility of representing the process of the work's making, which demystifies the object and engenders better understanding. From very early in his career, before his privileging of the moving image, Knight responded to new technologies. As a fashion photographer his work is heavily worked to create imagery that is dramatically extracted, and foreign to the everyday world.

There are different types of fashion films: the large-scale budget films for brands such as *Lady Blue Shanghai* directed by David Lynch, and the more edgy and experimental films, such as *Blackened Wings* by Josh Brandao, which won first place Coupe d'Or at the 2014 Fashion Film Festival Chicago (FFFC). Brandao's film was inspired by the Greek legend of the phoenix and takes place in a militarized Soviet world. *Blackened Wings* tells the tale of a young boy fighting to overcome bullying and oppression. The film showcases a collection of accessories and fashion artefacts by London College of Fashion Graduate Chiara Pavan, as well as garments by Givenchy, Westwood and Armani. Other sub-genres include what Gary Needham has described as a 'boutique' film associated with e-stores, the 'authored' film created by a known film director, such as Martin Scorsese's *Street of Dreams* for Dolce & Gabbana (D&G) starring Matthew McConaughey and Scarlett Johansson. Filmed in classic black-and-white cinematic style, *Street of Dreams* is a story about the power of love and dreams. Then there is the 'artist' film – which is a brand-funded feature created by an established artist, such as photographer Ellen von Unwerth's film *Sister Act* featuring models Anne Vyalitsyna and Irina Shayk for *Vs Magazine* – and the 'designer' film, best exemplified by *Brothers of Arcadia* by creative director Nicola Formichetti for Thierry Mugler, to be explored at the end of this chapter.

Moving fashion

As with any filmic genre, fashion film does not have defined edges, but it can be defined as a moving-image platform to show off contemporary fashion. Its length is defined according to what it can sustain; it is seldom over fifteen minutes (with exceptions, of course). It can be highly abstract, making full use of post-production effects, or it can be situated in a narrative that is suggested or suspended. Billing itself as 'the home of fashion film' and supporting 'the best of global fashion film', SHOWstudio is in many respects a point of connection between directors, designers, models and other fashion 'creatives'. In the fifteen years of its life it has been the portal and the facilitator of a long list of esteemed, if not also notorious and controversial, members of the fashion industry, ranging from Gareth Pugh to Lady Gaga. Björk, former partner of the celebrity artist Matthew Barney, has also played a part (she is also the subject of one of Knight's most iconic photographs). In his essay on her relationship to fashion, Dirk Gindt remarks that 'Björk strategically uses McQueen's and Knight's understanding of fashion as a performative process, that is, constantly in a state of becoming and transformation'.[29] Gindt concludes that the collaborative encounter, over a decade before McQueen's death, was

> a creative meeting between high art and popular culture, between the avant-garde and the commercially viable, between music, fashion, and visual culture . . . Moreover, there was an identifiable subversive potential in their output that articulated issues of cultural marginalization and independence.[30]

This was enabled in large part to the suppleness and malleability of the medium of the moving image, and penetrability of the Internet.

Fashion film is a significant example of what arrives after what art and media theorists have termed 'post-photography'. This emerges with the so-called death of photography and the birth of what Kevin Robins calls 'a post-photographic culture'. With the development of digital technologies 'the domain of the image has become autonomous, even in which the very existence of the "real world" is called into question'.[31] With analogue photography there was still some indexical stake in the material world, the world of things and of lived time, for the analogue photograph is literally an imprint (*graphos*) of light (*photo*) taken from a particular moment. With digital technology, this is an altogether new configuration and the result of an algorithm. The image is received with startling immediacy, can be adjusted just as quickly and replicated and disseminated in numerous ways. In recent years, the use of the moving image has become part of the everyday vernacular; one is even able to see the moving face of a friend while talking on the telephone. Still images can be taken from the moving image, and image stills can be taken with the same interface that can also take film. The old separation of still photography and moving image is no longer as self-evident. The transition of the fashion image toward moving images is therefore a logical, inevitable and natural development.

While, as we have seen already in this book, SHOWstudio is not responsible for an absolute beginning, it has certainly accelerated the phenomenon and done the most work so that fashion film be recognized as its own separate genre. It has also resulted in countless other efforts by eminent and/or prominent celebrities, directors and designers. Nathalie Khan distinguishes fashion films into two categories: edgy experimental films and large-scale budget fashion films produced by major fashion brands like Chanel and Dior that employ big-name Hollywood directors such as David Lynch for Dior. If Duran Duran's 'Girl Panic' can be seen as an effective merging of music video and fashion film (and other genres besides), there have been a number of unfortunate forays into this genre. One example is David Lynch's *Lady Blue Shanghai* (2010) for Dior, which begins with the usual Lynchianisms of mysterious music, fractured psychological landscapes, dramatic angles, 1920s nostalgia, unrequited love and a seemingly empty hotel, with unconvincing musings on the part of the heroine Marion Cotillard, Dior's ambassador, over a mysterious bag (The Lady Dior bag). Filmed in Shanghai in 2009 and streamlined on the Dior website in May 2010, *Lady Blue Shanghai* is the third instalment in a film series related by product placement and Cotillard following *The Lady Noire Affair* (Dahan, 2009) and *Lady Rouge* (Åkerlund, 2009). The film's location was chosen by the then creative director, John Galliano, to coincide with the reopening of the Dior store in Shanghai and the World Expo and is described by John Berra as an example of media convergence, where 'two seemingly distinct yet possibly intertwined audiences – Lynch admirers and Dior consumers – are courted through new media'.[32]

Mildly more successful and just as amusing is Karl Lagerfeld's film for the Fendi 2013 fur-filled collection that sets up a horror-movie scenario in which Cara Delevingne and another woman are led into a vast mansion at night to the sound of 1970s suspense music and braying dogs in the distance. They dress for dinner, which allows for a change of look. On the sight of a tall mysterious man they escape the dining room into another chamber, an excuse for a scene of the two models sitting on soiled mattresses on the floor incongruously wrapped in their fur coats. Another handsome man climbs the ironwork to the balcony and in a sexy French accent instructs them to escape. A more salutary example that involves no plot whatsoever is the exquisitely sinister but beautiful film by Tim Walker for *Vogue Italia* in 2011, *Mechanical Dolls*, featuring Audrey Marnay and Kirsi Pyrhonen. Here the camera pans a spacious but dilapidated house with flaking paint and peeling wallpaper that is populated with a cohort of life-sized mechanical dolls. Some wearing fake beards and marvellous headdresses and severe make-up, they move as if powered by clock-movements, or sit motionless next to real dolls. Both ghostly and irrepressibly charming, the film is resonant in bringing the world of childhood together with childhood desires and fears.

The trouble with these films is that they rely on thin plotlines and their appeal to recognizable filmic genres tips them dangerously in the mawkish and tawdry. But what they succeed in doing is to display fashion in a state of movement, and in the simulacrum of real life. Although the sets and narratives are all of course contrivances, models do not pose in the same way. As Kiku Adatto observes, 'the act of taking photographs can impinge on the freedom of the subject. . . . the freedom of one's own action and being'.[33] This is primarily an issue of being within the photographic 'frame', which then objectifies the subject (the French for 'lens' is conveniently *objectif*) and places him or her within an array of interpretations that he or she does not necessarily share with others or the person doing the photographing. While the fashion model willingly assents to this alteration – it is their job to do so – to place them within an imaginary scenario and within variable frames in which they move gives the illusion of agency and verisimilitude. The contrivance of the still and that of the moving image are perceived differently. The photographic still of fashion photography, removed and separated from real life, is always distant and forbidden, while we immerse ourselves in the implausibilities of the moving image with a suspension of disbelief. The integration of movement provides a new rapport of intimacy and of proximity to the garment and the commodity. In order to understand the impact of fashion film as a distinct genre, it is essential they we turn to the ways in which modern or contemporary fashion as a mode of communication has been constructed and disseminated in the last two centuries.

The democratization of fashion

Fashion's democratization came into being with the advent of the couture industry in Paris in the second half of the nineteenth century. This is not to suggest that fashion did not exist before, however from its early beginnings in the fourteenth century fashion was regulated by strict sumptuary laws and craft guilds and only the wealthy could afford to attend salons and purchase made-to-measure garments. Fashion was the domain of the aristocratic elite who set styles and trends that were copied by the masses. Core artisan skills such as drapery, pattern making and illustration were required skills for tailors and seamstresses employed in the garment trades. Characteristic of the fashion of this period were full skirts and clearly visible corsets around the waist accompanied by elaborate hairstyles and hats. In Britain, Beau Brummell introduced trousers, perfect tailoring and immaculate linen as the ideals of men's fashion. In France, Frederic Worth (1860) and Paul Poiret (1903) designed garments for the newly emancipated woman, and department stores such as Bon Marché (1834) in Paris were established as retail outlets for the sale of designer clothing. The nineteenth century also witnessed the revolutionary new technology photography, which gave audiences a peek into 'fashion in action', and its impact on everyday life and society. In an age that had limited means of communication compared with the twentieth century, ideas of fashion were primary disseminated via hand-rendered illustrations in fashion booklets such as *The Robes of Paul Poiret*, illustrated by Paul Iribe.

Since the industrial period of mass production, fashion witnessed a collapsing of the boundaries between haute couture and ready to wear, with clothing becoming increasingly affordable to the masses as fashion entered the modern era. It was the century in which women first liberated themselves from constricting fashions and began to wear more comfortable clothes (such as short skirts or trousers). Men likewise abandoned overly formal clothes and began to wear sports clothes for the first time. Proponents of the 'new' leisure style included The Prince of Wales and Chanel, who wore signature styles eventually imitated by millions of women and men. By the 1920s the role of the couturier as fashion dictator and trendsetter was firmly established, including Schiaparelli, Madame Gres, Callot Soeurs and Vionnet.

Most other fashion designers worked for large-scale ready-to-wear manufacturers in the early part of the twentieth century. Ready-to-wear garments were important to the working class because they were inexpensive and did not require the time commitment of sewing the garment or the cost of visiting a tailor or seamstress. Department stores with ornate interiors, such as Macy's in New York, often described as 'palaces', provided the latest American and Parisian fashions for women with disposable incomes to acquire fashionable dress. Nordstrom also provided in-house designers for private-label goods as well as purchased samples of Parisian garments for reproduction. Fashion magazines were a primary force in communicating fashion ideas. Originating as catalogues, they were inexpensive and readily available and often included articles as well as illustrations and photography. *Vogue* (1909) magazine transformed fashion communication and *Women's Wear Daily* was established in 1910 with full editorial and commentary heralding the birth of the fashion editor/commentator. Mail-order catalogues provided another source of fashion communication because they featured a variety of details about fashionable styles and silhouettes, fabrics and trims.

The increased popularity of photography and the use of photographs in magazines increased the pace at which fashion trends were disseminated. Rather than illustrations, magazines such as *Vogue*, *Harper's Bazaar* and *Esquire* carried photographs of major social events, society balls and weddings, including the marriage of the Prince of Wales to Wallis Simpson in 1937. Photographs were incorporated into mail-order catalogues, such as *Sears*, and were mass distributed. Photographs of Hollywood 'starlets' were also popular to collect and provided clear and complete details on the latest fashions and trends. Film stars such as Clara Bow, Gloria Swanson and Joan Crawford made appearances in catalogues endorsing the latest fashion. Another new medium, film also played a pivotal role in fashion communication in the 1920s and 1930s. Movie houses or cinemas opened across the world and 'going to the shows' became a favourite pastime of young and old, all of whom were directly influenced by the fashions and mores projected onto the 'silver screen'. Fashion designers such as Salvatore Ferragamo realized the power of cinema and its mass appeal, and Ferragamo was the pioneer designer brand to take advantage of product placement. Ferragamo donated thousands of pairs of sandals to extras in *The Ten Commandments* (1923), directed by Cecil B. DeMille, and shoes for films like *The Thief of Bagdad* (1924). Cinema became a powerful generator of fashion advertising and, more importantly, brand advertising, and many designers were to follow Ferragamo's lead such as Givenchy's collaboration with Edith Head for *Sabrina* (1954), Yves Saint Laurent's creations for *Belle de Jour* (1967), Giorgio Armani's suits worn in *American Gigolo* (1980) and *The Untouchables* (1987) and Ralph Lauren for *The Great Gatsby* (1974). To be more specific, in the twentieth century, factors that contributed to fashion's *second* democratization included: the mass production of clothing (the American ready-to-wear industry); the copying of haute couture models and samples; the accessibility of fashion images in magazines that could be duplicated; and the display and availability of ready-to-wear fashion in department stores and cinema. The fashion industry has since continued its trajectory toward the democratization of style through the technology of the Internet.

Where the democratization of fashion was responsible for the collapse of social-class differentiations in the twentieth century, in the twenty-first century the democratization of fashion appears to be directed toward the collapse of geographical style distinctions. Fashion has become increasingly accessible to global markets as a result of new media. The Internet has offered an arena to make industry fashion trends more readily available to consumers. More significantly, the Internet underlines the social aspects of fashion and demonstrates that the democratization of fashion in the twenty-first century has allowed consumers to provide the narrative and meaning for fashion that had previously been the domain of the traditional fashion media. The rise of fashion blogs, social networking, online retail and online live streaming of fashion shows has exponentially increased the availability of fashion products and images globally, enabling a further multiplication of styles and looks. At the same time, new genres such as fashion film are increasingly blurring the line between fashion and industry, creativity and control. Widespread interest in this phenomenon is reflected in the range of cultural institutions such as museums and national libraries that have chosen to either exhibit or critique fashion films in the last few years. Although the relationship between film and fashion has existed throughout the twentieth century, recently we've seen this develop from fashion being a *part of film* to fashion being a *major focus point of the film*. The popular television series *Sex and the City* (1998–2004) is a well-known example of where the fashion and fashion designers are as important as the characters themselves. Fashion designer Tom Ford's *A Single Man* (2009) was a milestone where the designer diversified his creative pursuits toward recreating Christopher Isherwood's 1964 eponymous novel. Fashion film brings together designers and filmmakers, providing a platform for these two mediums to exist. Elegance moves seamlessly with melancholy drama, creating a cinematic crystal whose beauty is ethereal and moody.

In the last two years, Khamis and Munt write that Chanel, Prada and Dior have enlisted *auteurs* of modern cinema to create what is now known as 'fragrance films'; films that do not just sell perfume, but tell a story – branding as narrative, not merely allusion. In their big-budget collaborations with celebrities of modern cinema, these films suggest that, as the media sphere becomes more fragmented, and consumer interest more precious, such projects and markets are needed for brands to 'cut through', that is, hold audience interest, and maintain cultural cachet.[34]

Brothers of Arcadia: Homotography, or the meeting of fashion film and pornochic

As we noted in Chapter Five, from the 1980s, when marketers constructed the New Man as a consumer of fashion and luxury goods, depictions of masculinity in fashion imagery have deployed pornographic visual codes to create homoerotic images of men that appeal to a wider audience, but are characteristic of ways of looking in gay male spectatorship. This homoerotic style, which invites the audience to enjoy erotized images of men, takes its materiality from gay pornography and is reworked via postures and images that also evoke classical Greco-Roman sculpture. No other fashion film serves better to portray the meeting of fashion, gay porno chic and S/M chic than *Brothers of Arcadia*, a film directed by Branislav Jankic and styled by Nicola Formichetti, creative director of Thierry Mugler for his menswear Spring/Summer range 2012.

'I was interested in the idea of fantasy, dreams and voyeurism,' Formichetti says:

> I was looking at Italian Neo-Realist cinema and then, post-that, where Fellini and Pasolini become more about myth and fantasy. At the same time, I loved the idea and accessibility of pornography and everyday voyeurism on Xtube. Fashion is always referencing pornography, so there was an element in doing this film of just 'cutting out the middleman,' but it is an erotic fashion film nonetheless.[35]

Formichetti's film is set in the Greek mythic land of Arcadia, an earthly paradise of shepherds and nymphs situated on the mountainous Peloponnese peninsula. Fittingly, Arcadia was the home of Pan, the god of woods, fields, flocks and music. Half-goat, half-human, Pan was known for his sexual prowess and was often depicted in Greek mosaics and sculpture with a large erect penis. This wild and untamed natural setting is appropriate for a fashion film that has been described as pornographic with 'explicit sex scenes left in it'.[36] Set to Franz Schubert's Piano Trio No. 2 in E flat major, and Jessica 6's song 'White Horse', and shot in grainy black and white to capture early neo-realist Italian cinema, the film opens on an empty rocky beach somewhere in Arcadia. The camera slowly pans along the shoreline to rest on the figures of three semi-naked men dressed in Mugler underwear rising from the bottom of the screen mimicking erect Corinthian columns. The models represent Adonis, the Greek symbol of male beauty and desire, and are examples of the ideal in homosexual spectatorship. In his article 'Considerations on a Gentleman's Posterior', Shaun Cole writes that from the 1980s onwards men's underwear advertisements increasingly pictured semi-naked men objectifying and sexualizing their 'hairless, highly developed, super-muscular male bodies' that were understood as a 'metaphor of masculine sexual power and transcendence through the symbolic language of High Classicism'.[37] As Richard Dyer argues, the visualization of the male muscular body acts as a 'natural' signifier of 'male power and dominance'.[38] The men dive into the water and frolic amongst each other on the beach whilst the camera pans into close-up shots of their crotch, arms, legs and torso and buttocks. The spectator's gaze cuts the men's bodies into pieces, headless limbs, and dismembered figures of desire. The film invites the audience (men and women) to consume, almost in vampiric fashion, the bodies of the men who are displayed in classically exhibitionist and provocative poses. In the process of identification and desire the male audience desires to *be* the model and desires to *have* the model. The subject comes into being through a network of complex identifiers, narcissism, desire and eroticism.

In an act of SM chic, the men pull seductively on chains and maritime ropes that are wrapped around their bodies as the camera pans across the full rear nudity of a model to rest on his naked buttocks. Desmond Morris writes that 'the Greeks of classical antiquity considered the buttocks as an unusually beautiful part of the body, partly because of its pleasing curvature'.[39] The viewing position of the naked rear body with exposed buttocks places the model in a passive sexual position and situates the spectorial gaze on the rear view of the male object, what Anne Hollander describes as 'unconscious charm, a sign of submissive and receptive sexuality'.[40] Models of masculine perfection, the men adorn gold medals around their neck as though Olympian gods, or athletes. 'This project is a combination of the two things,' says Formichetti, 'there are surfers, footballers and classical gods all rolled into one in this film.'[41]

Formichetti's use of the term 'brothers' in the film's title is intentional and applied to evoke an exclusive 'club' or an environment for men only, one that prohibits women. The word 'brother' is a form of identification and acceptance in motorcycle subculture and in groups whose social structure consists of a masculine hierarchy such as the mafia, the army or men's prisons. The lack of women's presence in this film also heightens the homosexual content. An exemplar of pornochic, *Brothers of Arcadia* contains imagery that exposes the body, fragmenting it by cropping and foregrounding the culturally eroticized parts of it, and uses stereotypically gendered, eroticized tropes. Bodies appear as *ideal* bodies placed in *ideal* environments, in this case along a deserted shoreline in a mythical and idyllic Arcadia. This homoerotic style of photography takes its materiality of sex and desire from the language of gay pornography and is reworked via postures and images that also evoke classical Greco-Roman sculpture.

'I think a lot of people now think that the porn around at the moment is "real", but it is not,' says Formichetti.

> It is total fantasy, these people are like Olympian athletes of sex. What has changed is the look of pornography. I wanted to bring some of that excessive drama and the look of fantasy back to porn – to acknowledge something as over-the-top as Tinto Brass' *Caligula* with the explicit sex scenes left in.[42]

Three and a half seconds into the six-minute fashion film, the models begin to playfully wrestle amongst each other. The film moves from grainy black and white into colour and the musical beat and tempo increases as the soundtrack shifts to 'White Horse' by the nu-disco band Jessica 6. Characteristic of the types of fashion photography of the 1990s, raw and gritty, the audience is transported to the set of a B-grade pornographic film where we are introduced to Nomi Ruiz lead singer of Jessica 6 whose role on the set is that of a porn star. An interesting sequence of events follows, so much so that the dynamics and spectatorship positions shift from a primarily homosexual film to that of male heterosexual viewing positions as the models gather around Ruiz pouring champagne and what looks like milk all over her face, bathing in the excessive liquid that acts as a trope for ejaculation. This act is known as the 'money shot' or the 'cum shot' in pornography parlance, where a man ejaculates on a woman's body, either on her face or in her eyes. Michael Thomas Carroll writes that some people would explain this pornographic scene in terms of sexism. 'In heterosexual cum-shot porn,' Carroll argues, chauvinism is evident in the 'domination of the standing male/kneeling woman stance that is one of the most popular forms of this image, but also in the implied degradation of the phallus "spitting" on the woman's face – that part of the body which is most closely associated with one's individual dignity and personality'.[43] It's worth noting that a similar dominant-subservient dynamic plays out in gay porn, especially in *Brothers of Arcadia*, where in this particular scene the models are wearing army combat boots, an accessory that is prevalent in gay male pornography. The models then proceed to bath and shave each other in a homoerotic scene whilst looking at pornographic magazines and ejaculating. The film reverts to black and white and ends on the deserted Arcadian beach, empty, the men have disappeared, the wet-dream fantasy is over.

Notes

1 Nilgin Yusuf, *Fashion's Front Line*, London: Bloomsbury, 2015.

2 Laura Clout and Stephen Adams, 'Yves St Laurent Dies at 71: Tributes Pour in to French King of Haute Couture', *The Telegraph*, http://www.telegraph.co.uk/news/worldnews/europe/france/2064246/Yves-Saint-Laurent-dead-at-71-Tributes-pour-in-to-French-king-of-haute-couture.html, accessed 17 December 2014.

3 Gary Needham, 'The Digital Fashion Film', in Stella Bruzzi and Pamela Church Gibson, *Fashion Cultures Revisited*, London: Routledge, 2013, 104.

4 Suzy Menkes, 'The Circus of Fashion', *The New York Times*, 10 February 2013, http://tmagazine.blogs.nytimes.com/2013/02/10/the-circus-of-fashion/?_r=0, accessed 7 December 2014.

5 Agnes Rocamora, 'New Fashion Times: Fashion and Digital Media', in Stella Bruzzi and Pamela Church Gibson, *Fashion Cultures Revisited*, London: Routledge, 2013, 69.

6 Menkes, 'The Circus of Fashion'.

7 See, for example, Bettina Friedl, 'The Hybrid Art of Fashion Photography: American Photographers in Post-World War II Europe', *American Studies*, 52 (1), 2007, 48.

8 Marketa Uhlirova, 'The Fashion Film Effect', in Djurdja Bartlett, Shaun Cole and Agnes Rocamora, *Fashion Media: Past and Present*, London: Bloomsbury, 2013, 119.

9 Ibid., 119.

10 See showstudio.com and http://showstudio.com/projects/tag/fashion_films.

11 Marketa Uhlirova, '100 Years of the Fashion Film: Frameworks and Histories', *Fashion Theory*, 17 (2), 139–140.

12 See Uhlirova, ibid., 140; Caroline Evans, 'Multiple, Movement, Model, Mode: The Mannequin Parade 1900–1929', in Christopher Breward and Caroline Evans, eds., *Fashion and Modernity*, 133; and David Robinson, *George Méliès: Father of Film Fantasy*, London: Museum of the Moving Image, 1993, 45.

13 See Caroline Evans, 'The Walkies', in Adrienne Munich, ed., *Fashion in Film*, Bloomington and Indianapolis: Indiana U.P., 2011, 110–134; and Uhlirova, ibid., 142.

14 Marketa Uhlirova, 'The Fashion Film Effect', in Djurdja Bartlett, Shaun Cole and Agnes Rocamora, *Fashion Media: Past and Present*, London: Bloomsbury, 2013, 119.

15 See Eirik Frisvold Hanssen, 'Symptoms of Desire: Colour, Costume and Commodities in Fashion Newsreels of the 1910s and 1920s', *Film History*, 21 (2), 2009, 107–121.

16 Uhlirova, 'The Fashion Film Effect', 143.

17 Ibid., 144.

18 Nick Knight, cited by Marketa Uhlirova, ibid., 122.

19 Ibid., 143–144.

20 Mila Ganeva, 'Weimar Film as Fashion Show: *Konfektionskomödien* or Fashion Farces from Lubitsch to the End of the Silent Era', *German Studies Review*, 30 (2), May 2007, 289–290.

21 Ibid., 293.

22 Ibid., 299.

23 Ibid., 305–306.

24 Uhlirova, '100 Years of the Fashion Film', 145.

25 Nita Rollins, 'Greenaway-Gaultier: Old Masters, Fashion Slaves', *Cinema Journal* 35 (1), Autumn 1995, 71.

26 Ibid., 76.

27 Nick Knight, 'SHOWstudio: Thoughts on Fashion Film', http://www.youtube.com/watch?v=BOBZMS9Bhr0.

28 Ibid.

29 Dirk Gindt, 'Performative Processes: Björk's Creative Collaborations in the World of Fashion', *Fashion Theory* 15 (4), 2011, 426.

30 Ibid., 444.

31 Kevin Robins, *Into the Image: Culture and Politics in the Field of Vision*, London and New York: Routledge, 1996.

32 John Berra, 'Lady Blue Shanghai: The Strange Case of David Lynch and Dior', *Fashion, Film and Consumption,* 1 (3), 2012, 247.

33 Kiku Adatto, *Picture Perfect: Life in the Age of the Photo Op*, Princeton and Oxford: Princeton U.P., 2008, 244.

34 Suzie Khamis and Alex Munt, 'The Three Cs of Fashion Media Today: Convergence, Creativity & Control. The Journal of Media, Arts Culture, http://scan.net.au/scan/journal/display.php?journal id=155', accessed 25 June 2015.

35 Nicola Formichetti, http://kentonmagazine.com/thierry-mugler-brothers-of-arcadia/, accessed 19 December 2014.

36 Nicola Formichetti, http://kontraplan.com/site/2011/06/24/brothers-of-arcadia/, accessed 20 December 20 2014.

37 Geraldine Biddle-Perry, cited by Shaun Cole, 'Considerations on a Gentleman's Posterior', *Fashion Theory*, 16 (2), 218.

38 Richard Dyer, cited by Sarah Gilligan, 'Fragmenting the Black Male Body: Will Smith, Muscularity, Clothing and Desire', *Fashion Theory*, 16 (2), 2012, 178.

39 Desmond Morris cited by Shaun Cole, 'Considerations on a Gentleman's Posterior', 218.

40 Anne Hollander cited by Shaun Cole, ibid., 214.

41 Nicola Formichetti, http://kontraplan.com/site/2011/06/24/brothers-of-arcadia/, assessed 20 December 2014.

42 Ibid.

43 http://www.salon.com/2012/02/21/explaining_the_money_shot/, accessed 20 December 2014.

CONCLUSION

Conditions of impossibility

In the early pages of Dostoevsky's novella *The Double*, the protagonist Golyadkin is spotted by a neighbouring carriage containing two fellow colleagues, clerks who work in the same government department. In one of those contretemps of sudden recognition, Golyadkin shrinks in embarrassment at seeing eye-to-eye his office superior in a different and unexpected context. Not knowing how to react, he says to himself that he'll 'pretend that I am not myself, but somebody else strikingly like me, and look as though nothing were the matter. Simply not I, not I – and that's all.'[1] With the cover of the story in mind, this comic scene inserted at the beginning is intentionally ironic and anticipatory, for he will eventually meet the person who looks 'strikingly like' him and yet is 'not I'. Golyadkin is an archetypal try-hard and parvenu who tries, vainly, to gain advancement. He is an erratic bumbler who sees the world with a mixture of paranoia and desperation. He meets his double, who also happens to have the same name as him, distinguished by 'Jr.'. The double, or doppelgänger, is the very obverse of Golyadkin, and the very person he strives to be. Charming and outgoing, the new arrival manages in the same workplace where Golyadkin Sr. had only bungled. Understandably, the 'original' Golyadkin begins to feel oppressed and anxious, suspicious that his counterpart will overtake his position and finally his life. His nervous agitation exacerbates, and in a fit of neurasthenic exhaustion he begins to see replicas of himself, whereupon he is carted off to an insane asylum. Dostoevsky's story is not an isolated one, lifting from superstition and folklore. Like many similar tales, their persistence and retelling owe themselves to their relevance, self-image and social relations.

What makes this relevant for the study of fashion imagery, all related ways in which fashion is featured in visual media, artistic or commercial, is two-fold. First, the external double – what we choose to identify with respect to the way we see ourselves – is always better than us; everything is enviably in place; the chips have not fallen randomly, but providentially. Second, there not just one double, but many. As soon as we elect to make strong investments of identity in figures of the outside world, we become addicted. It is a way of implanting ourselves with physicality and credulity into the world of things so as to make them more at home to us. It is a process that has a disturbingly dual effect. While we have the soothing sense of having some imprint in the world in which we live, some stake that seems unerring and indelible, this imprint does not comply with the evolution of our lives, and in fact exposes the variability of our personality and ourselves. In this regard the double has the power of the uncanny, divorcing us from our feeling of homeliness (*un-heimlich* = 'unhomely') by transporting us to some ethereal, disembodied realm to a place we have never visited, not ever can. The effect of this is not necessarily as devastating as it was for Dostoevsky's Golyadkin, but it certainly casts into doubt where the most trusted reality lies. For especially when we choose to be in fashion, as opposed to wearing just clothes, we are always looking over our shoulder to who is behind us and a few steps forward to where we could be.

If fashion is an embodied practice, fashion imagery has a vital, if problematic presence within this. For what fashion imagery reveals is the extent to which this embodiment of physically wearing a garment is but one co-ordinate in a dense web of suppositions, expectations and unconscious whims. Thanks to anecdotes about celebrity, images in photography and film, associations bound to music and television, and finally, thanks to what we search for over the Internet, fashion is a vast surface of meanings and associations. It has been one of the aims of this book to show not only the seamlessness between physical garment and image, but, more subtly, that the image is internal to the garment, as if woven within it. But the dynamic does not stop there, for while the image is sewn into the garment, it is precisely its dominant presence that reveals some other order of disjuncture. This is not some Platonic order of real and counterfeit, but rather one where the right and the correct are confounded. As we found with the unconventional manipulation of the fetish, one is lost within an oscillating dynamic between what is there and what is not. So if one were to ask the cryptic question, 'where is fashion located?', then one would have to answer that it is within this oscillation between embodiment and disembodiment, surfeit and lack. The fashion image is worthless if no one aspires to be fashionable or wears fashionable clothing, and the fashionable aspiration cannot exist without the image.

But neither came first. As we have shown, from the inception of fashion as a concept of high social prestige in the middle of the nineteenth century, fashion and its representation were tightly bound. Painters painted gowns that were already inspired by, or copied from, painting. Fashion's birth is therefore from within a room of mirrors. The play of representations only becomes more intricate, risqué and diverse, but the impenetrable relay of reflections continues its course, ad infinitum – or until people stop looking and stop wearing clothes.

Note

1 Fyodor Dostoevsky, *The Double: A St Petersburg Poem*, trans. Constance Garnett, Electronic Classics Series Publication, Pennsylvania: Pennsylvania State University, 2006–2013, 8.

BIBLIOGRAPHY

Adatto, Kiku, *Picture Perfect: Life in the Age of the Photo Op*, Princeton and Oxford: Princeton U.P., 2008.

Arnold, Rebecca, 'The Brutalised Body', *Fashion Theory: The Journal of Dress, Body and Culture,* 3 (4), 1999, 487–502.

Avedon, Richard, 'Borrowed Dogs', *Grand Street* 7 (1), Autumn 1987, 52–64.

Bakhtin, Mikhail, *Rabelais and His World*, Bloomington: Indiana U.P., 1984.

Barthes, Roland, *The Fashion System* (1967), trans. Matthey Ward and Richard Howard, Los Angeles and London: California U.P., (1983) 1990.

Barthes, Roland, *The Language of Fashion*, trans. Andy Stafford, Andy Stafford and Michael Carter, eds, Sydney: Power Publications, 2006.

Bataille, Georges, *Erotism*, trans. not cited, New York: City Lights, 1986.

Baudrillard, Jean, *L'échange symbolique et la mort*, Paris: Gallimard, 1976.

Beene, Geoffrey, Tom Kalin, Grace Mirabella and Matthew Yokobosky, 'Fashion and Film: A Symposium', *PAJ: A Journal of Performance Art*, 20 (3), September 1998, 12–21.

Benjamin, Andrew, *Style and Time*, Evanston, IL: Northwestern U.P., 2006.

Benjamin, Walter, *The Arcades Project*, ed. Rolf Tiedemann, trans. Howard Eiland and Kevin McLaughlin, New York: Belknap Press, 2002.

Berra, John, 'Lady Blue Shanghai: The Strange Case of David Lynch and Dior', *Fashion, Film and Consumption,* 1 (3), 2012.

Black, J. Anderson and Madge Garland, *A History of Fashion*, New York: William Morrow and Company, 1980.

Bonnefoy, Yves, *Poèmes*, Paris: Gallimard, 1978.

Breward, Christopher and Caroline Evans, eds, *Fashion and Modernity*, Oxford and New York: Berg, 2005.

Brookes, Rosetta, 'Fashion Photography: The Double-Page Spread: Helmut Newton, Guy Bourdin and Deborah Turbeville', in Malcolm Barnard, *Fashion Theory: A Reader*, London and New York: Routledge, 2007, 520–526.

Bruzzi, Stella, *Undressing Cinema: Clothing and Identity in the Movies*, London and New York: Routledge, 1997.

Bruzzi, Stella and Church Gibson, Pamela, eds, *Fashion Cultures: Theories, Exploration and Analysis*, New York: Routledge, 2000.

Bruzzi, Stella and Church Gibson, Pamela, *Fashion Cultures Revisited*, New York: Routledge, 2013.

Burnett, Ron, *How Images Think*, Cambridge, MA: MIT Press, 2005.

Calefato, Patrizia, *Luxury: Fashion, Lifestyle and Excess*, London: Bloomsbury, 2014.

Capote, Truman, *Breakfast at Tiffany's*, (1958) e-book 2008.

Carter, Michael, 'Fashion Photography: The Long, Slow Dissolve', *Photofile*, 4 (4), 1987, 5–7.

Chadwick, Whitney, 'Fetishizing Fashion/Fetishizing Culture: Man Ray's "Noire et blanche"', *Oxford Art Journal*, 18 (2), 1995, 3–17.

Church Gibson, Pamela, *Fashion and Celebrity Culture*, London: Bloomsbury, 2011.

Church Gibson, Pamela and Vicki Karaminas, 'Letter from the Editors', *Fashion Theory*, Fashion and Porn Special Issue, 18 (2), April 2014, 116–122.

Cole, Shaun, 'Considerations on a Gentleman's Posterior', *Fashion Theory*, 16 (2), 211–234.

Collins, Suzanne, *The Hunger Games*, New York: Scholastic Press, 2008.

Collins, Suzanne, *Catching Fire*, New York: Scholastic Press, 2009.

Collins, Suzanne, *Mockingjay*, New York: Scholastic Press, 2010.

Conekin, Becky, 'Lee Miller: Model, Photographer and War Correspondent in *Vogue* 1927–1953', *Fashion Theory*, 10 (1–2), March–June 2006, 97–125.

Cook, Susan, 'Subversion Without Limits: From *Secretary*'s Transgressive S/M to "Exquisite Corpse's" Subversive Sadomasochism', *Discourse*, 28 (1), Winter 2006, 121–141.

Craik, Jennifer, *The Face of Fashion: Cultural Studies in Fashion*, London and New York: Routledge, 1993.

Dorré, Gina, 'Horses and Corsets: "Black Beauty", Dress Reform and the Fashioning of the Victorian Woman', *Victorian Literature and Culture*, 30 (1), 2002, 157–178.

Dostoevsky, Fyodor, *The Double: A St Petersburg Poem*, trans. Constance Garnett, Electronic Classics Series Publication, Pennsylvania: Pennsylvania State University, 2006–2013.

Eagleton, Terry, *The Event of Literature*, New Haven and London: Yale U.P., 2012.

Edelman, Amy Homan, *The Little Black Dress*, New York: Simon and Schuster, 1997.

Evans, Caroline, *Fashion at the Edge: Spectacle, Modernity, Deathliness*, New Haven and London: Yale U.P., 2003.

Evans, Caroline, *The Mechanical Smile: Modernism and the First Fashion Shows in France and America, 1900–1929*, New Haven and London: Yale U.P., 2013.

Faiers, Jonathan, *Dressing Dangerously: Dysfunctional Fashion in Film*, New Haven and London: Yale U.P., 2013.

Foucault, Michel, *Discipline and Punish: The Birth of the Prison,* London: Penguin, 1991.

Francis, Martin, 'Cecil Beaton's Romantic Toryism and Symbolic Economy of Wartime Britain', *Journal of British Studies*, 45 (1), January 2006, 90–117.

Friedl, Bettina, 'The Hybrid Art of Fashion Photography: American Photographers in Post-World War II Europe', *American Studies*, 52 (1), 2007, 47–62.

Frisvold Hanssen, Eirik, 'Symptoms of Desire: Colour, Costume and Commodities in Fashion Newsreels of the 1910s and 1920s', *Film History*, 21 (2), 2009, 107–121.

Ganeva, Mila, 'Fashion Photography and Women's Modernity in Weimar Germany: The Case of Yva', *NWSA Journal*, 15 (3), Autumn 2003, 1–25.

Ganeva, Mila, 'Weimar Film as Fashion Show: *Konfektionskomödien* or Fashion Farces from Lubitsch to the End of the Silent Era', *German Studies Review*, 30 (2), May 2007, 288–310.

Garber, Marjorie, 'Fetish Envy', *October* 54, Autumn 1990, 45–56.

Geczy, Adam, *Fashion and Orientalism: Dress, Textiles and Culture from the 17th to the 21st Century*, London and New York: Bloomsbury, 2013.

Geczy, Adam and Vicki Karaminas, *Queer Style*, London: Bloomsbury, 2013.

Geczy, Adam and Vicki Karaminas, 'The Metastable Bodily Ideal: The Vicissitudes of Body and Dress in the Twentieth Century and Beyond', in Alexandra Palmer, ed., *A Cultural History of Fashion in the 20th Century*, London and New York: Bloomsbury, 2015.

Gill, Rosalind, 'Empowerment/Sexism: Figuring Female Sexual Agency in Contemporary Advertising', *Feminism and Psychology*, 18 (35), 36–60.

Gilligan, Sarah, 'Gwyneth Paltrow', in Stella Bruzzi and Pamela Church Gibson, eds, *Fashion Cultures: Theories, Exploration and Analysis*, New York: Routledge, 2000.

Gilligan, Sarah, 'Get me an Exit: Mobile Phones and Transforming Masculinity in the *Matrix* Trilogy', in Ruby Cheung and David Fleming, eds., *Cinema, Identities and Beyond*, Newcastle-Upon-Tyne: Cambridge Scholars Publishing, 2009.

Gilligan, Sarah, 'Becoming Neo: Costume and Transforming Masculinities in the *Matrix* Films', Peter McNeil, Vicki Karaminas and Catherine Cole, *Fashion and Fiction: Text and Clothing in Literature, Film and Television,* Oxford: Berg, 2009.

Gilligan, Sarah, 'Fashioning Masculinity and Desire in *Torchwood*', in Andrew Ireland, ed., *Illuminating 'Torchwood': Essays on Narrative, Character and Sexuality in the BBC Series*. Critical Explorations in Science Fiction and Fantasy, London: McFarlane, 2010.

Gilligan, Sarah, 'Branding the New Bond: Daniel Craig and Designer Fashion', in Rob Weiner and Jack Becker, eds, *James Bond, History and Popular Culture: The Films Are Not Enough*, Newcastle-Upon-Tyne: Cambridge Scholars Publishing, 2010.

Gilligan, Sarah, 'Fragmenting the Black Male Body: Will Smith, Muscularity, Clothing and Desire', *Fashion Theory*, 16 (2), 2012.

Gilligan, Sarah, *Fashion and Film: Gender, Costume and Stardom in Contemporary Cinema*, London: Bloomsbury, 2016 (forthcoming).

Gindt, Dirk, 'Performative Processes: Björk's Creative Collaborations in the World of Fashion', *Fashion Theory*, 15 (4), 2011, 425–450.

Gunning, Tom, 'Making Fashion Out of Nothing. The Invisible Criminal', Marketa Uhlirova, ed., *If Looks Could Kill*, London: Koenig, 2008.

Haenlein, Carl, ed., *Anton Josef Trcka, Edward Weston, Helmut Newton*, exn cat., Zurich and New York: Kestner Gesellchaft, 1998.

Harding, James, *Artistes Pompiers*, London: Academy Editions, 1979.

Hills, Patricia, ed., *John Singer Sargent*, exn cat., Whitney and New York: Abrams, 1987.

Hinton, Laura, '(G)Aping Women; Or, When a Man Plays the Fetish', *The Journal of Cinema and Media*, 48 (2), Fall 2007, 174–200.

Horst, Horst P., *Salute to the Thirties*, New York: Studio, 1971.

Innes Homer, William, 'Edward Steichen as Painter and Photographer 1897–1908', *American Art Journal*, 6 (2), November 1974, 45–55.

Kawamura, Yuniya, *The Japanese Revolution in Paris Fashion*, Oxford and New York: Berg, 2004.

Kazmaier, Martin, *Horst: Photographien aus sechs Jahrzehnten*, Munich, Paris and London: Schirmer-Mosel, 1991.

Khamis, Suzie and Alex Munt, 'The Three Cs of Fashion Media Today: Convergence, Creativity & Control, *The Journal of Media, Arts Culture*, http://scan.net.au/scan/journal/display.php?journal_id=155'.

Klossowski, Pierre, *Un si funeste désir*, Paris: Gallimard, 1963.

Kofman, Sarah, *L'Énigme de femme: La Femme dans les textes de Freud*, Paris: Galilée 1980.

Krauss, Rosalind, 'On Photography and the Simulacral', *October* 31, Winter 1984, 49–68.

Kromm, Jane and Susan Benforado Bakewell, eds, *A History of Visual Culture: Western Civilization from the 18th to the 21st Century*, Oxford and New York: Berg, 2010.

Kulp, Denise, 'Music Videos: Friday Night Sexism', *Off Our Backs*, 14 (4), 1984, 21.

Kwass, Michael, 'Ordering the World of Goods: Consumer Revolution and Classification of Objects in Eighteenth-Century France,' *Representations*, 82 (2003): 93.

Laver, James, 'Winterhalter', *Burlington Magazine for Connoisseurs*, 70 (406), January 1937, 44–45.

Lawford, Valentine, *Horst: His Work and His World*, New York: Knopf, 1984.

Lewis, Reina and Katrina Rolley, 'Ad(dressing) the Dyke: Lesbian Looks and Lesbian Looking' in Peter Horne and Reina Lewis, eds, *Outlooks: Lesbian and Gay Sexualities and Visual Cultures*, London: Routledge, 1996.

Lipovetsky, Gilles. *The Empire of Fashion: Dressing Modern Democracy*, trans. Catherine Porter, with a Foreword by Richard Sennet, Princeton, NJ: Princeton U.P., 1994.

Lunning, Frenchy, *Fetish Style*, New York and London: Bloomsbury, 2013.

Lynch, Annette, *Porn Style: Exploring the Contours of Raunch Eroticism*, London and New York: Bloomsbury, 2012.

Marks, Craig and Rob Tannenbaum, eds, *I Want My MTV: The Uncensored History of the Music Video Revolution,* New York: Dutton, 2011.

Marly, Diana de, *Worth: Father of Haute Couture*, London: Elm Tree Books, 1980.

Maynard, Margaret, 'The Mystery of the Fashion Photograph', in Peter McNeil, Vicki Karaminas and Catherine Cole, *Fashion in Fiction*, Berg: Oxford, 2007.

McNair, Brian, *Striptease Culture: Sex, Media and the Democratisation of Desire*, New York: Routledge, 2002.

Mears, Ashley, *Pricing Beauty: The Making of a Fashion Model*, Berkeley and London: California U.P., 2011.

Miller, Janice, *Fashion and Music*, Oxford and New York: Berg, 2011.

Misselbeck, Reinhold, Rainer Wick and Richard Tardiff, eds, *Horst P. Horst*, exh cat., Cologne: Art Forum, 1992.

Mitchell, Juliet and Jacqueline Rose, eds, *Feminine Sexuality: Jacques Lacan and the école freudienne*, trans. Jacqueline Rose, New York: Norton, 1982.

Montague, Ken, 'The Aesthetics of Hygiene: Aesthetic Dress, Modernity, and the Body as Sign', *Journal of Design History*, 7 (2), 1994, 91–112.

Mulvey, Laura, 'Some Thoughts on Theories of Fetishism in Contemporary Culture', *October* 65, Summer 1993, 3–20.

Munich, Adrienne, ed., *Fashion in Film*, Bloomington and Indianapolis: Indiana U.P., 2011.

Myers, Kathy, 'Fashion 'n' Passion: A Working Paper', in Angela McRobbie, ed., *Zootsuits and Second Hand Dresses: An Anthology of Fashion and Music*, London: Macmillan, 1989.

Needham, Gary, 'The Digital Fashion Film', in Stella Bruzzi and Pamela Church Gibson, *Fashion Cultures Revisited*, London: Routledge, 2013, 104.

Newton, Helmut, *47 Nudes*, London: Thames and Hudson, 1981.

Newton, Helmut, *Polaroids*, Cologne: Taschen, 2011.

Newton, Helmut, *Portraits*, Munich: Schirmer Art Books, (1987) 1993.

Newton, Helmut, *World Without Men*, Cologne: Taschen 2013.

Niven, Penelope, *Steichen: A Biography*, New York: Clarkson Potter 1997.

Olson, Stanley, *John Singer Sargent*, London: Macmillan 1986.

Ormond, Richard and Carol Blackett-Ord, eds, *Franz-Xaver Winterhalter and the Courts of Europe 1830–1870*, exn cat., London: National Portrait Gallery, 1988.

Paulicelli, Eugenia, *Writing Fashion in Early Modern Italy: From Sprezzatura to Satire*, Surrey and Burlington: Ashgate, 2014.

Phillips, Christopher, 'The Judgment Seat of Photography', *October*, 22, Autumn 1982, 27–63.

Ratcliff, Carter, *John Singer Sargent*, New York: Abbeville Press, 1982.

Reims, Bettina, *Les Espionnes*, Munich: Gina Kehayoff, 1992.

Ribeiro, Aileen, *Fashion in the French Revolution*, BT London: Batsford, 1988.

Rilke, Rainer Maria, *The Complete French Poems of Rainer Maria Rilke*, trans. A Poulin Jnr., New York: Graywolf Press, (1979) 1986.

Riviere, Joan, 'Womanliness as Masquerade', *International Journal of Psychoanalysis*, 10, 1929, 303–313.

Robins, Kevin, *Into the Image: Culture and Politics in the Field of Vision*, London and New York: Routledge, 1996.

Robinson, David, *George Méliès: Father of Film Fantasy*, London: Museum of the Moving Image, 1993.

Rollins, Nita, 'Greenaway-Gaultier: Old Masters, Fashion Slaves', *Cinema Journal*, 35 (1), Autumn 1995, 65–80.

Rubin Suleiman, Susan, ed., *The Female Body in Western Culture*, Cambridge, MA: Harvard U.P., 1985.

Rosset, Clément, *The reel et son double*, Paris: Gallimard, (1976) 1984.

Saxe, Lorena Leigh, 'Sadomasochism and Exclusion', *Hypatia*, 7 (4), Lesbian Philosophy, Autumn 1992, 59–72.

Schwarzenbach, Alexis, 'Royal Photographs: Emotions for the People', *Contemporary European History*, 13 (3), August 2004, 255–280.

Shinkle, Eugenie, ed., *Fashion and Photograph: Viewing and Reviewing Images of Fashion*, London and New York: I.B. Tauris, 2008.

Silberman, Richard, 'Richard Avedon: Evidence 1944–1994; New York and Cologne', *The Burlington Magazine*, 136 (1098), September 1994, 641–642.

Simpson, Marc, ed., *Uncanny Spectacle: The Public Career of the Young John Singer Sargent*, New Haven and London: Yale U.P. and Williamstown: Clark Institute, 1997.

Sklar, Monica, *Punk Style*, London and New York: Bloomsbury, 2013.

Smedley, Elliott, 'Escaping to Reality: Fashion Photography in the Nineties', in Stella Bruzzi and Pamela Church Gibson, *Fashion Cultures: Theories, Explorations and Analysis*. London and New York: Routledge, 2000.

Smith, Joel, *Edward Steichen: The Early Years*, New York and Princeton: Metropolitan Museum of Art and Princeton U.P., 1999.

Squiers, Carol, ed., *The Critical Image: Essays on Contemporary Photography*, Seattle: Bay Press, 1990.

Steele, Valerie, *Fashion and Eroticism*, Oxford and New York: Oxford U.P., 1985.

Steele, Valerie, 'Anti-fashion: The 1970s', *Fashion Theory: The Journal of Dress, Body and Culture,* 1 (3), 1997, 279–296.

Steele, Valerie, *Paris Fashion: A Cultural History*, Oxford and New York: Berg, (1988) 1998.

Steele, Valerie, *The Black Dress*, New York: Harper Collins, 2007.

Steichen, Edward, 'On Photography', *Daedalus*, 89 (1), Winter 1960, 136–137.

Steichen, Edward, *Selected Texts and Bibliography*, ed. Ronald Gedrin, Oxford: Clio Press, 1996.

Stern, Marc, *The Fitness Movement and Fitness Centre Industry 1960–2000*, Business History Conference, 2008, http://www.thebhc.org/publications/BEHonline/2008/stern.pdf.

Stone, Richard, 'Winterhalter: London and Paris', *The Burlington Magazine*, 139 (1019), February 1988, 151–152.

Triggs, Teal, 'Framing Masculinity: Herb Ritts, Bruce Weber and the Body Perfect', in
    Juliette Ash and Elizabeth Wilson, eds, *Chic Thrills: A Fashion Reader*, Berkeley and
    Los Angeles: University of California Press, 1993.
Troy, Nancy, *Couture Culture: A Study in Modern Art and Fashion*, Cambridge, MA: MIT
    Press, 2003.
Uhlirova, Marketa, '100 Years of the Fashion Film: Frameworks and Histories', *Fashion
    Theory*, 17 (2), 2013, 137–158.
Uhlirova, Marketa, 'The Fashion Film Effect', in Djurdja Bartlett, Shaun Cole and Agnes
    Rocamora, *Fashion Media: Past and Present*, London: Bloomsbury, 2013.
Veblen, Thorstein, *The Theory of the Leisure Class*, New Brunswick and London:
    Penguin, 1992.
Veblen, Thorstein, *The Theory of the Leisure Class*, London: Teddington, [1899], 2007.
Vernallis, Carol, *Experiencing Music Video: Aesthetics and Cultural Context*, New York:
    Columbia U.P., 2004.
Wilde, Oscar, *The Picture of Dorian Gray*, *Complete Works*, London and Glasgow:
    HarperCollins, (1948) 1991.
Yusuf, Nilgin, *Fashion's Front Line*, London: Bloomsbury, forthcoming, 2015.
Zizek, Slavoj, *The Sublime Object of Ideology*, London and New York: Verso, 1989.
Zizek, Slavoj, ed., *Mapping Ideology*, London and New York: Verso, 1994.
Zizek, Slavoj, *The Metastases of Enjoyment*, London and New York: Verso, (1994)
    2005.
Zizek, Slavoj, ed., *Everything You Always Wanted to Know About Lacan (But Were Afraid
    to Ask Hitchcock),* London and New York: Verso, (1992) 2010.
Zizek, Slavoj and Mladen Dolar, *Opera's Second Death*, New York and London:
    Routledge, 2002.
Zupancic, Alenka, *The Odd One In: On Comedy*, Cambridge, MA: MIT Press, 2008.

Conference papers

Church Gibson, Pamela, 'Fashioning Adaptations: *Anna Karenina* on Screen',
    conference paper, 'Fashion in Fiction: Style Stories and Transglobal Narratives', 2014.

Films

The Hunger Games, Lionsgate Films, dir. Gary Ross, 2012.
The Hunger Games: Catching Fire, Lionsgate Films dir. Francis Lawrence, 2013.
The Hunger Games: *Mockingjay, Part 1*, Lionsgate Films, dir. Francis Lawrence, 2014.

Internet sources and websites

Clout, Laura and Adams, Stephen, 'Yves St Laurent Dies at 71: Tributes Pour in to
    French King of Haute Couture', *The Telegraph*, http://www.telegraph.co.uk/news/
    worldnews/europe/france/2064246/Yves-Saint-Laurent-dead-at-71-Tributes-pour-in-
    to-French-king-of-haute-couture.html, accessed 17 December 2014.

'Duran Duran and Supermodels Spark Girl Panic', *The Telegraph*, 8 November 2011, http://fashion.telegraph.co.uk/videos/TMG8877048/Duran-Duran-and-supermodels-spark-Girl-Panic.html.

Harvey, Michelle, 'Sex. Desire. No Romance', *Blanche Magazine*, n.d. 2011, http://www.blanche-magazine.com/sex-desire-no-romance/.

'Helmut Newton: Sexist Fetish to Magazine Mainstream', at the Museum of Fine Arts, Budapest, *Artdrum*, 17 April 2013, http://artdrum.wordpress.com/2013/04/17/helmut-newton-sexist-fetish-to-magazine-mainstream/.

Knight, Nick, 'SHOWstudio: Thoughts on Fashion Film', http://www.youtube.com/watch?v=BOBZMS9Bhr0.

Lagerfeld, Karl, 'Cara Delevingne Stars in Karl Lagerfeld's Latest Fashion Film', http://www.youtube.com/watch?v=qyn4FxONWUs.

Leopardi, Giacomo, 'Dialogue Between Fashion and Dress', trans. Charles Edwardes, http://leopardi.letteraturaoperaomnia.org/translate_english/leopardi_dialogue_between_fashion_and_death.html.

Lynch, David, 'Dior Presents Our Lady Shanghai by David Lynch', http://www.youtube.com/watch?v=oepfkpkxjmA.

Menkes, Suzy, 'The Circus of Fashion', *The New York Times*, 10 February 2013, http://tmagazine.blogs.nytimes.com/2013/02/10/the-circus-of-fashion/?_r=0, accessed 7 December 2014.

Ranck, Rosemary, 'The First Supermodel', *The New York Times*, 9 February 1997, http://www.nytimes.com/1997/02/09/books/the-first-supermodel.html showstudio.com and http://showstudio.com/projects/tag/fashion_films.

Stone, Tim, 'In Focus: The First Photo Shoot and the Invention of Fashion Photography', http://www.abc.net.au/arts/blog/the-first-photo-shoot-and-the-invention-of-fashion-photography-120712/default.htm.

INDEX

Italicized numbers denote pages with illustrations

Abercrombie and Fitch (brand) 89
Absolutely Fabulous (television series) 53, 90–1
Acconci, Vito xvii
Adatto, Kiku 120
Adonis (Greek mythology) 124
Adrian *see* Greenberg, Adrian
Åkerlund, Jonas 96, 99, 119
L'Album de la Mode du Figaro (magazine) 18
Alcmena 21
Allure (magazine) 25
Althusser, Louis, Althusserian 55
   Ideological State Apparatuses 55
   Repressive State Apparatuses 55
Amazon (firm) 52
America's Next Top Model (television series) 53
American Gigolo (film) 122
American Revolution xv
Amphitryon 21
anarchism, anarchist 9
androgyny 69
Anna Karenina (2012 film) 44
anti-fashion 52
Antonioni, Michelangelo xxi
Arcadia 123–6
Archimedes, Archimedean point 15
Arena (magazine) 38
Armani, Giorgio 44, 117, 122
   Armani Privé (brand) 53
   Armani Sport (brand) 46
Arnold, Rebecca 36–7, 39
Art et Décoration (magazine) 23
Avedon, Richard 30, 32–4, 114, 116

Babin, Gustave 20
Bailey, David 114
Bakhtin, Mikhail 59
   Rabelais and his World 59
Bakst, Léon 20
Balanchine, George 29
Ballets Russes 20
Balthus (Balthusz Klossowski de Rola) 72
Balzac, Honoré de 49
   Illusions perdus 49
Banana Republic (firm) 44
Banks, Elizabeth 51
Banner, Lois 73
   American Beauty (film) 73
Banton, Travis 47
Barbier, Georges 20
Baring, Norah 43
Barney, Matthew 118
Baron, Fabien 100
Barrymore, John 27
Barthes, Roland xiv, xvii–xviii, 7
   The Fashion System xvii–xviii
Bataille, Georges 81–2
   Eroticism 81
Baudelaire, Charles 17, 47
Baudrillard, Jean xx
   'Fashion or the Enchanted Fairy Land of the Code' xix–xx
Bauhaus 28, 46
Bazille, Frédéric 6, 7–8
   Réunion de famille 7, 7
BDSM xxii, 66, 78, 87, 94, 96, 100, 103, 104
Beaton, Cecil 27, 30–2, 34–5, 66
Behind the Green Door (film) 88
Belle de Jour (film) 122

Benjamin, Andrew xviii–xix
Benjamin, Walter xix
   'A Short History of Photography' 17
   'The Work of Art in the Age of
      Mechanical Reproducibility' xviii
Bentham, Jeremy 54
Bentley, Wes 54
Bernhardt, Sarah 3
Berra, John 119
Bing, Siegfried 24
      L'Art Nouveau (gallery) 24
Björk (Björk Guðmundsdóttir) 118
black dress xxi, 10, 43–50
Blackened Wings (film) 117
Blason jewellery 101
bloomers, bloomerism 20
Blow Up (film) xxi
Bobergh, Otto 3
Bogart, Humphrey 33
bohemian 66
Boime, Albert 11
Boldini, Giovanni 5, 10, 12, 13
Bon Marché (department store) 121
bondage 87
   See also BDSM
Bonnat, Léon 12
Bono (Paul David Hewson) 98
Boucher, François 4
Bourdin, Guy 37, 68, 89, 114
Bow, Clara 122
Bowie, David 98
Brandao, Josh 117
Branton, Travis 44
Breakfast at Tiffany's (film) xxi, 45, *49*,
   47–50
Brinkley, Christie 28
Brookes, Rosetta 66, 75, 78
   'Fashion Photography' 75
Brothers of Arcadia (film) 118, 123–6
Browning, Tod xvi
Brownmiller, Susan 73
   Femininity 73
Brummell, Beau 121
Bruzzi, Stella 57, 61
   *Undressing Cinema: Clothing and
      Identity in the Movies* 61
Burnett, Ron xvii
Burton, Tim xvi
Butel-Dumont, Georges-Marie 57
   Théorie du luxe 57

Cabinet of Dr Caligari (film) xvi
Caillebotte, Gustave 6
Calefato, Patrizia 51, 59
   *Luxury: Fashion, Lifestyle and
      Excess* 59
Caligula (film) 125
Callot Soeurs 121
Calvin Klein (brand) 89
Camera Work (magazine) 23
Campbell, Naomi 38, 96, 97, *97*, 98–101,
   106
Capitol Couture (website, magazine) 43,
   50–62
Capote, Truman 48
   Breakfast at Tiffany's (novella) 48
   See also Breakfast at Tiffany's (film)
Caravaggio (Michelangelo Merisi da) 28
Carolus-Duran, Émile 8, 12
Carpaccio, Vittore 2–3
Carpeaux, Jean-Baptiste 5
Carroll, Michael 126
Carter, Michael 17–18, 72
Cartier-Bresson, Henri 32
Castiglione, Countess (Virginia Oldoïni) 3
Castle, Irene 27
Cavalli, Roberto 44
Chadwick, Whitney 106
Chalayan, Hussein 114, 116
   Absent Presence 116
   Anaesthetics 116
   Place of Passage 116
Chanel (brand/house) 53, 119, 123
Chanel, Gabrielle 'Coco' xvii, 20, 22, 28,
   30, 37, 46–7
Charlemagne xv
Charles X 3
Cheruit, Louise 20
Chloé (brand/house) 112
Christensen, Helena 38, 97, *97*, 100, 103
Church Gibson, Pamela 36, 68, 87–8
   *Dirty Looks: Women, Pornography,
      Power* 87
   *More Dirty Looks: Gender,
      Pornography and Power* 87
Cocteau, Jean 22, 28
   The Blood of a Poet 34
Cole, Shaun 124
Collins, Suzanne 45, 50
   The Hunger Games (book trilogy) 45,
   50

See also *The Hunger Games* (film trilogy)
commodity 2, 10, 12, 22, 26, 36, 60, 61, 78, 85, 87, 101, 103, 120
   commodity fetish 73, 82, 93
Compte-Calix, François-Claudius 5
Condé Nast (firm) 25
Condé Nast, Thomas 22–3, 30
Conekin, Becky 34
Cook, Susan 87
The Cook, The Thief, His Wife and Her Lover (film) 116
Corot, Camille 24
Cotillard, Marion 119
Courbet, Gustave 4, 6
Courrèges, André xvii, 44, 90
  'Space Age' collections 44, 90
Covergirl (magazine) 52
Cowan, John 114
Coward, Noël 28
Crawford, Cindy 38, 97, *97*, 105
Crawford, Joan 122
Crescent, Francine 66

D&G *see* Dolce & Gabbana 100
Dahan, Olivier 119
Daily Sketch (magazine) 31
Dali, Salvador 22, 28–9
Damiano, Gerard 68
Danaë 20, 82
dandy 95
Daubigny, Charles-François 24
Davis, Bette 28
De Beers (brand) 61
Debord, Guy 60
  The Society of the Spectacle 60
Debussy, Claude 27
Deep Throat (film) 68, 88
Degas, Edgar 8, 18
  Chez la modiste 8
Deleuze, Gilles and Félix Guattari xx
Delevingne, Cara 119
Delion (hats) 114
DeMille, Cecil 122
Derrida, Jacques 103
The Devil in Miss Jones (film) 88
The Devil Wears Prada (film) xxi
Dickens, Charles 59
  Great Expectations 59
Dickensian 59
diCorcia, Philip-Lorca 114

Dietrich, Marlene 25, 30, 44, 47
Dior (brand/house) 119, 123
Dior, Christian 44
Doeuillet, Georges 20
Dolce & Gabbana (D&G) 95, 100, 118
Dorré, Gina 91
Dostoevsky, Fyodor 129–30
  The Double 129–30
Dracula (1931 film) xvi
Duran Duran 86, 96–107, *97*, *98*
  'Girl Panic' 86, 96–107, 119
  'Girls on Film' 96, 99
  'Hungry Like the Wolf' 106
  'I Won't Cry for Yesterday' 100
  'Notorious' 100
  'Rio' 96, 100
Durran, Jacqueline 44
Dyck, Anthony van 2, 3, 4, 12
Dyer, Richard 124
dysfunctional fashion 91

Eagleton, Terry 16
eBay (firm) 52
Eckert, Charles 52
Ed Wood (film) xvi
Edwards, Blake 48
Eichberg, Richard 115
Eisenman, Peter 90
Elizabeth II, Queen 31
Elven, Paul Tetar van 5
Emmanuelle (film) 68, 89
Empress Eugénie 3, 4
Erasmus xiv
erotica, erotic, eroticism 72, 74, 81–2, 96
Esperanto 72
Esquire (magazine) 122
Etsy jewelry 52
Evangelista, Linda 38
Evans, Caroline 22, 23, 60

Facebook 52, 53, 112
Faiers, Jonathan 91–2
Faithfull, Marianne 86
Fashion farce 115
  See also Konfektionskomödie
fashion film 111–26
Fashion Film Festival Chicago 117
Fashion Theory, The Journal of Dress, Body and Culture 36
Fellini, Federico 94, 124

female gaze 104
Feminina (magazine) 18
feminism 74
Fendi (brand/house):
    2013 collection 119
Ferragamo, Salvatore 44, 122
fetish, fetishism 100, 102–3, 105
Le Figaro 10
film noir 94
fin-de-siècle 68
First World War 24, 31
Flanner, Janet 28
Flügel, J. C. 16
Fonssagrives, Lisa 29, *29*
Ford, Tom 123
Fordist production 22, 46
Forever 21 (brand) 112
    Rumi Neely 112
Formalism 70–3
Formichetti, Nicola 118, 123–6
Fortuny, Mariano 3
Foucard, Louis de 11
Foucault, Michel 54–5
    Discipline and Punish 54
Fox Talbot, Henry xvi
Fragonard, Jean-Honoré 4
French Revolution xv, 56, 57
Freud, Sigmund 102–3
Freudian 102–3
Friedl, Bettina 33
Der Fürst von Pappenheim (film) 115
Fürstenberg, Diane von 112

Galliano, John 101
Ganeva, Mila 115–16
Garavani, Valentino *see* Valentino
Garber, Marjorie 102
Garbo, Greta 25
Gaultier, Jean Paul 44, 93–4, 116
Gautreau, Pierre 9
Gautreau, Virginie 9–12,
    See also Sargent, John Singer
gay 38, 73–5, 124
    gay male clones 74
    See also homosexual, lesbian, queer
Gazette des Baeaux-Arts 11
La Gazette du Bon Ton 20, 22, 23
George V hotel 65
German Expressionism 94

Gérôme, Jean-Léon 5
Gesamtkunstwerk 24
Gilda (film) 47
Gill, Rosalind 104
Gilligan, Sarah 52
    *Fashion and Film: Gender, Costume
    and Stardom in Contemporary
    Cinema* 52
Gindt, Dirk 118
Gish, Lillian 27
Givenchy, Hubert de 45, 47, 117,
    122
Glamour (magazine) 25
The Golem (film) xvi
Golightly, Holly 48
Goncourt brothers 4
Gone With the Wind 44
Goude, Jean-Paul 72
GQ (magazine) 38
Grachvogel, Maria 61
The Great Depression 20
The Great Gatsby (1974 film) 122
Greenaway, Peter 116
Greenberg, Adrian 44
Greenberg, Clement 70–1
Guardian (newspaper) 38
Guattari, Félix *see* Deleuze, Gilles and
    Félix Guattari
Guinness, Daphne 53
Gundle, Stephen 44
Gunning, Tom 61
Gutenberg, Johannes xiv

H&M (fashion retailer) 112
Hans, Peters 34
Harper's Bazaar (magazine) 18, 24, 27,
    28, 32, 100, 122
Harrelson, Woody 51, 59
Hartnell, Norman 114
Hayworth, Rita 47
Head, Edith 44, 122
Hefner, Hugh 86
Hellenism 91
Hemsworth, Liam 59
Hepburn, Audrey 47
Herpen, Iris van 53
Herzigova, Eva 38, 97, *97, 98*
heterosexual 75
Hitchcock, Alfred xviii, 43, 44

Hollander, Anne 125
Hollywood cinema 104
homoeroticism 123–6
homosexual 74, 102, 123–6
    gay male clones 74
    See also gay, lesbian, queer
Horst (Horst Bohrmann) *29*, 27–30, 116
    Waxed Beauty 28
Horwell, Veronica 38
Hoyningen-Huene, Baron George 27–8,
    30, 116
The Hunger Games (film trilogy) xxi, 45,
    56, *60*, 50–62
Hustler (magazine) 67, 86
Hutcherson, Josh 51

L'Illustration (magazine) 20
Impressionism, Impressionist 5, 9
Impressionism, Fashion and Modernity
    (*L'impressionism et la mode*)
    (exhibition) 6
Instagram 112
Iribe, Paul 20, 121
Isherwood, Christopher 95, 123
    Goodbye to Berlin 95
    A Single Man 123
Italian Futurism 114

Jacobs, Marc 100, 112
    Bryanboy 112
Jaeckin, Just 89
Jagger, Mick 98
James, Henry 8, 11
Jardin des Modes (magazine) 23
Jennings, Humphrey 114
Jessica 6 124, 125
    'White Horse' 124, 125
Johansson, Scarlett 118
Jourdan, Charles 37
Journal des Modes (magazine) 18
Jun Rupé (brand) 116
Junior Bazaar (magazine) 32
Jupiter 21

Karaminas, Vicki 36, 68
Khan, Nathalie 119
Kiki of Montparnasse (Alice Prin) 106
kitsch 56, 59, 96
Klein, Steven 89

Klein, William 114
Klimt, Gustav 24, 33
Kling, Elin 112
Kneller, Godfrey 12
Knight, Nick xxi, 53, 89, 113, 115, 117
Knightley, Keira 44
Kodak 19
Kofman, Sarah 103
Konfektionskomödie 115
    See also fashion farce
Krauss, Rosalind 69–70
Kravitz, Lenny 51

Laaksonen, Touko *see* Tom of Finland
Lacan, Jacques, Lacanian 10, 15, 45,
    79, 102
LaChapelle, David 53
Lacroix, Christian 90
Lady Blue Shanghai (film) 117, 119
Lady Gaga 96, 118
    'Paparazzi' 96
    'Telephone' 96
Lady Noire Affair (film) 119
Lady Rouge (film) 119
Lagerfeld, Karl 68, 69, 73, 74, 119
Lancret, Nicolas 4
Landau, Martin xvi
Landshoff, Herman 114
Lanvin, Jeanne 37
Lartigue, Jacques-Henri 114
Lauren, Ralph 46, 122
Laver, James 5
Lawrence, Jennifer 51
Lawrence, Thomas 4, 12
Le Bon, Simon 97–101, 106
Le Bon, Yasmin *97*, 97–8
Le Corbusier (Charles-Édouard
    Jeanneret) 28
Lee, Vernon 10
Leibniz, Gottfried Wilhelm von xvi
Leigh, Vivien 44
Lelong, Lucien 46
Lepape, Georges 20
lesbian 37, 74,101–2, 105
    See also homosexual, gay, queer
lesbian gaze 77
Levy, Ariel 88
Lewis, Reina 77
L'Herbier, Marcel 115

Libeskind, Daniel 90
Liebovitz, Annie 100
Life (magazine) 32
Lionsgate (production company) 45, 59
London College of Fashion 117
Loo, Charles-André van 4
Louis XIV 13
Louis, Jean 47
Louis-Philippe, King 3
Louis Vuitton (brand/house) 100
    Autumn/winter collection 2011 100
Lubitsch, Ernst 116
Lugosi, Bela xvii
Lumley, Joanna 53
Lunning, Frenchy 103
    Fetish Style 103
Lutens, Serge 116
Luther, Martin xiv
Lynch, Annette 88, 105
    Porn Chic 105
Lynch, David 117, 119

Macdonald, Julien 61
    2001 Spring/Summer collection 61
Macy's (department store) 105, 121
Madame Gres (Germaine Émilie Krebs)
    121
Madame X see Sargent, John Singer
Madonna 86, 93–6, 105
    Blond Ambition Tour 93–6
    Erotica 95
    The Girlie Show Tour 95
    'Justify My Love' 86, 94, 95
    Material Girl (brand) 105
    Mistress Dita 95
    Sex 95
Making Fashion (film) 114
Makovsky, Judianna 56, 61
male gaze 37, 66, 74, 85, 102, 105
Man Ray 3, 29, 34, 37, 105–6
    Noire et blanche 105–6
Manet, Édouard 6, 7, 8, 9, 12, 70
    Olympia 70
Mannoni, Octave 103
Mapplethorpe, Robert 30, 89
Marey, Étienne-Jules 114
Margiela, Martin 114, 116
Marie-Amélie, Queen 4
Marie-Antoinette, Queen 4

Marie Claire (magazine) xvii
Marlborough, Duke of 12
Marly, Diana de 3
Marnay, Audrey 120
Martin, Homer 24
Marx, Karl, Marxist 103
masquerade 4, 76, 77, 103
Maverick Records 95
Maynard, Margaret 69
McConaughey 118
McLellan, Alasdair 89
McNair, Brian 87, 88, 89, 95
McQueen, Alexander 51, 56–7, 118
    Fall 2012 Collection 57
    Highland Rape collection 91
    Monarch Butterfly dress 57
    Plato's Atlantis collection 112
Mechanical Dolls (film) 120
Medici, Marie de 13
Meisel, Steven 39, 94
Melba, Dame Nellie 3
Méliès, George 114
Menkes, Suzy 112–13
    'The Circus of Fashion' 112–13
Mercury 21
Mergassov, Barbe Dmitrievna, Madame
    Rimsky-Korsakov 4, *5*
Mert and Marcus (Mert Alas and Marcus
    Piggott) 89
Metropolitan Museum of Art,
    New York 6
Metternich, Pauline von 3, 4
Metz, Christian 103
Meyer, 'Baron' Adolph de 27, 28, 31
Miller, Janice 86, 101
Miller, Lee 34–5
The Minotaur 51
Miu Miu (brand) 53
Miyake, Issey 90
Möbius, Paul Julius 78
    *On Physiological Deficiency of
    Women*, 78
La Mode Illustré (magazine) 18
Moholy-Nagy, László 28, 34
Molière (Jean-Baptiste Poquelin)
    21
Mondino, Jean-Baptiste 95
Mondrian dress xviii
    See also Saint-Laurent, Yves

Monet, Claude 6
Déjeuner sur l'herbe 6
Femmes au jardin 6, *6*
Monroe, Marilyn 33
Montesquiou, Comte Robert de 10
Moss, Kate 86
Mower, Sarah 39
MTV 86, 94, 95, 113
See also music video
Mucha, Alphonse *19*, 19–20
Mugler, Thierry 118, 123–6
Menswear spring/summer 2012
124
Mulvey, Laura 103–4
Munkacsi, Martin 114
Murder! (film) 43
Musée de la Mode 90
Musée des Arts Décoratifs 90
Musée D'Orsay 6
Museum of Modern Art, New York
(MoMA) 25, 26
music video xxi, 85–107
See also MTV
Muybridge, Eadweard 114
Myer, Stephanie 50
Myers, Kathy 37, 77
Mystère (brand/house) 114

N.E.R.D (band) 101
'Everyone Nose' 101
Napoleon III 1, 4
Nattier, Jean-Marc 4
Needham, Gary 111, 117–18
Neo-Realist cinema 124
'New Man' 38, 123
New Romantic(s) 86, 96
The New York Times 112
The New Yorker (magazine) 25
New York World Fair 115
Newhall, Beaumont 26
'Photography 1839–1937'
(exhibition) 26
Newton, Helmut xviii, xxi, 10, 17, 27, 36,
65–82, 89, 92–3, 114, 116
Domestic Nudes 75
photograph for YSL *67*
'Self-Portrait' with wife and models
80, *81*
Le Smoking 69

Newton, Isaac xv
Niépce brothers xvi
Niewekerke, Comte de 4
Niven, Penelope 23
noir film xviii
Nordstrom (fashion retailer) 121

The Observer (newspaper) 39
L'Officiel (magazine) 18
Olsen and Lamarque 16
Olson, Stanley 9–10
Olympus, Olympian 125
Orient, Oriental 1, 2, 24, 92

Paley, Natalia 116
Palma, Brian de xvi
Pan (Greek god) 124
Panic at the Disco (band) 99
'But It's Better if You Do' 99
Paquin, Jeanne 20
Paramount Pictures (production
company) 47
Pasolini, Pier Paolo 94, 124
Patou, Jean 20, 22, 46, 77
Coin de Sports (shop) 46
Le Sien (fragrance) 46
Pavan, Chiara 117
Penn, Irving 30, 33, 114
Penthouse (magazine) 67
Peppard, George 49
Petri, Ray 89
Photoshop 113
Piano, Renzo 90
Pierson, Pierre-Louis 3
Pissarro, Camille 9
Pistel, Stephanie *97, 98*
Plato, Platonic 130
Plautus 21
Playboy (magazine) 67, 86
La Plume d'Or (bookstore) 28
Poe, Edgar Allan
'William Wilson' xx
Poiret, Paul 20, 22, 24, 37, 77, 121
The Robes of Paul Poiret 121
The Thousand and Second Night 114
Pollock, Jackson 70
Polo Sport (brand) 46
pornochic xxi, 75, 85–107, 124–5
See also pornostyle

pornography 67–8, 70, 72, 88–9, 93–4,
124–5
pornostyle 87–8
See also pornochic
Porter, Cole 28
Potter, Harry 50
Prada, Miuccia 44, 123
Price, Antony 98
'primitive', primitivism 106
Prince (Prince Roger Nelson) 98
Protestantism xiv
Proust, Marcel 11
À la recherché du temps perdu 2–3
Pugh, Gareth 118
Pyrhonen, Kirsi 120

queer, queering 21, 66, 74, 105
See also gay, homosexual, lesbian

Raeburn, Henry 12
Raphael (Raphaello Sanzio da Urbino) 4
Ratcliff, Carter 8–9
raunch eroticism 88
See also pornochic, pornostyle
Ray, Billy 51
Redfern, John 20
Rembrandt (Rembrandt Harmenszoon
van Rijn) 28, 33
Renaissance xv, 2, 3
Renoir, Paul 6
Revlon (firm) 32
Reynolds, Joshua 2, 12
Rhodes, Nick 97–8, *98*, 99, 103
Ribeiro, Aileen 3–4, 57
Fashion in the French Revolution 57
Richards, Keith 100
Rilke, Rainer Maria 15
Ritts, Herb 38–9, 89
Riviere, Joan 76
'Womanliness as Masquerade' 76
RLX (brand) 46
Robbins, Kevin 118
Rocamora, Agnes 112
rock chic 86
Rococo 4
Rogers, Richard 90
Rolley, Katrina 77
Rollins, Nita 116
The Rolling Stones 98, 100

Romney, George 12
Rose, Barbara 68
'The Beautiful and the Damned'
68
Ross, Gary 50
Rossellini, Roberto 94
Rosset, Clément xiii
Roxy Music 86, 98
Rowling, J. K. 50 n.62
Royal Academy, London 10
Rubempré, Lucien de 49
Rubens, Peter-Paul 12, 13
Ruiz, Nomi 125–6
Rumpelstiltskin 82
Russian Avant-Garde 28
Russian Revolution 27

Sabrina (film) 122
Sade, Donatien Alphonse, Marquis
de 78
sadomasochism 87
See also BDSM
Saint-Laurent, Yves xviii, 65, *67*, 68, 111,
122
Pop Art collection 69
Le Smoking 68, *69*
Salò (film) 94
Salon, Paris 10
Samsung Electronics 52
Sander, Jil 44
Sargent, John Singer 8–12, 44,
72, 85
Madame Édouard Pailleron 8–9
Madame X 8–11, 19, 43–4, 85
Saunders, Jennifer 53
Saville, Peter 113
Savoy Hotel 96, 101, 104
Schiaparelli, Elsa 22, 28, 37, 56, 121
Schiele, Egon 33
Schneider, Dana 52
Schopenhauer, Arthur 79
veil of Maya 79
Schor, Naomi 103
Schubert, Franz 124
Trio No. 2 in E flat major 124
Schuman, Scott 112
Sartorialist (website) 113
Schwarzenbach, Alexis 31
Scorsese, Martin 118

Sears, Roebuck & Co. 18, 122
Second World War 27, 32, 35–40, 93
September 11 39
Sex and the City (television series) 123
Seymour Hoffman, Philip 54
Shadow of a Doubt (film) 43
Shanghai Express (film) 47
Shayk, Irina 118
Shields, Kathryn 98–9
    'Carnival of Mirrors: The Hermetic
        World of Music Video' 98
SHOWstudio xxi, 113–15, 118–19
Silberman, Richard 33
Silva Pereira, José da 49
Simmel, Georg 16
Simpson, Wallis 122
Sims, David 89
A Single Man (film) 123
Sire Studios 94
Sister Act (film) 118
S/M *see* BDSM
SM chic *see* pornochic
Smedley, Elliott 39–40
Socialism, socialist 9
Sosie, *sosie* 20–1
Stage Fright (film) 44
Steele, Valerie 37, 47, 73, 74, 77
    Fashion and Eroticism 73–4
Stefani, Gwen 101
    'Rich Girl' 101
Steichen, Edward *25*, 22–6, 27,
    31, 32
    The Pond 24
    Woods in the Rain 24
Stern, Marc 38
Sternberg, Josef von 47
Stieglitz, Alfred 23, 26
Stierle, Karlheinz 16
Stonewall riots 75, 86
Street of Dreams (film) 118
The Student of Prague (1913, 1926,
    1984 films) xvi
Surrealism, Surrealist 22, 28–9, 34, 37,
    66, 70
Sutherland, Donald 51
Swanson, Gloria 25, 122
Swarovski (brand/house) 100
    'Dead or Alive' skull 100
Sylvian, David 86

Takada, Kenzo 90
Taylor, John 97–8, 103
Taylor, Roger 97, 100
Teller, Juergen 39
The Ten Commandments (film) 122
Théâtre Robert-Houdin 114
Theseus 51
The Thief of Baghdad (film) 122
Tissot, James 12
Titian, Tiziano 2
Tom of Finland (Touko Laaksonen) 74
Tour, Georges de la 28
Troy, Nancy 22
Tryon, Dwight 24
Tucci, Stanley 61
The Twilight Saga 50 n.62
Twitter 52

U2 (band) 98
Uhlirova, Marketa 113–14
    The Fashion Film Effect 114
The Untouchables (film) 122
Unwerth, Ellen von 118

Valentino 44
Vampyros Lesbos (film) 96
Vanity Fair (magazine) 25, 27
Veblen, Thorstein 57–8
    Theory of the Leisure Class 57
Velázquez, Diego 8
Venturi, Robert 90
Vernallis, Carol 99
Veronese, Paolo 2
Versace, Gianni 32
    Versace (brand) 53
Vertigo (film) 43
Victoria, Queen 3
Vidor, Charles 47
Vietnam War 34
Vigée-Lebrun, Elisabeth 2, 4
Viktor and Rolfe 116
Vionnet, Madeleine 37, 121
Vogel, Lucien 20, 23
Vogue (magazine) *21*, 25, 27, 29, *29*, 32,
    34, 37, 116, 121, 122
    American 29, 46, 68
    British 30, 44
    French 28, 65–6, *67*, 68, *69*, 89, 106
    Italian 39, 120

Vs Magazine 118
Vyalitsyna, Anne 118

W Magazine 94
Wagner, Richard 24
Walker, Tim 120
Wangenheim, Chris von 66
Ward, Tony 94
Wasson, Craig xvi
Watteau, Antoine 2
Weber, Bruce 38–9, 89, 114
Weininger, Otto 78–9
   Sex and Character 78
Westwood, Vivienne 94, 101, 117
Whistler, James Abbott McNeill 24
Wilde, Oscar:
   The Picture of Dorian Gray 1
Wilding, Dorothy 31–2
Williams, Pharrell 101
Winterhalter, Franz-Xaver 1–5, 13
   Young Italian Girl by the Well 4

Wolfe, Tom 30
Women's Liberation Movement 68
Women's Wear Daily (magazine)
   121–2
Wong, Anna May 47
Woolf, Albert 10
Worth, Charles Frederick 1–5, 13, 18, 20,
   37, 121

Yamamoto, Yohji 90
YSL *see* Saint-Laurent, Yves
Yusuf, Nilgin 111

Zegna Sport (brand) 46
Zeitgeist 117
Zeus 20, 82
Zizek, Slavoj xiii, xx–xxi, n. xxii,
   78–80, 85
   'Otto Weininger, or, Woman Doesn't
    Exist' 78
Zupancic, Alenka 21–2